MW01444660

The Wireless Operator

The Wireless Operator

The Untold Story of the British Sailor Who Invented the Modern Drug Trade

David Tuch

Published in the UK and USA in 2025 by
Icon Books Ltd, Omnibus Business Centre,
39–41 North Road, London N7 9DP
email: info@iconbooks.com
www.iconbooks.com

ISBN: 978-183773-245-6
ebook: 978-183773-246-3

Text copyright © 2025 David Tuch

The author has asserted his moral rights.

No part of this book may be reproduced in any form, or by any means, without prior permission in writing from the publisher.

Typeset by SJmagic DESIGN SERVICES, India

Printed and bound in Great Britain

Appointed GPSR EU Representative: Easy Access System Europe Oü, 16879218
Address: Mustamäe tee 50, 10621, Tallinn, Estonia
Contact Details: gpsr.requests@easproject.com, +358 40 500 3575

Dedicated to MELOC

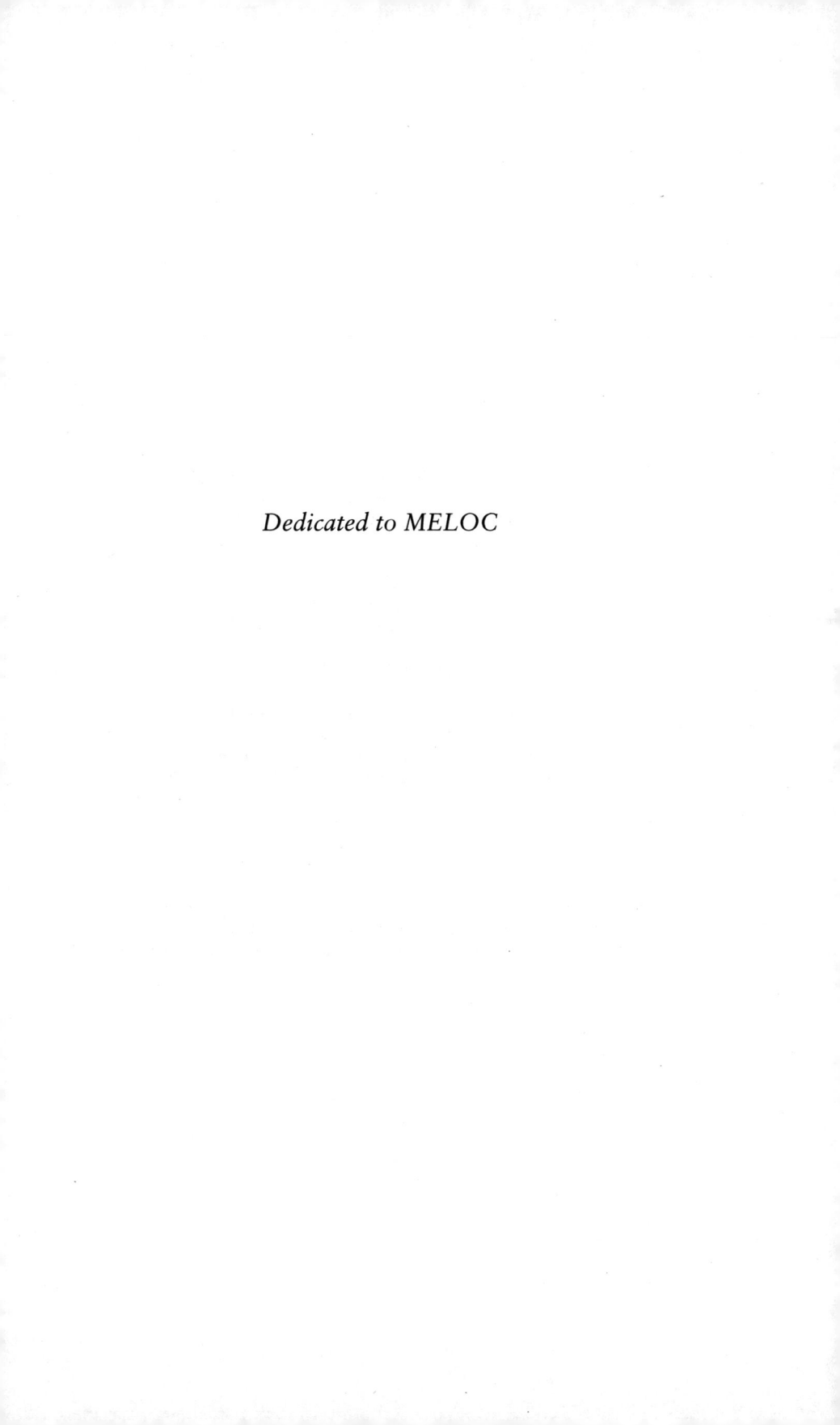

CONTENTS

Dramatis Personae xiii
Prologue xvii

PART I
1. Escape from Manchester 3
2. War 27
3. Questionable Ventures 39

PART II
4. The Three-Mile Limit 55
5. The New American Dream 63
6. The Freedom Ferry 77
7. We Will Not Be Stopped by Military Force 95
8. The Exile Runner 119
9. Love and Hate and Humanitarian Solutions ... 137

PART III
10. Shipping Interests 151
11. The Night Train 161
12. Operation Zebra 167
13. Vast Opportunities 181

Epilogue 193
Acknowledgements 199
List of Illustrations 203
Abbreviations 207
Bibliography 209
Notes 237

AUTHOR'S NOTE

While researching my family history, I discovered I had a British cousin named Harold Derber, reputed to have been a smuggler, gunrunner and soldier of fortune. Curious, I began researching old newspaper articles to see if there was any truth to the family lore. With each story confirming the rumors, I was drawn into a world far stranger and more dangerous than I ever could have imagined.

Unable to turn away, I interviewed his criminal associates, former undercover agents and distant relatives. I tracked down an unpublished memoir, long-lost folders in foreign archives, undercover photos and newly declassified intelligence reports. The tale that emerged – one of organized crime, espionage and survival – was so astonishing that I dedicated myself to chronicling Derber's life, culminating in the book you're reading now.

Writing about the intersection of espionage and crime presented unique challenges. My research was often hindered by intentional falsehoods, conflicting accounts, relatives sworn to secrecy, and government records that had been classified or destroyed. In such cases, I've presented the most plausible scenario based on the available information, always aiming to distinguish between established facts and informed speculation. I've corroborated extraordinary findings with at least two independent sources whenever possible.

I've taken some artistic liberties to enhance certain sensory details and minor scenes. These creative touches are designed to help readers more vividly imagine the events and emotions Derber may have experienced without compromising the fundamental truth of his unbelievable odyssey.

It is not down on any map; true places never are.
HERMAN MELVILLE, *MOBY DICK*

DRAMATIS PERSONAE

Principal Characters (in order of appearance)

HAROLD DERBER	'Soldier of Fortune.' Former radio officer with the British Merchant Navy. Born Hyman Tuchverderber in Manchester, England.
REHAVAM 'RAY' ADIEL	Derber's lifelong friend and occasional business associate.
SARAH COHEN	Derber's romantic partner. Aliases: Sari Lesley and Sari Cohen.
JACK NAGELEY	Derber's Miami attorney and a thorn in the side of the US State Department.
CAPTAIN VÍCTOR PINA	Director in the Cuban Transportation Ministry and co-founder of the Cuban intelligence service. Derber's ally in the Castro government.
JOHN D. STEELE	Derber's ground operator in America. Former mayor of Hallandale, Florida.

Supporting Characters (in order of appearance)

JOSEPH AND KATHE TUCHVERDERBER	Derber's parents. Later, Joseph and Kathy Derber.

ISIDOR AND SYBIL TUCHVERDERBER	Derber's brother and sister. Later, Jack and Sybil Derber.
FIDEL CASTRO	'El Comandante.'
JOHN F. KENNEDY	President and second-most hated man in Miami.
SUSAN COHEN	Sarah's identical twin sister. AKA: Susan Johnston. Alias: Susan Lesley.
MICHAEL MCLANEY	Casino magnate and 'Genial Hustler.'
MORRIS LANSBURGH	Hotel tycoon who backs Derber's cruise liner.
SAM BENTON	Private investigator and Mafia fixer.
MEYER LANSKY	'The Mob's Accountant.'
JAMES B. DONOVAN	Private negotiator for the Kennedy administration. 'The Metadiplomat.'
ROBERT F. KENNEDY	Attorney General and White House coordinator for Operation Mercy.
GORDON CHASE	Special Assistant for National Security Affairs.
MCGEORGE 'MAC' BUNDY	US National Security Advisor and 'Shadow Secretary of State' in the Kennedy administration.
IRENALDO GARCÍA BÁEZ	Ticket salesman for the ferry. Former Chief of Military Intelligence in the Batista regime.
EMIL STADELHOFER	Swiss Ambassador to Cuba.
PETER WHITEHEAD	Briton living in Jamaica. Provides Derber with the *Nana* ship used for the Cuba ferry.

Dramatis Personae

CAPTAIN ALAN C. TOUGH	Harbormaster at Port Royal, Jamaica. Originally from Scotland.
BRAULIO ALFONSO MARTINEZ	Labor organizer and Cuban intelligence agent. Aliases: Braulio Alfonso and Francisco De Ravirich.
HENRY KISSINGER	Secretary of State and chairman of the Cabinet Committee on International Narcotics Control.
TED AKEY	Florida Marine Patrol officer. Undercover alias: Kelly Summers.
WINCES VELASCO	Derber's Colombian supplier and import-export broker for the Medellín cartel.
FERNANDO RAVELO-RENEDO	Cuban Ambassador to Colombia. Architect of the Cuban-Colombian guns-for-drugs trade.
ROBERT E. BRENNAN	President of First Jersey Securities and Derber's stockbroker. 'The Penny stock king.'

Principal Boats

CALYPSO LINER	Luxury cruise ship.
CYPRIA	Norwegian merchant ship.
EMPRESS OF BAHAMAS	Luxury cruise ship. Formerly called the *Wappen von Hamburg*.
LILLIAN B	Trafficking boat.
NANA	Ship initially planned for the Cuba ferry.

NELSON II	Ship used for the Cuba ferry, also called the new *Nana*.
NIGHT TRAIN	The mothership.
VAN OSTADE	Dutch merchant ship. Formerly called the *Empire Toiler*.

Other Key Boats

CATCHALOT II	Undercover 'pickup' boat.
CLARA	Trafficking ship.
CORAL ROCK	Colombian fishing boat.
DAUNTLESS	United States Coast Guard endurance cutter. The 'nation's premier drug buster.'
GINA IV	Trafficking ship.
LOBSTER FARM	Colombian fishing boat.
MIL MAR I	Colombian fishing vessel.
ORANGE SUN	Cruise ship considered for return of the Bay of Pigs prisoners and for the Cuba ferry.
ORION	Cruise ship considered for the Cuba ferry.
RED MACHINE	Trafficking ship.

PROLOGUE

Mesic, North Carolina, 1975

Cordgrass and black needlerush swayed beside an old mobile trailer parked on the edge of Pamlico Sound, a vast brackish lagoon. Moonlight reflected off the mud-covered corrugated siding. Inside, three middle-aged men in salt-stained flannel shirts and worn jeans lay deep asleep. Their fishing trawler, carrying thirty tons of Colombian marijuana, was still hours from arriving.

Outside, a branch snapped. Night herons screeched and beat their wings. The flimsy trailer door flung open. Two armed men stormed in – one with a shotgun, the other a pistol. The first was gaunt, with wire-frame glasses and tight, kinky hair; the second was short, nearly obese, with an unlit cigar clenched between his teeth.

"Where's Derber?" one shouted.[1]

Not waiting for an answer, he fired his shotgun. The blast tore through a trafficker's skull, almost decapitating him. Without another word, the two hitmen slipped out the trailer door and vanished into the night.

The two survivors lay staring at the spreading pool of blood. When their breaths finally steadied, they exchanged a single, grim look. Then they moved.

They stripped the body down to its underwear and wrapped it in a plastic tarp and bedsheet. One grabbed a box cutter and sliced out the blood-soaked carpet. They loaded the body into the back of a truck and drove to nearby Bear Creek. In a secluded pine grove, they dug a shallow grave and buried the body, along with his clothes, a key and the stained carpet.[2,3]

It was easy to understand how the hitmen had mistaken the victim for Derber. The description matched almost perfectly: white, around 150 pounds, medium height, dark facial hair, late forties. The main difference was that the real Derber couldn't be killed that easily.

PART I

1. ESCAPE FROM MANCHESTER

Manchester, England, 1939–43

Hyman's head snapped back from another straight jab. His opponent's shoulder twitched, signaling an incoming cross. Hyman slipped the punch and fired back with a right hook to the floating rib. The large boy stumbled, then dropped one knee to the grass, wincing in pain.

On the ringside bench, a mother gasped, clutching her neighbor's arm. A father grimaced and wrung his cap with both hands. The cadet officers straightened in their seats.

Hyman Tuchverderber, the thirteen-year-old destined to become Harold Derber, worked his mouthguard free and spat it to the ground. He loosened his glove strings with his teeth and a twist of his swollen jaw.

The Manchester Jewish Lads' Brigade (JLB) had taught him well. Home to the finest cadet boxing club in the kingdom, it had won the prestigious Prince of Wales' Challenge Shield for several consecutive years.

Through boxing and paramilitary training, the JLB sought to 'iron out the Ghetto bend'[1] into the ramrod values of honor, self-respect and loyalty to the Crown. All these virtues were on display at the retreat, which was deliberately held on Saturday to clash with the holy Shabbat.

The cadet major called an end to the day's sparring and ordered the lads to change into their greens for rifle drills. Spilling out of the makeshift bell tent barracks, the cadets fell into a two-line formation.

Hyman and his fellow cadets made a splendid sight in their World War I-style serge wool uniforms, complete with peaked service caps adorned with the 'JLB' monogram encircled by an imperial laurel wreath.[2] Standing shoulder to shoulder with their bolt-action Enfield rifles, they presented a unified front – not as Polish, Russian, Hungarian or German Jews, but as 'Englishmen of the Mosaic persuasion.'

Manchester Jewish Lads' Brigade.

Yet, even among his peers, Hyman stood out. Intense, obsidian eyes hinted at a depth of understanding beyond his years. His face was etched with deep laugh lines, the left more pronounced, lending him a bemused smirk. His angular nose gave his youthful face a sharp edge, and his furious, scruffy black hair seemed perpetually in motion.

The cadet major marched Hyman and the lads to the firing range, where they assumed the line. On the command to aim, Hyman raised his rifle and rested his swollen cheek against the cold rifle stock. The placement was second nature; he had mastered the proper cheek weld at the age of ten.

He closed one eye and focused the other on the wooden plank fifty yards away. He inhaled the familiar scent of cleaning solvents, oil, sulfur, and saltpeter, and held his breath. The still pine branches in the distance meant no correction was needed. He made microscopic adjustments for the bullet drop and his reflexes.

At the command to fire, Hyman opened his closed eye and squeezed the trigger between heartbeats. The lads unleashed a cracking barrage of bullets. With the cadet major's command, 'Orders Down!', the rifle clicked back into place at the heels. Hyman's lips twitched into a subtle grin as he saw the empty spot where his target had been.

Following rifle drills, the cadets assembled for the colonel's address. He commended them for winning the Lucas Tooth Trophy for the most efficient cadet corps and then launched into an oration on the imperative of military preparedness. England's solemn pledge to defend Poland should rouse the fervor of every cadet, he said. These virtues, he insisted, were not mere slogans, but sacred principles worth fighting for.

Hyman clenched his jaw as the speech wore on. Five more years of this before he could enlist felt like a lifetime.

The buglers finally sounded the closing retreat, and the commander dismissed the battalion. Hyman grabbed his kit bag and hurried to catch the train back home to Cheetham Hill. On the walk home from the station, the Manchester Parks Officers were scrubbing the chalk slogans from the city walls again: "Stop the War, Stop the Warmongers!" and "Christians awake! Don't be slaughtered for Jewish finance."[3]

The vocation of slogan-cleaner seemed like steady, honest work.

Hyman passed by windows flickering with Sabbath candles, their gentle glow amplified by the blackouts. He reached his one-up, one-down red-brick terrace house on Herbert Street. After checking the rooms to ensure no one would catch him, he went straight for the wireless. He flicked the switch, and the radio hummed to life. He tuned to the BBC on the Moorside Edge frequency, the warmth of the tubes drawing him closer. Yet there was no news – no invasion, no movement. Herr's troops were still holding at the Polish border.

Later that night, as Hyman prepared for bed, the whispers of his parents, Joseph and Kathe, drifted through the open crack of his door. The hushed tones piqued Hyman's curiosity, proving the old saying that children only listen when parents try not to be heard.

Peeking out, he caught his mum waving a letter at his father. Hyman had no idea what it was about, except that it wasn't call-up papers. His dad was short, had broken teeth, a sideways-bent spine, and a history of epilepsy, hysteria and "heaviness of head."[4] He had struggled with these illnesses since childhood, but they worsened during his service in the last war. He now ran a leather goods stall in Accrington Market Hall, selling shoes and handbags despite a surname that meant "cloth spoiler." Work-related correspondence never came home, though, so the letter remained a mystery.

The next morning, Hyman half-heartedly dressed for school, throwing on his cardigan and shadow-colored jacket. He tucked his unruly dark hair beneath his black cap adorned with the school's 'M' logo, for Manchester Jews' School (MJS).

The school was an imposing red-brick Victorian building with gabled wings and a verdigris copper atrium. Inside, the students settled at their desks for the morning register. Hyman's inscrutable surname always brought a classroom snicker. Most of his classmates' names had been anglicized by the school long ago – Cohen to Cowan, Hillel to Hill, Levi to Lewis – but, for some reason, Hyman's absurd last name remained unchanged.

Classes covered the quintessential three Rs and the geography and history of Britain and her empire. The lessons on this day covered Dickens's reflections on social reform, moral conscience and the ceaseless struggle between the aristocracy and the downtrodden. Other days were reserved for Shakespeare's timeless tales of the towering ambitions of rulers and the sacred bonds of loyalty.

The teachers stressed the unique beauty of the English language, compared to the 'uncivilised, uneducated jargon' of Yiddish, which the school had thoroughly banned due to the waves of unwashed refugees arriving from the continent.[5] Forbidden from speaking Yiddish and struggling with English, the new students were quiet, which suited Hyman fine.

Recess offered a medley of games. On some days, the yard rang with the crisp *pock* of leather cricket balls hitting willow bats. Other afternoons brought the clickety-clack of croquet mallets or the thunderous gallop of football. Today, the children strapped on their gas masks and ran practice sprints to the pretend air raid

Class from Manchester Jews' School. Hyman is likely the boy second row from the back and second from the right.

shelters in the equipment sheds. The visors fogged over, sending the students veering off in comical directions, while other pupils collapsed, writhing with phlegmatic laughter.

Hyman paused, his breath catching – the old tightness in his chest, a lingering scar from childhood tuberculosis. Memories surged: his mother's panicked screams at the first sight of blood in his cough, the murmuring doctors, the agonizing months in sanatoria, staring at the white ceilings of Pendlebury and Booth Hall children's hospitals, each strained breath bubbling and clicking in his chest.[6,7]

After school, Hyman trudged home to find his mum reciting the daily litany of angst to his dad: the children need to evacuate in case the Nazis bomb the factories; the Blackshirts set up headquarters down the road; the clothes rations will mean the end of the market stall; Home Office administrators are pounding on Jews' doors; the cousins in Berlin have stopped sending letters.

But Kathe's sermon could only hold back the malevolent spirit for so long. The BBC wireless rasped the following morning:

> These are today's main events. Germany has invaded Poland and has bombed many towns. General mobilisation has been ordered in Britain and France. Parliament will summon for six o'clock this evening. Orders completing the mobilisation of the Navy, Army and Air Force were signed by the King at a meeting this afternoon of the Privy Council.

Hyman turned to his four-year-old sister, Sybil, with her black hair and precocious rosy cheeks, engaged with her toy blocks. His fifteen-year-old brother, Jack, born Isidor, returned to his business, whistling a jaunty tune. Hyman had also had a younger brother, Basil, but he'd succumbed as a three-month-old when Hyman was only six.

The following Sunday, the family huddled around the dining room wireless set. Hyman pressed his ear against the speaker as he counted down to the ultimatum deadline. Fifteen minutes past the cut-off, the Prime Minister made the announcement:

> This morning, the British Ambassador in Berlin handed the German Government a final Note stating that unless we heard from them by eleven o'clock that they were prepared at once to withdraw their troops from Poland, a state of war would exist between us. I have to tell you now that no such undertaking has been received, and that consequently this country is at war with Germany.

When 'God Save the King' played at the end, the family exchanged uncertain glances, wondering if they should stand. The house was silent, except for the metallic clanging outside where city workers were dismantling an iron fence and loading it onto a truck bound for the smelting furnaces.

While his family attended to their affairs, Hyman sat captivated, marveling at the magic of wireless. This mystical box, made of walnut veneer and gleaming Bakelite, housed glowing glass tubes, spiraled copper coils, and reverberating magnetic membranes. It plucked invisible waves from the ether, bringing word from the other side of the world.

Testament to its dark wonder came a few hours later when the radio choked out the somber news: off the northwest coast of Ireland, a German U-boat had mistakenly torpedoed the SS *Athenia*, an unarmed passenger liner carrying people fleeing the war. Over a hundred souls perished – American tourists, European refugees and British child evacuees, many from the north.

Hyman's mind filled with flashes of icy water gushing through torpedo holes, panic-stricken passengers clawing at lifeboats, bodies already blue. Maritime regulations were supposed to protect civilian ships, but rules were always the first to go.

Knowing what was coming, Hyman's mum finally explained the purpose of the mystery letter she had been angrily waving at his dad. She had packed everything listed on the note in a worn, oversized haversack: fresh undergarments, nightclothes, plimsolls, spare socks, toothbrush, comb, towel, soap, face cloth, handkerchiefs, a Mackintosh and his gas mask, neatly tucked in its cardboard box with his name scrawled on it. She prepared a twine-wrapped paper parcel containing a cheese sandwich and dry biscuits for the trip. Lastly, she fastened a hefty cardboard tag with his name and address to his lapel.

She didn't know where he was going or who the family would be. If Hyman despised them, her heart would break from despair; if he loved his new parents, her heart would ache with jealousy. The family wouldn't be kosher, but it wouldn't be a sin if there was a war. His brother and sister would remain in Manchester with her. Maybe he'd be home soon – rumors said the war would end by Christmas, although she wasn't sure. The only thing she knew for certain was that his train was leaving the following morning.

The next day, Hyman and his classmates gathered in the MJS classroom, some bouncing with anticipation, others from fright. Whenever the teacher's back was turned, the mischievous ones sniggered and swapped name tags. The teacher, clipboard in hand, explained the evacuation procedures for Pied Piper Day. They would quietly queue outside by standard and board trams bound for Manchester Victoria Station, where evacuation trains would take them to Blackpool for wartime billeting.

The classroom erupted into cheers at the news they were going to Blackpool, home of the famous Pleasure Beach amusement park. With a wry smile, the teacher reminded them not to get too carried away – the war would be over by Christmas, and they'd be back before they knew it.

The eager students gathered outside and boarded the rickety trams. As it rattled through the streets, Hyman slumped forward, resting his forehead on his folded arms. Pleasure Beach was hardly the warfront he'd had in mind.

Stepping into Victoria Station, the platform was mobbed with animated schoolchildren, some as young as five. The children carried rucksacks and makeshift valises from pillowcases. Tearful mothers handed their children chocolates, urging them to hurry aboard for a good seat. Expectant mothers, the elderly, the disabled, and civil servants were the last to board.

The platform whistle screamed as the steam train began to chug forward. Hyman found a seat and pressed his forehead against the glass as the parents, waving handkerchiefs, disappeared around the bend.

After an hour-long journey, the train shuddered to a halt at Blackpool Central Station. The door chute slid open, unleashing a stampede of students onto the platforms. In a scene resembling a frenzied cattle market, eager adults snatched children as they alighted from the train. Foster mothers elbowed their husbands to pick this one – no, wait, that one. Brothers and sisters screamed as they were wrenched from each other's arms.

Amid the commotion, the teachers scrambled to record the names of the foster parents and ensure an equitable distribution of children. As the new foster parents spirited the students away, teachers stuffed pre-paid postcards into the children's jacket pockets so they could inform their parents back home of their new address.

After the foster parents picked all the best children, the teacher took Hyman and the leftover children on a door-to-door appeal. Hyman and his classmates straggled in crocodile formation through Blackpool center. The teacher politely knocked from door to door and inquired if the lady of the house would be so kind as to foster a deloused, bed-trained evacuee from 'Derby Street School' – no oil sheets required.[8] The students stood upright at the outset, eager to get a billet, but sagged closer to the pavement as the evening dragged on.

Around dusk, when Hyman had all but given up, his teacher found him a home on Highfield Road. His new foster father stood in the doorway – a dour, unmarried Irish butcher in his early thirties wearing a blood-stained smock.[9] The Ministry of Health would compensate him eight pounds sixpence a week to look after an unaccompanied child under fourteen.

Hyman slumped his shoulders and entered his new home, which smelled of raw meat and disinfectant. Meeting his foster father's stern gaze, he gripped his sack tighter, exchanged a few soft murmurs of gratitude, and climbed the creaking stairs. That night, he lay on the bed facing the barren wall, staring into his future.

The following morning, Hyman and the other evacuees trudged to the local school for their first day of classes. The unfamiliar teachers droned on in tiresome half-day lectures while Hyman's gaze drifted out the classroom window. Outside, children played carefree in the yard. Reports began filtering in from Manchester: Nazi troops were not goose-stepping down Market Street. Town Hall hadn't been razed. Only the odd stray bomb landed in a suburb.

With no actual fighting happening, they should have called it the Phony War or perhaps the Bore War. *Sitzkrieg* had a nice ring to it. And thinking about names, 'Pied Piper' seemed fitting for the evacuation scheme; after all, the piper hadn't led the rats to safety but to drown them in the river.

As the days passed, the teachers began to resemble amateur actors in an ill-rehearsed play. Their constant reminders about the evacuation's importance rang hollow, as if they were trying to convince themselves as much as the students.

With no imminent invasion, the evacuation was pointless. There was no reason to have children living with strangers so far from home. Yet none of the adults were willing to make the call to bring them back. Left with no choice, Hyman took matters into his own hands.

After three miserable weeks in Blackpool, he'd had enough. He declared an end to the phony war, packed his belongings into his haversack, and caught the next train back to Manchester. He'd face the firebombs rather than stay with the wretched butcher one more day.

As the train rolled into Manchester, the familiar industrial skyline welcomed Hyman home. The red brick buildings and bustling streets were a comforting sight after the desolation of his foster home. His parents barely looked up when he walked through the door, offering little more than a nod as if his return was just another routine part of the day.

Hyman resumed classes at MJS proper, joining a mix of classmates who had either defied evacuation or stayed behind for religious reasons. Gradually, more evacuees returned. Some spoke of loving foster families who even offered to adopt them, while others had endured misery and attempted the fifty-mile journey back to Manchester on foot. Many returned haunted, flinching at touch, victims of unspeakable abuse behind closed doors. Like many children, Hyman rarely spoke of what happened to him in Blackpool.

Months passed, and the day of the entrance exams arrived. True to his own path, Hyman didn't sit for Manchester or Salford Grammar. On Leavers' Day, at fourteen, he left MJS without a backward glance. Done with school but still too young to join up, he spent his days helping at the market stall and knocking about with his corner mates.

One day, Hyman returned home to find his parents and grandfather, Alter Tuchverderber, gathered at the kitchen table. They were discussing a letter from the Home Office internment tribunal, which had just cleared Alter. The British government, under Churchill's order, was rounding up thousands of British residents of German and Austrian descent, predominately Jews, and forcing them into detention camps across the country. The fear was that, in the event of a Nazi invasion, they might form a fifth column and align with Hitler's forces. Detainees from Manchester were sent to the Warth Mills cotton mill factory in Bury, Lancashire, which had been converted into one of the largest internment camps in the country.[10]

In his broken English, Alter had explained to the tribunal that he had fled Tarnów, Poland, to Manchester in the 1890s to escape the boycotts. He served some prison time when he first arrived, but now he lived within the law.[11]

Thankfully, the tribunal had classified Alter and his wife, Rebecca, as Category C, meaning they were not deemed 'enemy aliens' and were spared from internment.[12] They also avoided Category B, which would have confined them to within five miles. Category A went straight to the camps.

Despite Alter's reprieve, a cloud loomed over the family. If a 75-year-old retired grocer who had lived in Manchester for five decades was a potential enemy of the Crown, then the outlook for the rest of the family was bleak.

The streets of Cheetham offered no refuge. One autumn afternoon, as Hyman ran errands, a faint, rhythmic click-clack echoed off the cobblestones. He glanced over his shoulder. A group of men in sharp business suits was closing in, too polished to be mistaken for socialists. The black dress shirts worn by some gave them away – a subtle nod to the now-banned uniform of the British Union of Fascists.

The fascist procession marched past Hyman, exchanging stares. They were headed to the New Hippodrome to hear their leader, Sir Oswald Mosley.[3] The troops paraded past a cordon of local shopkeepers, schoolteachers and housewives lining the pavement. The onlookers extended their right arms in a Nazi salute as the marchers passed. Behind them, supporters and protestors jostled and shoved, tearing at each other's jackets. England was at war.

On the Sunday evening before Christmas 1940, a gentle knock came on the door. Hyman peered through the window and exhaled upon seeing two young female Air Wardens rather than Home Office bureaucrats or Mosley's henchmen. When he swung the door open, the undulating wail of the air raid sirens flooded the house. Neighbors were streaming onto the streets. This was no drill – the German bombers were on their way.

The Wardens pointed Hyman and his family to the nearest shelter, a quarter of a mile away. The family shouted over each other, scrambling to shut the lights, turn off the gas mains, and draw the heavy blackout curtains. They grabbed their winter jackets and sprinted to the shelter, the children's cardboard gas mask boxes bouncing off their thighs.

Overhead, the rhythmic drone of several-hundred planes reverberated like an industrial transformer. The first wave of Luftwaffe flew unscathed through the crisscrossing searchlights, releasing incandescent flares. The new stars hung low in the atmosphere, casting an eerie reddish-white glow over the city's factories, train stations and hospitals, lighting the targets for the incoming Junkers and Heinkel bombers. The flares multiplied until all the illumination fused, turning the evening night into unnatural day.

Hyman and his family sprinted the last few yards to the air raid shelter, tumbled inside and collapsed against the stone wall. All was quiet except for their heaving breaths.

The prolonged silence was broken by the distant staccato of anti-aircraft fire. Faint whistles followed, growing louder and sharper, until they erupted in a ground-shaking quake. Stones and dirt rained on the cowering occupants. Parents huddled over their children as their terrified screams pierced the air.

With heads bent and eyes closed, they prayed silently, their faces lit by dim emergency lights. Distant thuds echoed, each rumble shaking loose bits of masonry that fell softly around them. No one dared to sleep.

When the all-clear signal sounded at dawn, the shelter occupants stirred and coughed, emitting clouds of dust. Hyman rose and climbed out of the shelter exit, squinting against the daylight and acrid smoke. Black ash covered every surface like an eerie, inverted snowfall. On the horizon, an apocalyptic pall hung over central Manchester.[13]

Hyman staggered through the ruins, weaving past smoking debris, gaping craters, and overturned, flaming cars. Sparks rained from parachutes draped over tram cables, showering down onto his head. Every few paces, he doubled over, coughing and retching from the stinging vaporized glass and brick.

Only a few hundred feet from his home, the Victoria Memorial Jewish Hospital nurses' quarters were a jumble of jagged beams and debris. Searchers stood amid the debris in a fugue state, rummaging for trapped survivors and salvageable metal.

Hyman rounded the corner, the broken glass crunching beneath his feet. Amid the devastation, his home stood, miraculously unscathed. He stumbled forward, reaching out with a trembling hand to touch the rough, warm brickwork.

He turned to face the burning skyline. Tears cascaded down his face, blackening as they trailed through the soot on his cheeks. He wept for a city in utter ruins. But he also cried from a secret, rapturous joy at witnessing the dreariness of his old mundane life consumed in a purifying, all-consuming firestorm. Wiping the ash and tears with the backs of his hands, he tilted his head back, basking in a supreme, blissful calm.

Victoria Memorial Jewish Hospital after the Christmas Blitz.

The next day, the *Manchester Evening News* reported the scale of the devastation. The Christmas Blitz left several hundred dead, thousands injured and countless others trapped beneath the wreckage. Dozens of cherished buildings were reduced to meaningless rubble. And then, in a horrifying echo, the bombers returned the following evening.

Over the following days, Hyman learned of the friends who had perished. His once bustling street corner turned desolate. The relentless rain turned the rubble into a muddy quagmire. The smell of smoldering brick and plaster gave way to the ferment of mold and refuse. The city was shrouded in darkness at night from the blackouts. Distant shouts of looting filled the air.

The Rest Centre on Cheetham Hill Road, just around the corner from his house, provided breakfast, shelter and clothing to those left homeless by the bombings. Exhausted people stretched around the building, their faces marked by fatigue and despair.

Within weeks the Luftwaffe struck again – and then again.

By sixteen, Hyman had witnessed his share of devastation. The war scarred every aspect of life, from ruined streets to empty shelves. His old school, the MJS, had been gutted by a fire caused by the bombings.

With his dad's leather goods stall empty due to the clothing rations, Hyman became responsible for supporting the family. No one ever assigned the duty, but it was implied whenever his parents asked if anyone had any milk spaces left in their Junior Ration Book or why the gas bill had not magically disappeared from the kitchen counter.

Seeking some way to support his family, Hyman donned his beige tweed suit and matching trousers and headed to the garment district. Steam plumes billowed from the factory chimneys as workers scuttled in, shoulders hunched, while the proprietors strode past in their ribboned homburg hats. The thought of joining either side of the procession made his stomach turn. There had to be another way.

Thumbing through the 'Clerks, Assistants Wanted' section of the *Manchester Evening News*, he came across an advertisement:

> The Best Foundation for a Future Career. Wise Parents are having sons of school-leaving age trained now for positions as Radio Officers in the Merchant Navy. On joining the service such boys are given officers' status and accommodation, and £21 17s. 6d. per month. A sound investment for your son's future, now and after the war. —Call, 'phone, or write, The Wireless Telegraph College, 25, John Dalton-street, M/c 2. BLA. 7501.[14]

He had also seen the recruitment posters plastered on factory and train station walls. One of the more cinematic ads showed a silhouetted wireless operator encased in a transparent orb, transmitting concentric rings of radio waves out to scenes of electrical towers without wires, tanks bounding up flaming hills, diving bombers and distant battleship convoys, all far beyond the market stalls of Cheetham. The poster read: 'Wireless War: Post office Engineers and Operators are in the forefront of radio developments.'[15]

Radio. Radio was the medium to transmit himself the hell out of Manchester. At sixteen years old, though, he was too young to enlist in the Royal Navy, so the British Merchant Navy (BMN) would have to do. He already knew the 'Guns and Butter' of the BMN. Although considered the poor relation of His Majesty's Royal Navy, the BMN was the lifeline for the Allied world, delivering everything from fresh fruit on reefer boats and unkempt refugees on passenger liners to blockbuster bombs on hulking cargo ships.

Hyman's eyes gleamed as his brilliant escape plan took form. He would attain his 2nd Class Postmaster General Certificate in Wireless Telegraphy and work for Marconi. He'd send his seaman's wage home to his skint family, have grateful women meet him in every port, and help save what was left of the free world.

When Hyman shared his plans with his family, his mother gasped. His father leaned in, forehead creased with concern. His brother laid out the dangers bluntly. Merchant sailors faced the same dangers as the Royal Navy – U-boats prowled the seas in wolfpacks, acoustic mines were scattered across shipping lanes, and patrol aircraft circled everywhere. Without defenses or armor, merchant ships didn't stand a chance. Just look at the *Athenia*. Worse, the Germans deliberately targeted merchant ships as part of their strategy to starve England. U-boat commanders measured their success not in kills but in cargo weight destroyed.

Despite the warnings, Hyman remained resolute. And so, at sixteen, Hyman Tuchverderber enrolled in wireless college with the breathless goal of becoming a wireless operator in the British Merchant Navy.

In early 1942, Hyman arrived early for his first day at the College of International Marine Radio Telegraphic Communication, housed in a stately building on Mosley Street.[16] Sitting in the back of the room, he surveyed his new classmates. They were mostly twice his age – ex-servicemen, landline operators seeking their first sea posting, and engine room ratings training for new roles. The few closer to his age had the pale complexions of ham enthusiasts who loved building their own crystal sets at home. Hyman was surprised to see so many other Hebrews, but it made perfect sense considering, as he saw it, all the codes and secret meanings.

With graying hair and charcoal eyes, the head instructor explained that the curriculum would lead to Special, 2nd Class, and 1st Class PMG Certificates of Proficiency in Wireless Telegraphy. He called the students 'Sparks,' after the occult blue electrical arcs that leapt from the silver-coated spark-gap transmitters used in the original telegraphs.

Morse instruction began, covering both plain language and code. To pass, students needed to achieve 25 words per minute for plain text and 15 for coded groups. They started with distress signals. Each letter symbolized a threat: AAAA an aircraft attack, while MMMM indicated a mine hit and SSSS warned of a submarine attack. During drills, the instructor heightened the urgency by kicking chair legs or dropping books to simulate bulkheads cracking and portholes blowing out.

Next, they learned the Q-codes – three-letter signals that condensed messages, enabling communication between operators without needing a common language. For instance, 'QRK?' asked, 'How do you receive me?' And 'QRV?' meant, 'Are you ready?'[17]

Hyman's classmates quickly mastered the tapping, while he struggled, his shoulder and forearm burning. Pressing on, he refined the minimal flex at his wrist until the rhythmic pattern finally clicked into place.

After transmission came the principles of reception. The class dialed into the Portishead radio station, with its unmistakable raspy GKA call sign and buzzing tone.

Compared to sending, Hyman had a natural flair for receiving. He could hold ten words in his head while touch-typing, then twenty, then thirty, even with increased levels of simulated interference.

Exam day finally arrived for the coveted PMG Certificate. The test covered wireless telegraphy, radiotelephony, and knowledge of rules in practical and written form. Hyman left the exam room with a sigh and a nagging doubt about whether he had passed.

A few weeks later, the results arrived in the post. Hyman ripped open the letter. His expression fell as his eyes scanned down the page. He crumpled into a nearby chair, burying his face in his arms. After months of relentless studying, he had failed the exam miserably.[16]

Hyman composed himself and retreated to his room. There was no way forward without the certificate; it was his only chance to escape. Resolute, he opened his codebook and dove back into his studies.

He sat the PMG exam again ten months later, hoping his hard work would finally pay off. When the telegram from the wireless college arrived, Hyman leaned back and exhaled as he read the words: 'Congratulations success meantime confidential.' It was official – he was going to be a wireless operator.

By spring 1943, Hyman received his Postmaster General's Certificate and his British Radio Officers' Union card. But there was one more hurdle – the medical exam. Given his past battle with tuberculosis, the outcome was far from certain.

When the letter with his medical exam results arrived, he tore it open with trembling hands. His eyes focused on a single word: 'clear.' At last, he had put his childhood illness behind him.

With a clean bill of health, Hyman's next challenge was securing employment. Unlike merchant sailors, who were hired directly by the shipping companies, wireless operators were employed by specialized radio companies, such as Marconi.

Wasting no time, Hyman sent off his applications. Each morning, he sifted through the mail, his pulse quickening as he opened each envelope. Then, one day, a telegram arrived from the radio company. His hands shook as he read the message: he'd been offered a position as 3rd Wireless Operator on the Dutch cargo steamship SS *van Ostade*. She was docked in Leith, Edinburgh, bound for Boston in America. Departure was set for June 1, 1943 – just weeks away.[18]

Hyman ran his thumb along the edge of the telegram, picturing the Dutch crew with their foreign language, hardened habits and the scars of years spent fighting in the war. He took comfort knowing the *van Ostade* was British by birth. She was formerly the HMS *Empire Toiler* before the Ministry of War gifted her to the Dutch government-in-exile encamped at Stratton House in Piccadilly.

Many foreign merchant vessels used British radio operators. Due to security concerns, foreign ships visiting British ports were prohibited from having their nationals in the radio room. Also, boats from occupied countries, like the Netherlands, couldn't train their own operators.

As dawn broke over Manchester, Hyman stood at his family's doorstep, a bulging kit bag slung over his shoulder. His mum adjusted his collar while his dad grasped his shoulder. With one last look, Hyman turned and headed toward the train station.

Upon arriving in Edinburgh, he headed to Leith port. Passing the charred, bombed-out warehouses, he reached the waterfront, where Allied ships lined the docks, their assorted flags whipping and snapping in the wind. Moored among them was the *van Ostade*. Her radio room was conspicuous from the tall aerials and prominent position near the bridge as if raising its hand to be a target. Crew members were loading steel and lumber cargo which was a mixed blessing; in case of a torpedo hit, the steel would drag the ship down, but the timber could serve as makeshift life rafts.

The SS van Ostade.

Tuchverderber	Hyman	1 yr.	3rd W.O.	31/5/43	Leith	-	yes	17	Male	Hebrew
Meyer	Adrianus Anthonis	23 yrs.	Ch.Steward	10/5/43	Leith	-	yes	41	Male	Dutch
Wouters	Martinus Josef	20 yrs.	Ch.Cook	10/5/43	Leith	-	yes	48	Male	Dutch
Dessing	Nicolaas	6 yrs.	2nd Cook	10/5/43	Leith	-	yes	24	Male	Dutch

Hyman's entry in the van Ostade *crew list.*

Hyman reported to the shipping office, where the clerk handed him his onboarding forms. His monthly salary was confirmed at £8.10.0, including a 25 percent Foreign Flag Allowance bonus. It was much less than the wireless college had promised, but still more than he had ever earned. He arranged to send £8 home to his mother each month, leaving himself 10 shillings for shore leave expenses.[18]

The clerk reminded him his wages would stop when his ship went down and wouldn't resume until he pulled himself onto a new one. He smiled, thinking she was joking, until she added, 'There's no pay for recreational swimming – no ship, no wages.'

When the form asked for his religion, he left it blank – perhaps out of concern for anti-Jewish sentiment or a desire to distance himself from his past. With no hesitation, he signed the registration form, securing his position as the *van Ostade*'s 3rd wireless operator.

Reporting dockside for muster roll, Hyman craned his neck at the fair-haired Dutch sailors, their dungarees and wool sweaters covered in oil and tar. The first mate gurgled the call: van den Berg, van Hoeke, van Meurs, van Velsen, van Vliet.[19] When his name was called, Hyman straightened up, lifted his chin and met the stares. The sailors fixed their steel-blue gazes on the newcomer.

Hyman slung his kit bag over his shoulder and leapt on deck, his feet landing with a solid thud. The sailors' piercing eyes followed the foreigner crossing into their world.

The Master, Cornelis Prins, greeted him with a grudging smile. Prins was a battle-hardened mariner with three decades at sea. He introduced Hyman, a first-tripper, to the Chief Wireless Operator, Antonius Johannes van den Blink, who had a scar running diagonally across his face.

Chief Blink showed Hyman to his cabin, which they would share with the 2nd operator. The cabin had two tiers of bunks welded to the heads. Above the top bunks, a maze of hissing and clanking steam pipes ran across the ceiling. The smell was a foul mix of brine, oil, shag tobacco and long-standing piss. Shattered bottles, thighs from torn girlie mags, and soiled laundry were strewn across the grime-caked floor, where a thriving civilization of roaches claimed a corner as their own.

From the cabin, van den Blink led Hyman to the radio shack. They squeezed into the eight-by-ten-foot room, where Blink introduced Hyman to the second operator, Alex Gibson, a fellow Brit, who nodded and smiled. Since the war began, each ship required three Sparks to monitor around the clock for U-boat sightings and distress calls. As the 3rd, Hyman got the least desirable shift.

Thankfully, the equipment labels were in English, a vestige of the ship's British origins. Solid banks of radio equipment lined the walls, with steel tables resting on the floor cabinets. The short-wave and medium-wave transmitters and receivers were in fine shape, as was the emergency crystal receiver. The acid battery needed a clean and top-up, but everything else looked in order.

Chief Blink gave a brief induction. U-boats surface at night and will fire their quadruple-mounted 20mm Flak guns to try to disable the radio room first, cutting off any chance for the Sparks to call in for depth charges. They then torpedo the engine room and the midship to cripple the boat. If the Germans capture or sink the ship, toss all the logs and codebooks into the weighted bag and throw it overboard. Once in the water, breaststroke is best – it helps clear the burning oil and keeps one's head high enough to spot any floating lumber, but not so high as to attract machine-gun fire. In the Atlantic, you have about twenty minutes before you freeze to death.

Hyman nodded, acknowledging his first-day welcome. He sat in the banker-style chair and lowered the height until his feet were flat on the deck. After adjusting the large headphones, he calibrated the receivers. With a light twist, he fine-tuned the gap screw and the tension spring until the key gave the desired kick.

After a few moments, the *van Ostade*'s horn blared, and the deck rumbled beneath his feet. The ship cast off, calling first at Glasgow before escaping into the glistening unknown of the Western Ocean.

2. WAR

Atlantic Ocean and Caribbean Sea, 1943–45

When the *van Ostade* crossed into the Great Quiet Zone, Hyman clicked off the transmitter. Any signal, no matter how brief, could expose their position to the Germans. The only sound was the faint crackle of atmospherics.

Days passed in near silence until one morning, the telegraph burst to life with a distress call. Frantic coordinates and casualty numbers followed. Hyman voice-tubed the message to the bridge. He waited for the rescue instructions, but the only reply was a hollow, reverberating echo. His gaze fell on the soul tally in the logbook. Alone in the swaying radio room, he closed his eyes, straining to catch any hint of a response. But there was only silence as the ship continued its course.

When the next distress stuttered over the telegraph, Hyman hesitated, his hand hovering over the voice tube. This time, he logged the entry without notifying the bridge. And in that moment, the childhood belief in the sanctity of life dissolved into the quiet zone.

Along the voyage, Hyman spent his days decoding Morse and aiding the navigator. In quiet moments, he would press the phones against his ears, straining to catch any BBC interference on the distress frequency. On other days, he would try to identify the operators on the other ships from their 'fists,' the unique rhythm and cadence of their Morse. He attuned to the subtle differences in how they bounced their dots and dragged their dashes. Hyman smiled to himself as he imagined the face of the operator, a fellow Spark he had never met but had a kinship with. It was a small comfort in an otherwise isolated role.

Meals were always a dreaded affair. Radio operators were a relatively new addition to ships, and their place in the ship's hierarchy was far from clear. Moreover, since they were employed by the radio company rather than the shipping company, they weren't considered 'company men.'[1]

Hyman scanned the galley, tray clutched tightly in his hands, searching for an open seat. Deck officers exuded a confident professionalism, but the engineers' technical discussions were always more interesting. He was caught between two worlds, belonging to neither.

He slipped into an empty spot at the corner of the table, grabbed his fork, and pushed the unappetizing food around: pork loaf with the consistency of plasticine, carrot puree flecked with black metallic shards, fruit mess reeking of rubbing alcohol.

While he picked at his meal, Hyman strained to make sense of the incomprehensible, throat-clearing babble filling the mess. He closed one eye, hoping to catch any similarities to Yiddish, but the effort only deepened his sense of otherness.

On lucky days, Hyman's mess time overlapped with the other two Brits – James Swinton, a cheerful cook's boy with a knack for spinning outlandish tales, and Ronald Dennis, a quiet but steady ordinary seaman. Between bites, they would tease James about the rank food or natter about the small trinkets they'd brought for the eager ladies waiting in Boston.

On June 8, 1943, the *van Ostade* joined the Outbound North Slow convoy ONS-10.[2] Feeder convoys joined them along the route until the armada swelled to dozens of ships stretching out to the horizon.

Five tense days into the voyage, southwest of Iceland, the telegraph erupted with urgency: a Cobra escort plane had spotted a surfaced U-boat. Hyman steadied his hand, transcribed the message and alerted the bridge.

The plane dove for the kill, engines roaring. Under heavy flak, the aircraft dropped to 100 feet and released four depth charges. Thunderous explosions sounded, sending geysers into the air. The message came back: target destroyed.[3]

Hyman shot up, his chair clattering to the deck. The electric hum of the radio pulsed through the room. He stood there, catching his breath, the adrenaline coursing through his veins. The rush flooded him; he craved the next wave already.

On his next shift, a Liberator bomber took out another U-boat. Hyman stared at the dials, his fingers drumming on the desk. The rush was fading, leaving him restless, wondering what else was out there.

On June 30, 1943, after two grueling weeks at sea, the *van Ostade* cleared the danger zone and sailed into Boston Harbor. Hyman and the crew disembarked onto the bustling dock, filled with rumbling flatbeds, blaring whistles and towering cranes loading crates larger than cars.

Clad in filthy dock clothes, the crew emerged from the navy yard into the sunlit streets of downtown Boston. Women in shirtwaist dresses strolled by, arms linked. Sunbeams glinted off a supersized car as it passed, swing music drifting from the open window.

It was surreal and alien to stand in a city untouched by war. The colonial red-brick buildings bore no shrapnel scars or scorch marks. This intact, carefree world was oblivious to the horrors back home – U-boats, internment camps, Blackshirts, and air raid sirens were all a distant reality. For the first time in years, he was free.

With only ten days of shore leave, Hyman dove into everything Boston could offer a seventeen-year-old sailor abroad for the first time. The Terrace Room at the Silver Dollar featured nonstop jazz, dancing girls, and 'the longest bar in the world' which seemed to stretch to Boston Harbor. The night began with a redheaded colleen singing Irish standards. For the intermission, a brilliant pony who graduated from MIT did arithmetic with its hoof. Up to the last call, an enchanting pair of white and black girls dressed as piano keys harmonized duets on an upright.

Over the next week, the crew tore through every taproom, servicemen's club, and cabaret, from the Oval Room at Copley Plaza to Buddies Club on Boston Common. Yet through the sloshing pints and rowdy chants, Hyman remained on the periphery, distanced by his youth, slight build, swarthy complexion and lack of Dutch. There were no overt sneers or insults, just an invisible separation that no amount of alcohol or laughter could breach.

Breaking away from the crew one night, Hyman stumbled through the North End on his way back to the harbor. Neon lights flickered above Italian bakeries, still bustling with late-night customers. Golden light spilled from Irish pubs onto the cobbles, where men hunched over their pints. From side streets came the clatter of plates and bursts of laughter from Polish restaurants.

America, with its swirl of foreign voices and customs, was a far cry from the suffocating traditions of British life. Here, he could finally sever the ties to his past and reinvent himself. He pledged that if he survived the war, he'd return to America and begin again.

With only a few days of shore leave remaining, the crew took in *Heroes Without Uniforms*, a film starring Humphrey Bogart as an Italian-American captain that showcased the bravery of the American merchant navy: "Through the perilous Atlantic steams the grim gray armada on whose battle-scarred decks ride the precious cargos for victory that must get through, and dedicating their lives to getting them through are the valiant men of our merchant marine." The movie ended with a stirring speech from President FDR, commending the merchant marines for their courage and sacrifice. The audience erupted in applause and whistles. In that moment, all their sacrifices felt justified.

The next day, the *van Ostade* cast off and returned to Plymouth, England. At port, Hyman informed Captain Prins he wished to leave the ship, citing insufficient shore leave. He wanted to see more of the world before he got machine-gunned in a pool of oil. The captain obliged and noted in Hyman's service record, 'wishes to sign off, 10 days' leave is too few.'[4]

Hyman turned to the Norwegian fleet, attracted by their modern ships and generous shore leave. It didn't take long for him to secure a position with Nortraship as a 2nd *Telegrafist* aboard the MS *Cypria*.[5] She was docked in Liverpool, set to depart for St John, New Brunswick.[6]

Arriving at Liverpool station, he stepped off the train into a war-torn landscape. The station walls were cracked and charred, bearing the scars of relentless bombing and strafing. Outside, the city was a wasteland of half-collapsed buildings and scorched streets.

MS Cypria.

After hailing a black cab to the dock, Hyman watched the city go by as the cabbie maneuvered around water-filled craters and fallen beams, the remnants of the Luftwaffe's wrath. Block after block blurred past, each stretch revealing more destruction.

At port, Hyman found half the berths reduced to piles of twisted metal and warehouses stripped to skeletal frames. But amid the chaos, the *Cypria* stood apart. Cabins had been added on her boat deck to accommodate ten gunners, and the cement blocks around her wheelhouse and charthouse had been replaced by sturdier asphalt ones. She was ready for the journey.

On deck, Hyman was greeted by Capitan Syvertsen and the 1st wireless, Ivar Moe. Scanning the rest of the crew, Hyman was again one of the youngest and one of only a handful of foreigners. Moe introduced him to the 3rd operator, James Arthur Cameron, who, thankfully, was a fellow Manc. James offered a few tips, warning him about the ship's brandy and explaining that 'Sparks' in Norwegian was 'ga-NEE-stehr.'

The *Cypria* pushed off from Liverpool on August 27, 1943. In his first days at sea, Hyman kept to himself, much like the youngest child in a large family. He spent long hours in the radio room, absorbed in his duties. The constant listening and solitude only deepened his natural reserve.

After four uneventful weeks at sea, the *Cypria* slipped from convoy ON-199 and arrived at St John, New Brunswick, where she loaded her cargo of newsprint and steel. After a few days, she pushed off back to Liverpool, and joined dozens of merchant ships and military escorts in the fast convoy HX-259.[7] Its sister convoy, SC-143, sailed alongside further north.

On the morning of October 7, 1943, while on the return trip to Liverpool, Hyman received a radio message from Western Approaches Command (WAC), the Royal Navy unit responsible for defending British vessels along the Atlantic shipping routes. WAC had decrypted intelligence that the *Rossbach* wolfpack

HX convoy gathering in Nova Scotia.

of U-boats was stationed on a reconnaissance line at the western edge of the Greenland Air Gap, the undefended area of the Atlantic out of reach of Allied air cover. The *Rossbach* had orders from the U-boat supreme command, BdU: on first sight of the Allied convoy, the wolfpack should 'OPERATE AGAINST IT AT TOP SPEED.'

Only hours later, the U-boats spotted Hyman's sister convoy, SC-143. BdU ordered the *Rossbach* wolfpack to chase them at flank speed and prevent them from escaping: 'THERE IS ONLY A SHORT SPACE LEFT TO EASTWARD.' Dread filled the *Cypria* as the men became aware they were the prey.

With the U-boats closing in, the British Admiralty used SC-143 as bait to stall the wolfpack, providing Hyman's convoy with a precious window to escape. To bolster SC-143's defenses, the Admiralty dispatched the 10th Support Group, including the destroyers *Musketeer*, *Oribi* and *Orwell*, and the free Polish destroyer *Orkan*. Hyman's convoy was ordered to reroute south and then try to flee east.[8]

The *Cypria* surged forward at full speed, with the wolfpack closing in. The first torpedo wake streaked past the convoy; a geyser of water erupted astern of the escort destroyer *Orkan*. When the spray settled, the ship emerged unscathed – the torpedo had detonated harmlessly off her wake.

Dots and dashes escalated into a cacophony of distress signals, and 'who' and 'where' and QRT/pipe the fuck down. Amid the chaos, two more acoustic torpedoes detonated, this time striking the *Orkan*. Fires exploded on the bridge and funnel, sending thick black balls of smoke billowing into the sky. The Polish destroyer foundered stern first.

With the main convoys nowhere in sight, BdU realized the ships were a diversion. The German commands came in: 'THE DESTROYERS ARE A DECOY GROUP.' 'MUST BE THE ESCORT OF AN EASTBOUND CONVOY. CONTINUE THE SEARCH IN WIDE SWEEPS.' Hyman's convoy continued fleeing east with the wolfpack in close pursuit.

Allied aircraft spotted the *Rossbach* and pummeled them with depth charges and machine gun fire. The bombardment staggered the wolfpack's advance long enough for the *Cypria* to escape.[9]

When the *Cypria* achieved a safe distance, Hyman released his grip from the corners of the desk. The loss count arrived over the telegraph: nearly 200 souls perished on the *Orkan*, marking the largest tragedy in Polish Navy history. Many of them hailed from eastern Poland like Hyman's family. At just seventeen, he had survived his third brush with death.[10]

In January 1944, the *Cypria* returned from Liverpool to Philadelphia. Though the battles were behind him, fate had other trials in store. During shore leave, Hyman slipped on the winter ice and fractured his right ankle. The injury required several weeks of hospitalization and led to severe ankylosis, causing his ankle bones to fuse.[11] For the rest of his life he would walk with a distinctive spring-like gait, as if propelled by an unseen force.

With his ankle on the mend, Hyman rejoined the British Merchant Navy in the spring of 1944, securing a position aboard the Norwegian tanker *Østhav* and, later, the *Titania* and *Havprins*.[5,12] He spent the next several months sailing throughout the Caribbean, South America and Africa, nursing his ankle in the tropical warmth. On shore leave, he swam in the crystal-clear waters of Guantanamo Bay, strolled through the vibrant streets of Cristóbal in Panama, and admired the colonial architecture of Puerto La Cruz, Venezuela. He voyaged along the African coast, visiting the golden beaches of Lobito in Portuguese Angola, the white sands of Takoradi in the British Gold Coast, and the raging waterfalls of Matadi in the Belgian Congo.[13,14] By eighteen, he had seen more of the world than most would in several lifetimes.

While on the *Østhav* in October 1944, Hyman received the terrifying news from LGB/Bergen Radio: the Royal Air Force had bombed Laksevåg, a neighborhood in Bergen, resulting in the death of 200 civilians, including dozens of elementary school children. The bombing was only the latest Allied devastation of Norway. Earlier, Bristol Beaufighters had sunk a defenseless Norwegian passenger ship, killing 75 civilians, and a fleet of American Flying Fortresses had bombed the hydroelectric plant in Rjukan, taking the lives of 20 Norwegians.

For the Norwegian sailors, the knowledge that their fleet was carrying bombs to devastate their own country only deepened their anguish. They had to convince themselves the bombs were destined for Berlin and not Bergen to carry on with their duties.

Hyman shared their sorrow, grieving in silence for his Norwegian crewmates. He understood all too well the agony of one's homeland being bombed into ruins. But he kept his condolences to himself, unsure how to express his sympathy.

Upon returning to New York in November 1944, Hyman received an unexpected letter from home. His father had legally changed the family name from Tuchverderber to Derber and Hyman's first name to Harold.[15]

The name change was long overdue. 'Tuchverderber' had always sounded ludicrously Germanic, while his new name was simple and distinguished. With this change, he could finally break with the old world and adopt a modern identity as Harold Derber.

It was a fitting change with which to enter a new era. During his layover in New York, the *Times* headline announced, "THE WAR IN EUROPE IS ENDED! SURRENDER IS UNCONDITIONAL; V-E WILL BE PROCLAIMED TODAY." As luck would have it, he had secured a prime spot for the most fabulous party the world had ever seen.

On May 8, 1945, more than a million people packed into a rain-soaked Times Square to celebrate Europe's victory. Patriotic songs blared over honking horns as revelers climbed onto car rooftops. Ticker tape and office paper rained down from skyscrapers, sprinkling partygoers' shoulders and hair.

Wild street parties raged for days, celebrating years of sacrifice coming to an end. But as the revelry waned, the reality set in that although Europe was victorious, the war was not over. Derber's shore leave drew close, and the merchant navy beckoned again.

In June 1945, Derber rejoined his fellow sailors aboard the Norwegian tanker *Havprins* bound for Sheerness, England.[16] They celebrated the Allied triumph and the prospect of returning to a free Norway. Yet beneath their joy lay a deep grief. The Axis had killed one in eight Norwegian merchant seamen, a casualty rate almost unmatched by any armed service. Amid the shared sorrow, Derber was grateful simply to be alive.

Returning to New York in August, Derber sat in his midtown hotel room as British Prime Minister Clement Attlee announced on the BBC, "Japan has today surrendered. The last of our

War

MT Havprins.

enemies is laid low ... Peace has once again come to the world. Let us thank God for this great deliverance and his mercies. Long live the King." The war was finally over.

That night, Derber stood in Times Square for the V-J Day celebration, surrounded by a swirling crowd. Confetti fluttered through the air, caught in the headlights of passing cars, and glasses clinked as laughter echoed. He moved deliberately, hands tucked in his pockets, fingers tracing the seams of his coat, his shoulders brushing against strangers. He stepped aside to let a group of pissed servicemen pass by. The city around him danced and shouted, but the cheers reached him muffled, as if from far away. Faces blurred in the electric glow, yet Hyman's gaze remained fixed ahead, distant and unfocused. The war was over. The world had changed – and so had he.

3. QUESTIONABLE VENTURES

The World, 1946–61; Israel, 1948–1950s

In April 1946, Derber stepped off the *Havprins* into a Liverpool scarred by the war. He navigated the pocked cobblestones to the shipping office, where the clerk took his name and, after some rummaging, handed him his two service medals – a 1939–45 Star and an Atlantic Star.[1] With a shrug, the clerk noted that Derber didn't qualify for a Merchant Navy lapel pin because he hadn't served on a British ship during the war. If he was set on acquiring one of those 'Monkey Nuts' trinkets, he could always find one at a surplus store.

He emerged into the cold drizzle and boarded the bus to the flophouse. He reached into his pocket for the reduced veteran's fare, but the driver waved him off, pointing out that he didn't have a veteran's badge. Derber fished for the extra coins, attracting stares from the Royal Navy officers in their immaculate white uniforms adorned with rows of clinking, colored medals. Derber paid the full fare and found a seat at the back.

As the bus rattled over Liverpool's battered roads, Derber watched the passing ruins and questioned why he'd even come back. England held nothing for him. He would stay on with the British Merchant Navy, and avoid the country's postwar desolation.

In December 1947, Derber reported to the shipping office for his next assignment. Much to his surprise, he had been promoted to radio officer at the exceptionally young age of 21,[2] entitling him the same status and provisions as a deck officer.

Stepping into the supply room, he shed his dock clothes and slipped on the iconic midnight-blue double-breasted reefer jacket. He flicked his sleeves, flashing the golden, wavy cuff braids that signaled his new title as an R/O. After clipping on his service bars, he adjusted his cap, bearing the stylized monogram of his radio company surrounded by an embroidered laurel wreath. He grabbed his kit and stepped aboard his next ship, the Norwegian DS *Nandi*.[2]

Life in the peace-time Merchant Navy was tranquil. He passed his hours in the radio room, using his abundant spare time to earn his Master Mariner license, entitling him to the title of captain, and navigator's certificate. (Years later, he would boast of having been the youngest certified navigator in the "British Navy.")[3]

In the years after the war, the repetitive click of teletype gradually replaced the magic of Morse. Automated direction finders took over from radio compasses, and improved cranes and derricks cut down on shore leave. Air freight competition made the Merchant Navy efficient and predictable, while routine traffic reports replaced U-boat sightings and depth-charge instructions.

Derber spent his days flipping through dog-eared paperbacks he'd read countless times. He would transcribe weather reports predicting endless clear skies and tap out radiograms to crew members' families about home repairs and alimony payments.

While Derber waited for his life to begin again, half a world away a new nation was being born. On May 14, 1948, shortly after the British Mandate over Palestine expired, Israel proclaimed statehood. The following day, an alliance of five Arab nations invaded the nascent state, igniting the 1948 Arab–Israeli War. The UN and the US and British governments imposed an arms embargo on Israel and the neighboring Arab states, hoping to drive a stalemate and a negotiated peace.

Massively outgunned, the newly formed Israeli government dedicated itself to building a national arsenal, despite the international arms embargoes. What followed was one of the largest illegal arms smuggling operations in world history.

To build its fledgling navy, Israel called on sailors from across the Jewish diaspora. Among the volunteers were large numbers of British seamen – both Jews and gentiles – who ultimately made up more than half of the foreign recruits. To avoid the legal repercussions of serving in a foreign military, these volunteers adopted pseudonyms and false nationalities. Their mission was to outrun the arms blockade maintained by the British Royal Navy – including officers they had served alongside only a few years earlier.

Responding to the call, Derber volunteered to fight in the War of Independence.[4] He was not likely motivated by lofty ideals such as Zionism or anti-Imperialism but rather by the exhilaration of navigating treacherous waters once again. The opportunity to outsmart the condescending Royal Navy squids was a bonus.

British sailors such as Derber volunteered in the Israeli navy by visiting a Jewish Agency office, like the one in Russell Square, London. Following a brief ten-minute induction, the agency sent them to the Jewish Agency headquarters in Paris, where they were assigned a pseudonym, a service number and instructions for the next stage of the journey. Radio operators went to either the covert radio school in Marseille or directly to the front line in Israel.[5]

On October 12, 1948, Derber stepped off the plane in Haifa and was greeted by the acrid smell of burning wood and the hurried footsteps of soldiers.[6] Without pause, he joined Israel's fledgling radio operator corps, the Gideonim. His mastery of wireless operations and navigation made him indispensable to the clandestine network. The outsider had now come in.

The secret group was initially formed by the provisional Israeli government to illegally smuggle Jewish refugees into Mandatory

Palestine in defiance of the British immigration blockade. Now, the Gideonim coordinated the illegal arms shipments through the blockade, carefully avoiding detection by Arab, British and American patrol boats.[7]

Israel's antiquated ships lacked proper radio cabins, so Gideonim operators would rig a suitcase radio in a concealed nook of the ship. If capture seemed imminent, they were instructed to swap frequency crystals, hide the transmitter, jettison the codebooks and blend in with the refugees on board.[7]

With the help of the Gideonim, Israel's newly formed navy successfully smuggled thousands of tons of surplus World War II weapons, many sourced from illegal stockpiles in the United States and France, and Nazi surplus in Czechoslovakia, including Mauser rifles still marked with Nazi insignia. The illegal firepower was critical in shifting the tide of the war and forcing the Arab states to the negotiation table. After a bitter conflict that raged for over a year, in 1949 Israel signed a series of armistice agreements with its Arab neighbors, bringing the war to an end.

Although British volunteer sailors played a crucial role in the War of Independence, many, like Derber, went unrecognized due to the illegal nature of their service and signed secrecy agreements. The official list of the Gideonim shows no non-Israelis. While Derber's family confirmed he served in the War of Independence,[4] extensive archive searches found no record of his service. All traces of Derber's role had vanished like a mirage on the Mediterranean horizon.

With the war over, Derber lingered in Israel, captaining ships under the Mediterranean sun. He took on various maritime assignments that remain shrouded in mystery. In his future US visa application, he would simply mention that he had "business interests" in Israel at the time, while a US report more cryptically stated that he had "captained Israeli vessels in possibly questionable ventures."[8]

With Israel's political landscape stabilizing, the euphoria of being part of its birth began to ebb for Derber, replaced by a simmering restlessness. In search of his next adventure, he left Israel and returned to the British Merchant Navy.

At the Merchant Navy shipping office in the early 1950s, Derber braced himself for questions about his illegal foreign service. However, the clerk barely glanced at him, stamped his papers and welcomed him back as if he had never left.

Weeks stretched into months without any scrutiny of his illicit activities. There were no abrupt knocks on his door from the War Office, no stern summonses to the Board of Trade, nothing. The government had more pressing concerns than the moonlighting activities of a merchant mariner. The Cold War was on the horizon.

As tensions grew between the Western powers and the Soviet Union, new forces were at work in the merchant navy. The demand for blackmarket commodities, like oil and weapons, exploded. With its far-reaching routes and adaptable sailors, the Merchant Navy became a vital player in moving these contraband goods across borders, supplying those willing to pay the price.

For those merchant seamen willing to take the risk, the rewards were undeniable. Sailors who had once scraped together coins for a flophouse bed were now buying rounds for the entire crew. The allure of fast money and the thrill of danger called to Derber. He was no stranger to arms smuggling after his service for Israel. But whether that was a one-time necessity, a moral stand, or the gateway to something darker was undecided. All he needed was a nudge.

That shove came in September 1949 when the UK Chancellor of the Exchequer made a stunning announcement: crushed under wartime debt, the British government would de-peg the pound from the dollar. Overnight, the pound's value plummeted 30 percent. For most Britons, the devaluation was a financial shock; for merchant seamen like Derber, whose wages were paid in pounds but expenses in foreign currencies, it was devastating. His paycheck had effectively been cut by a third. Already struggling to make ends meet, Derber now faced financial ruin.

With money running out, he had no choice: he had to turn to illegal smuggling to survive. The decision would devastate his family if they ever found out about it, but it wasn't a sin if there was a war, and the world was now constantly at war.

AT FIRST, IT WAS as simple as accepting assignments on ships carrying contraband. In March 1952, he took an assignment with the North American Shipping and Trading Company, which was covertly smuggling fuel to the Soviet bloc, brazenly defying US export controls.[9] His fledgling trafficking career, however, suffered an early setback.

On returning to New York in May 1952, just as he was planning his next illegal venture, Derber received a knock on his Bronx apartment door. Standing in the hallway were Immigration and Naturalization Service (INS) officers. They informed him that he had violated the terms of his seaman's status. Within days, he was on a bus, deported to Canada.[10] Undeterred, he slipped back into New York two months later posing as a tourist.

Rumors swirled among his seafaring comrades about untapped gold and diamond deposits in the remote interior of South America. In February 1954, he assembled a makeshift prospecting team comprising two fellow Brits and an American. They journeyed to the frontier land at the border between Brazil and British Guiana,[11] where they made promising discoveries of small gemstones.[12]

Their fortune, however, was short-lived. Local authorities apprehended the group, confiscating their mining equipment and fining Derber and his associates. Additionally, authorities accused them of being communist agents.[13, 14] Despite the setback, Derber continued to return to Brazil for prospecting, making one such trip in March 1957.[15] The tale that he owned gold and diamond mines in the country would follow him throughout his life, as would the suspicion that he was a Soviet spy.

Returning to America, Derber discovered an immigration loophole that allowed foreign seamen such as himself to stay in America indefinitely as long as they were seeking a vessel assignment. Throughout the mid-1950s, he had his contacts in the shipping industry mislead the INS with letters of support claiming he was actively looking for a position but unable to find one due to labor disputes or business slowdowns. Settling in the Bronx and Brooklyn, he listed the British Consulate in New York as his official address to further avoid the INS. This ruse let him remain in the country but with the constant fear of being discovered and forcibly deported.

Derber's entry visa to Brazil.

From time to time, he would bolster his immigration status by taking legitimate shipping assignments such as on the *Galloway*,[16] *Ocean Skipper*,[17] *Texita*,[18] and *Lomaland*.[19] On a voyage aboard the *Texita* in January 1957, Derber traveled to Cienfuegos, Cuba, the Pearl of the South. The dock at Cienfuegos teemed with stevedores and porters grunting as they heaved sacks of freshly cured tobacco and raw sugar from the inland plantations onto fishing skiffs. Walking beyond the dockside bars and boat repair shops, Derber arrived in the heart of the barrio. Overcrowded shanty slums, cobbled together from scavenged wood, corrugated metal and cardboard, spilled onto the streets. Refuse and sewage trickled through the narrow, unpaved alleys. Barefoot, gaunt children clothed in rags roamed amid the squalor.

Just beyond the barrio, the idyllic Parque José Martí offered a scene from another world. French Neoclassical buildings flanked the streets, with their grand columns, intricate pediments and ornate balustrades. Landscaped boulevards were lined with royal palms, fine restaurants and boutique shops. The warm breeze carried the lilting chatter of lovers and the well-to-do, who discussed sailing and dinner plans.

Yet amid the bustle of the park, passers-by exchanged fearful whispers about the terrifying advances of the rebels in the mountains. The revolutionaries had executed a daring raid on a small army barracks, seizing the outpost with only a few dozen weapons. This marked their first military victory and equipped them with the firepower needed to propagate their dangerous ideology. The name of their leader, Castro – a privileged lawyer turned fervent revolutionary – hung in the air, portending the change that was to come.

Derber was making career changes of his own. In 1958, after fifteen years of meager pay and deplorable conditions, he left the British Merchant Navy to pursue his criminal career full-time. No longer content with a life of monotony and limited rewards, he set his sights on a far more lucrative and dangerous path in America.

Questionable Ventures

Ironically, Derber's first opportunity came from his former enemy. After the war, Germany was awash with surplus weapons, and revolutionaries and dictators worldwide were willing to pay top dollar. Derber reached out to his underworld contacts to find potential buyers. It wasn't long before he received a response from an unexpected source: the authoritarian government of the Dominican Republic.[8, 20]

Months passed in a blur of coded messages, secret negotiations and tense meetings brokered through a daisy chain of shadowy intermediaries. Derber had mastered the delicate art of maintaining distance. But beneath the surface, every deal carried the unspoken fear that it could all unravel in an instant.

And then, without warning, the Dominican arms deal collapsed. Whether triggered by paranoia, betrayal or unseen interference, the reasons were irrelevant. The deal was dead, leaving Derber scrambling for his next venture.

He turned next to business fraud, purchasing 75,000 acres of Tennessee timberland for $50,000, with $5,000 in cash and the remainder in notes. However, he failed to pay the first note and subsequently declared he would not honor the payments. Furthermore, he took corporate records and books to his apartment, threatening to name himself president through a resolution. He refused to return the records or make further payments and allegedly planned to sell the land unlawfully in England.[21] But he failed to pay the first installment and soon declared he had no intention of honoring the remaining debt. He then removed the company's books and records to his apartment, threatening to pass a resolution appointing himself president. He refused to return the documents or make further payments, and allegedly planned to sell the land illegally in England. Still lacking key paperwork, he plotted to break into the company's headquarters on Broad Street, in the heart of the city's financial district.

While casing the building from Battery Park, Derber stumbled upon the Wireless Operators Monument surrounded by poplar trees. The somber granite cenotaph bore an inscription surrounded by an engraved garland of seashells and foliage: "Erected in memory of wireless officers lost at sea at the post of duty." Derber read the names etched into the stone. He sat on the reflection bench, closing his eyes to pay his respects to the fallen seamen and then to mentally prepare for the break-in.

One evening in May 1960, Derber bribed the cleaning staff with sweets and cigarettes to gain access to the top floors. Under the cover of dim office lighting, he rummaged through files, drawers and cabinets, intent on finding all the documents for the lumber property.[22] Over the following weeks, he repeated the process, carefully stealing only the documents he needed, including maps and deeds. When the company president discovered Derber's theft and reported him to the New York Police Department and INS, no action was taken, leaving Derber surprisingly unscathed.

For his next venture in 1961, Derber delved into the world of stock fraud. With America having recently launched its first satellite, investor interest in satellite technology companies had reached a frenzy. Seizing the opportunity, through an unregistered private offering, Derber illegally acquired a substantial stake in a purported satellite technology company, American Orbitronics.[23, 24]

The Securities and Exchange Commission (SEC), the federal agency responsible for regulating securities law, cited the company for several violations, including failing to disclose the private share sale and making misleading statements.[25, 26] Despite its name, the company had no connection to the satellite industry. It was an elaborate facade designed to capitalize on the space race fever.

The commission filed an injunction against Derber and a dozen other defendants, including the company's executives. The federal court prohibited Derber from selling his shares, implying that he was more likely a perpetrator than a victim in the fraud.[27]

Recovering from the SEC fraud case, Derber unwound in New York's dimly lit bars. Each evening, he drifted from one crowded venue to the next, feeling the pressure ease with each drink. Through the haze of one such evening, a raspy voice cut through the noise – an unmistakable Hebrew accent. The voice belonged to a tall man, impeccably dressed. Recognizing a kindred spirit, Derber struck up a conversation. The man introduced himself as Ray Adiel. He was a former military pilot from Tel Aviv who, like Derber, had fought in the War of Independence.[28] He now led a quieter life, teaching Hebrew in Dobbs Ferry.

They settled side by side at the weathered wooden bar, speaking with the ease that only veterans of the same war can share. Derber, who had long kept his involvement in the war locked away, found an unexpected solace in finally having someone to confide in. Over glasses of rye whiskey and Old Fashioned cocktails, they toasted *l'chaim* to having created a new nation in their twenties. As the night deepened and the bar fell quiet, they drew closer, bound by memories few others truly understood.

Ray Adiel.

When the bartender made the last call, Derber and Adiel rose from their stools and stepped into the cold night. They clapped each other on the back and promised to meet again soon, both sensing it was only the beginning of a rare, lifelong friendship.

Over time, Derber and Adiel became close as they enjoyed the bustling social scene of early 1960s New York. Morningside Heights became their playground, offering jazz at the West End Bar, coffee at the Hungarian Pastry Shop and double features at the Thalia Theater. Derber eventually moved into Adiel's apartment at 519 West 121st Street on the Upper West Side.[29] The building's name, "Miami", etched above the entrance in golden Old English font, promised a sunnier life full of warmth and new beginnings.

Their shared love of film soon sparked a creative collaboration. Adiel befriended a young film student aspiring to become a director. Eager to support his ambitions, Adiel and Derber produced his first two films: a voyeuristic sexploitation short and a softcore cowboy Western. The student's name was Francis Ford Coppola.[30]

With ambitions of his own, Derber set his sights on building a new career in America. He applied for a US residence visa, taking advantage of the generous quota for British nationals. It remained unclear how the break-in, fraud charges and deportation might affect his application. Only time would tell if his checkered past would scupper his plans.

On his visa application, he said he planned to "take up employment in engineering or radio." Where the form asked about any past arrests, Derber provided a vague, legalistic explanation of his apprehension in Guiana, suggesting a jurisdictional misunderstanding rather than facing accusations of illegal mining and being a communist spy.[31]

Just as he had on his Merchant Navy registration, he scrubbed all references to his Jewish identity. Manchester Jews' School became "Derby Street School" and the Jewish Lads' Brigade the "Lads Army Brigade." He may have concealed his Jewish identity to avoid antisemitism or ensure his eligibility under the British quota. Or maybe he was severing ties with values that no longer served him.

Despite his omissions and obfuscations, he managed to secure glowing character references. One friend wrote, "I regard Mr. Derber as a person of good standing and think very highly of his morals and abilities ... Mr. Derber is in full agreement with the principles for which this Country stands."[32]

PART II

4. THE THREE-MILE LIMIT

Miami, 1962

In late 1961, Derber's coveted US visa arrived. A few months later, he left New York for Miami, lured by the Magic City's thriving underworld and prosperous cruise-ship industry. His friend Adiel joined him, equally enticed by the sun-drenched beaches and carefree lifestyle.

However, their timing could not have been worse. The failed Bay of Pigs invasion in the spring had raised tensions between the U.S. and Cuba, casting a shadow over the region. Just a month after Derber and Adiel arrived, President Kennedy escalated the crisis by slapping a trade embargo on Cuba. Tourists avoided Miami in droves, fearing the Cold War might spill into the Caribbean.

Never one to let a crisis go to waste, Derber spotted the opportunity of a lifetime: luxury cruise liners were selling at a fraction of their value. He pieced together financing from a stock swindler and a dubious business loan and, along with Adiel, signed a multi-million-dollar charter with Canaveral International for a magnificent cruise ship, the MS *Calypso Liner*.[1-5]

It was a personal triumph. Only a few years earlier, Derber had been toiling on a rusted tramp ship, and now, at 36, he had a luxury cruise liner under his command.

Derber wasted no time installing slot machines on the ship,[6] taking full advantage of the lucrative loophole that permitted

MS Calypso Liner.

gambling in international waters beyond the three-mile limit. That thin, invisible boundary between law and lawlessness was a line he navigated with ease.

He swapped his sailor's reefer jacket for a tailored gray pinstripe suit, geometric art deco tie and white pocket square, folded into a triangle. His wavy, dark hair was groomed in the executive contour style with a subtle side part. He cultivated his moustache into a refined pencil line reminiscent of the iconic leading men of the Hollywood Golden Age, such as Errol Flynn and Clark Gable. Black, circular sunglasses and a dark ring completed his debonair look.

Assuming the role of a guide to the British Caribbean, Derber would stand at the top of the gangway to welcome the passengers. When guests complimented his cultivated demeanor, Derber would attribute it to his background as a former "British Navy" captain, conveniently omitting the merchant part. He toured them through the vibrant seaquarium an the exclusive Paris Freeport

The Three-Mile Limit

boutique. The dining salon served delicacies like conch chowder, crab, and callaloo, while the cocktail lounge poured Bajan Rum Punch Mamas and Cuban Breezes. The Bahamian house band, wearing oversized straw beachcomber hats, played lively goombay music.[7] Special entertainment featured performances by Tony Bennett, the Ardells, Miss Universe contestants, and black-tie fundraising events.[8]

Despite the ship's luxury, few tourists were visiting Miami, still fearful of the looming Cold War in the Caribbean. To lure more customers, Derber placed ads in the *Miami Herald*, promising an "Exciting Sea Voyage to a land so near, so foreign, so British! Cast off your cares!!! To Bimini. A foreign land of native charm some 50 miles from the Florida coast, a sun-drenched tropical isle, nestled in the crystal sea at the eastern edge of the blue Gulf Stream."[9] Other ads promoted the ship's "weekly moonlight cruises to nowhere (beyond the three-mile limit)."

Passengers began trickling in. First came the casual gamblers, followed by the high rollers and, eventually, the Miami mob, notably Angelo 'The Gentle Don' Bruno, a Philadelphia boss from the Gambino crime family.[10]

It wasn't long before the mob's presence attracted the FBI's attention. Bureau agents noticed that most passengers on the *Calypso* had complimentary tickets and no luggage, suggesting they were more interested in the slot machines than in a romantic Bahamian getaway. One agent remarked dryly, "There was nothing to observe in Bimini but two old hotels and a straw market."[6] The report wasn't far from the truth. North Bimini had one road, a few bait shacks, some calypso joints and curio shops, and beaches on a par with Miami's.

Although gambling was legal once the ship crossed into international waters, the agents saw an opportunity. By keeping the *Calypso* under surveillance, they could monitor the movements of the Miami mob.

Still struggling to lure passengers, Derber placed a help wanted ad in the *Miami Herald* seeking "Young ladies (2) attractive, smart" to serve as onboard entertainers. Soon enough, two stunning, red-headed identical twins – Sari and Susan Lesley – strolled into the *Calypso* ticket office. They were hired on the spot.

Susan and Sari Lesley, the 'Calypso Twins.'

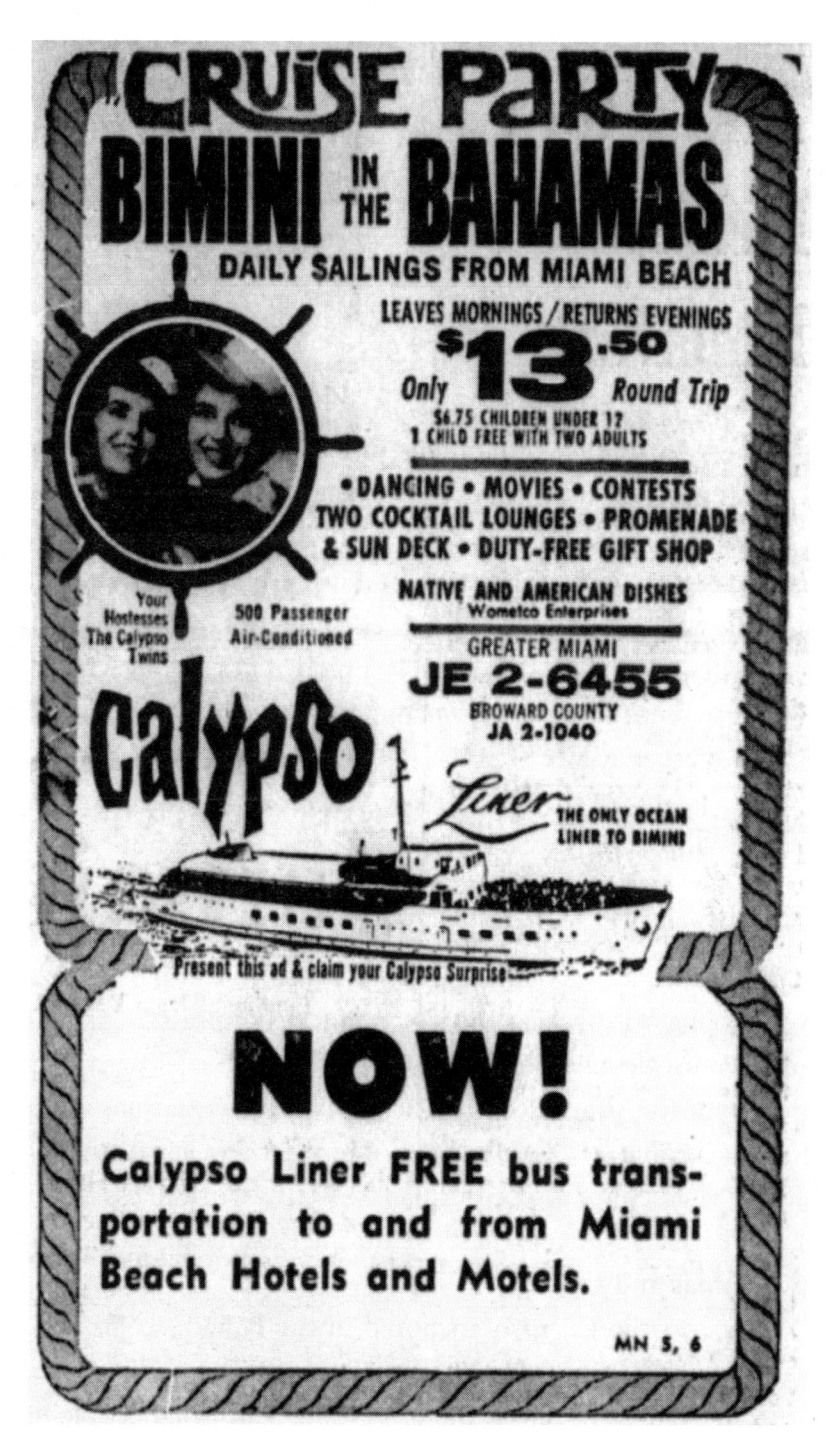

Advertisement for the Calypso Liner *in the* Miami Herald.

On their first day aboard the *Calypso*, the pair were outfitted with identical sheen dresses, rakishly tilted skimmer hats and beauty pageant sashes bearing their new title: the 'Calypso Twins.' The sisters brought the *Calypso* to life, cavorting across the lounge, hip-checking the squares, and kicking off their heels to teach the passengers the Cha-cha-cha.

Whenever Sari greeted Derber with her Southern ingénue lilt, he managed a composed reply, despite a racing heart. The mere act of looking at her felt reckless.

At first, Sari didn't think much of Derber. He wasn't tall, and his dark eyes were hard to read. The deep crease on his left cheek gave him a bemused smirk, as if he found the world endlessly entertaining. He had a soft voice, and his reserved British demeanor came across as aloof. She had encountered men before who played at being detached to suggest a hidden depth, but with him it was different. There was something about him, something she couldn't quite place.

Morning hellos in the narrow corridors became lingering, over-the-shoulder glances. Playful banter led to after-hours drinks in the ship's lounge. There, they discovered their shared fondness for repartee and their mutual disdain for that dreadful American custom known as ice. She matched his dry, ironic humor with her own piercing wit, teasing the sailor that his impressive drinking stamina must be due to his hollow wooden leg.[11]

Beneath the ship's deck lights, cocktail conversations drifted into lazy evening strolls. He spoke of his journeys across the seas, painting vivid pictures of far-off lands. With a worldliness beyond her 22 years, she spoke of her love for the Caribbean, particularly the Bahamas and Cuba.

Whenever the *Calypso* anchored in the Bahamas, she'd step away to do modeling work on the island.[12, 13] But Cuba was different. Its history, its spirit, the unyielding soul of its people had a grip on her. Her eyes crinkled and her pendant swayed as she condemned the government's disastrous embargo against Cuba. With no commercial transportation off the island, refugees were risking their lives on small boats to cross the Florida Straits, often perishing in the attempt. Parents were facing unimaginable dangers to save their children. This was not just a political issue; it was the most pressing moral crisis of their time. Derber understood, the urgency lingering between them like a silent pact.

In the weeks that followed, life aboard the *Calypso* settled into a familiar rhythm – scheduled crossings, cocktail hours, and evening shows for the guests. But Derber's moments with Sari began to deepen. After one of her return trips from the Bahamas, she spotted him on deck and ran to him, throwing her arms around him as if fleeing a fire. It was the first clear sign that she cared, and the first clue that her life wasn't as carefree as she let on.

That moment marked a turning point between them, opening up a quieter and more vulnerable connection. On late-night walks, he told stories he had never shared with anyone else. His eyes grew distant when he spoke about growing up during the war: the evacuation, the Blackshirts, the bombings. She didn't press him but let the walls come down on their own.

His courage gave her the confidence to finally share her own story. Her name wasn't really Sari Lesley. It was Sarah Cohen. Sari Lesley was her alias, combining her Hebrew first name with a Scottish last name. She fled her former life in Bradenton, Florida, a pleasant enough city outside of Tampa. In her senior year of high school, she 'became in the family way' with her high school sweetheart, the star center of the football team, and dropped out of school. They had a shotgun wedding, and her wealthy father gave them a house in Green Acres on the condition that she never spoke to him again.

Sari and her husband ended up having three children within two years. As with many young parents, the strain was too much and they divorced. Florida did not allow no-fault divorce, so there was an offense, but the details were never discussed, even among friends. Her husband got custody, and the kids moved in with their grandparents. Sari blinked away the glisten in her eyes.

After the divorce, Sari and her twin sister, Susan, moved to Miami looking for a fresh start. At 22, Sari was divorced, stripped of her young children, estranged from her parents and living under an alias in a new city. She was working as a drive-in carhop when she responded to the ad for the *Calypso*. And now, here she was, finding company with an eccentric British sailor, adrift on a ship.

Derber's eyes glassed. He also knew what it meant to be pressed into service at a young age, to be estranged from one's family, to change a name, to begin again. It was as if their lives had played out in parallel, thousands of miles apart, only to converge at that moment.

And yet the silence hung between them. Despite their growing trust, Sari couldn't reveal her business in the Bahamas. Her lingering gaze conveyed the unspoken understanding: no matter how close they became, some truths couldn't be shared.

5. THE NEW AMERICAN DREAM

Miami, 1962

When the *Calypso* docked in the Bahamas, Sari descended the gangway with her usual grace and headed straight to her modeling assignment. Once the cameras stopped flashing, she slipped away on a boat bound for Havana. Upon arrival, she flirted past the customs agents and traveled with her bodyguards to a nondescript safe house. Her contact greeted her there with a packet stuffed with cash and a folder containing documents. With the contraband securely hidden, Sari returned to the Bahamas and reboarded the *Calypso*, resuming her role as a cruise ship entertainer. Back in Miami, she discreetly delivered the materials to her secret handler.

Her glamorous facade was the perfect cover – so perfect that no one, not even Derber, suspected she was working as a freelance contractor for the CIA or a covert private consortium. Her mission was twofold: to smuggle cash and sensitive documents out of Havana and to gather intelligence on activities in Cuba.[1,2] Castro was seizing billions in American corporate assets, and companies desperately needed someone to rescue their funds before it was too late. That person was Sari Cohen.

As she continued undetected, her boldness grew. She increased her trips to twice a week, amassing a bankroll of $100,000. But with each mission, the risks mounted. One afternoon, convinced that a car was tailing her, Sari raced home and bolted upstairs to the apartment she shared with her sister, Susan. Desperate to throw off her pursuer, the twins swapped dresses. Susan took Sari's car and drove off. Though she often doubted Sari's fears as paranoia, Susan confirmed the unsettling truth – a car was following her.[1]

The question loomed: was the tail her handler ensuring the cash drop-offs proceeded as planned, Cuban agents suspicious of her frequent Havana visits, or G-Men tracking the *Empress* staff? Whatever the answer, she knew that a single misstep could unravel the entire operation.

While Sari undertook her dangerous covert work, Derber faced mounting problems of his own. With tensions in Cuba escalating, Miami tourism was vanishing fast. The *Calypso*'s once-grand dining room, the tables set for a lavish occasion, remained largely empty. The house band played to a deserted lounge while the staff exchanged nervous glances. Payments to vendors, staff and Canaveral International were delayed.

In October 1962, Derber received the inevitable news – Canaveral was canceling the charter and reclaiming the *Calypso*.[3] It was a setback, but far from the end. He would simply secure a new, even grander ship. He called Adiel, and together they launched a new cruise company, Empress Lines Ltd. For funding, Derber turned to the usual mobsters and fraudsters, hoping his gamble would pay off this time.

Derber and Adiel signed a charter for the *Wappen von Hamburg*, a magnificent cruise ship owned by the German ferry company HADAG. As Germany's first vessel built after the war, she was the pinnacle of nautical engineering. The stunning 340-foot cruise ship was powered by the pioneering Maybach diesel-electric propulsion system. Below deck, she housed three sumptuous restaurants, several opulent cocktail lounges and a solarium, all lavishly adorned with rich wood paneling and

The New American Dream

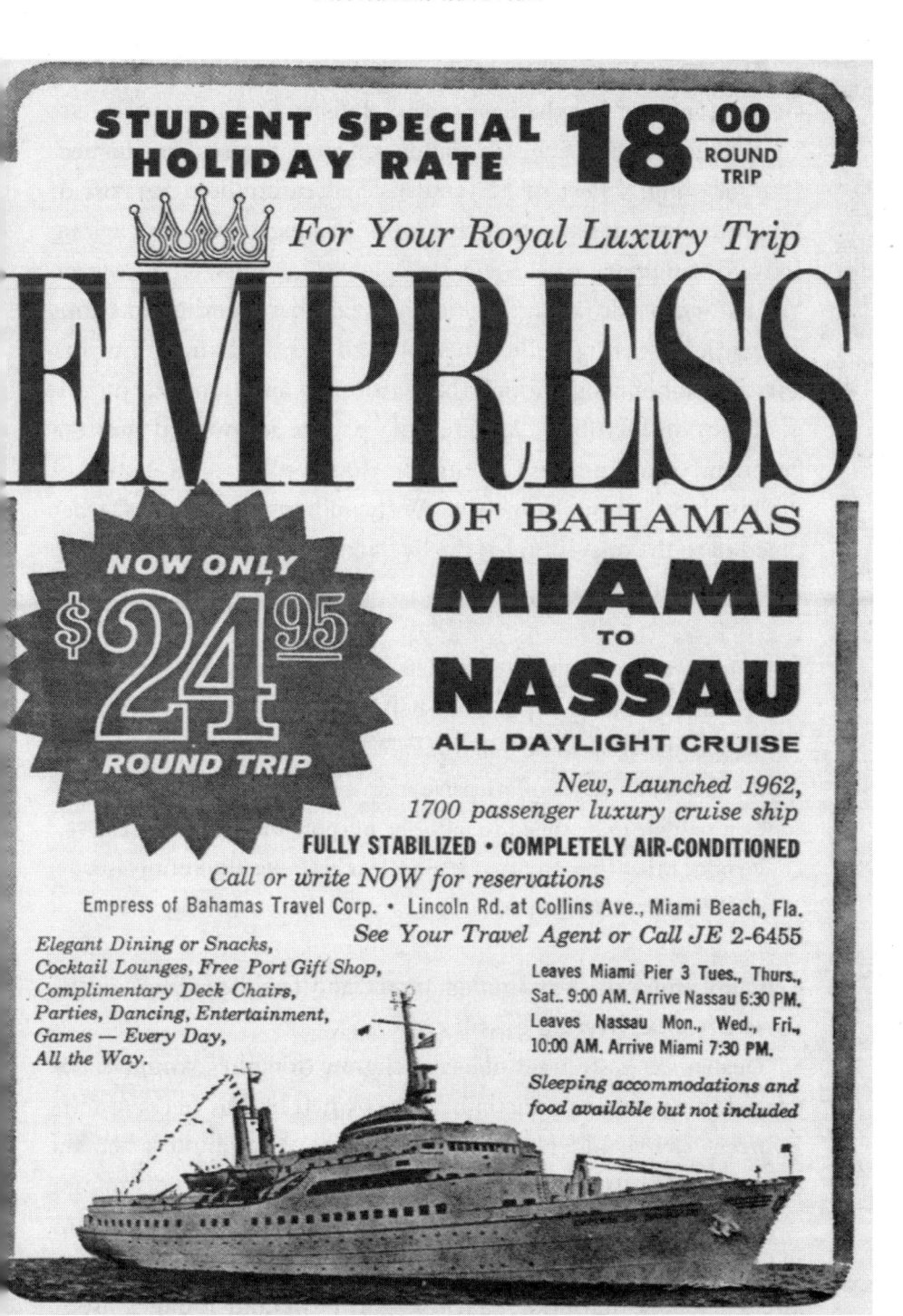

Empress of Bahamas *advertisement in the* Miami Hurricane.

modern furnishings.[4] To give her a title worthy of her grandeur, Derber renamed her the *Empress of Bahamas*.

Yet beyond the *Empress*'s grandeur, a mounting tension loomed. One morning, a fleet of Navy boats and cutters left the Port of Miami in unison. Later that day, while driving along US 1, a long convoy of military trucks rumbled past in the opposite direction. Yellow and black fallout shelter signs began appearing on banks and garages, stirring chilling memories of air raid shelters. The military was mobilizing, though the reason remained a mystery.

Then, on October 22, 1962, the papers announced that the President would address the nation that evening on a matter of the "highest national urgency." With millions of others, Derber tuned in to the television for the live address. President Kennedy's words echoed through his room:

> This government, as promised, has maintained the closest surveillance of the Soviet military buildup on the island of Cuba. Within the past week, unmistakable evidence has established the fact that a series of offensive missile sites is now in preparation on that imprisoned island. The purpose of these bases can be none other than to provide a nuclear strike capability against the Western Hemisphere.

Kennedy announced an immediate naval blockade to prevent the Soviets from delivering missiles to Cuba.

Derber sat in stunned silence, the glow of the black-and-white television casting an eerie light across his face. His plans for the *Empress* were suddenly meaningless. The country was headed toward nuclear war.

The following morning, thousands of troops descended into Florida. Fighter jets and bombers streaked over Miami. Anti-aircraft missile batteries, machine-gun nests and radar stations were installed on the beaches, now enclosed by barbed wire.

People began building fallout shelters and stockpiling food, sparking panic buying at the markets. Families gathered, preparing to face the end together, while Cuban refugees whispered about internment camps.

What little remained of Miami tourism collapsed completely. Hotels emptied overnight, the few remaining visitors fled, and the once-vibrant streets of Collins Avenue became eerily quiet.

By midweek, Soviet vessels were closing in on the blockade. In Washington, officials prepared for a potential clash at sea, while rumors of an imminent attack spread. Derber anxiously followed the radio broadcasts, his mind fluctuating between the escalating crisis and his faltering business. Photos of Soviet missiles in Cuba aimed at the US flooded the media. The public was now painfully aware of how close they were to disaster, and so was Derber. As US Ambassador Adlai Stevenson confronted his Soviet counterpart at the UN, Derber, like everyone else, braced for the possibility that the unthinkable could happen at any moment.

The crisis escalated when news arrived that a US spy plane had been shot down over Cuba. The prospect of nuclear war was now real. Everything – his plans, his city, the world – was on the brink of collapse.

And then, on October 28, 1962, a breakthrough finally came. Nikita Khrushchev, leader of the Soviet Union, conceded and agreed to withdraw the missiles in exchange for a US commitment not to invade Cuba. Nuclear disaster was averted and Derber exhaled, along with the rest of America.

Tourists began trickling back into Miami; hotels and restaurants returned to life.[5] Derber's vision for the *Empress*, which had seemed like an impossible dream just days before, now had a chance.

For the *Empress*'s maiden launch, the Mayor of West Palm Beach and a sash-wearing Miss Miami Beach presented the skipper with the keys to the city. They popped champagne and toasted the Queen of Cruise Ships and the return of Miami tourism.

Ticket sales on the *Empress* trickled in as affluent vacationers returned to Miami, ready to celebrate the end of the crisis. The ship was far from crowded, but pockets of prosperous real-estate developers, self-made entrepreneurs, well-connected insiders, and household-name actors began to appear on deck. Conversations buzzed with penny stock tips, recommendations for the latest hotspots, and gossip about the exploitable quirks of local politicians.

Despite attracting affluent passengers, the *Empress* struggled to reach the 350 passengers a day needed to stay financially afloat. Crew members and vendors began filing lawsuits. The ship's owner, HADAG, demanded the overdue payments. Time was running out, and Derber faced losing another cruise ship, this time on a grander scale.

In desperate need of revenue, Derber sought to install high-stakes betting equipment on the *Empress*, several steps above the *Calypso*'s dime and quarter slots. He had already made one deal with the devil; now he was just negotiating better terms. The only thing he needed was a financial backer.

Seeking a trustworthy partner with deep pockets, Derber approached Mike McLaney, a hotel and casino magnate known for his generosity and influential friends, including Robert F. Kennedy and J. Edgar Hoover. Before becoming a gambling tycoon, the New Orleans-born McLaney was a low-handicap golfer and a nationally ranked tennis player. He was known to hustle unsuspecting opponents on the greens and courts, earning him the nickname "the genial hustler." During the Batista era, he ran casinos in Havana, including the Casino Internacional at the Hotel Nacional de Cuba. After Castro came to power and nationalized the casinos, McLaney was jailed and then deported along with the Havana mob.[6,7]

When Derber and Adiel approached McLaney to finance the gambling operation, he considered taking over the entire charter.

However, McLaney ultimately declined, citing the ship's growing financial and legal trouble. He also didn't trust Derber and Adiel, remarking that even though they were "nice, charming guys, they were terrible liars, and he could not depend on anything they said."[8] Instead, McLaney introduced them to hotel and casino magnate Morris Lansburgh, who had fewer reservations.

Morris Lansburgh was the largest luxury resort developer in the country, with an empire that included the iconic Deauville and Eden Roc hotels in Miami Beach and the legendary Flamingo Hotel in Las Vegas, the city's first high-end casino. He was also feared and respected as the public face of the 'Mob's Accountant,' Meyer Lansky.

Lansburgh saw gambling on the *Empress* as a lucrative opportunity, with minimal competition in Florida and a way to offset Vegas' slower winter season. Due to Derber and Adiel's reputation, Lansburgh required them to secure the loan with their lumber property, ensuring foreclosure if they defaulted.[9]

With Lansburgh's backing, the *Empress* transformed into a lavish floating casino designed to cater to every gambler's whim. The ship was outfitted with dozens of single and double slots, bird cages, a Big Six, four roulettes, and blackjack and shimmy tables.[10]

Once word spread that the *Empress* was open for gambling business, Derber was inundated with approaches from the mob, including the mafia head Santo Trafficante and the Gambino enforcer Joseph 'Scootch' Indelicato.[11,12] One fateful day, a sun-bronzed Meyer Lansky boarded the ship. Meyer's brother, Jake Lansky, took the captain to lunch so Meyer and Derber could discuss business privately.[11] Their conversation remained a secret, but it was universally understood that refusing Lansky's support was unwise.

With the mob encroaching on the *Empress*, Derber hired Miami-based private detective Sam Benton to handle security.

Benton was an impressive figure, tall with horn-rimmed glasses perched on his finch-like face and a pearl-handled revolver always ready. On the *Empress*, his job description was to "be on the alert for professional gamblers, hoodlums or other undesirable persons who might come aboard."[13]

His résumé was perfect for the job. Born Finkelman, Benton escaped Poland as a child stowaway on a Panama-bound liner, only to be deported to Havana by Panamanian authorities. The US granted him entry on the condition that he serve in the Army Intelligence Corps during World War II. After the war, he returned to Cuba to head security at McLaney's Casino Internacional. His tenure was short-lived. After the revolution, the Cuban government arrested and expelled him along with the rest of the Havana mob. Now, back in Miami, Benton teamed up once again with McLaney, in the covert Castro assassination movement.[14]

As one of Trafficante and Lansky's key lieutenants, Benton served as a crucial liaison between the mafia and anti-Castro Cuban exiles. He specialized in arranging assassinations and sourcing explosives, or as he described it, he was a "commission broker in Latin American commodities."[15] In his spare time, after shifts on the *Empress*, he kept busy blowing up private yachts for insurance money, crafting assassination plots against Castro for the CIA, and conspiring with McLaney to blow up the Shell Oil refinery in Havana.[16] His mere presence on the *Empress* kept the other mobsters on their best behavior.

Benton was not the only one keeping an eye on the *Empress*'s clientele. The FBI began to take notice of the mob-sponsored gambling aboard the ship.[17] Although gambling in international waters was legal, transporting gambling equipment to places where it was illegal, like Nassau, was against the law. So the FBI closely watched the *Empress* to ensure the equipment wasn't being transported onward. It also allowed them to monitor the comings and goings of the Miami mob.

The Bureau also became curious how a retired British navy officer with tenuous ties to Miami secured funding for the gem of the luxury cruise ship industry. Captain Edwin Le May, the boat's shipping agent and an FBI informant, tipped them off that Morris Lansburgh had provided a $125,000 loan to fund Derber's initial charter, raising further suspicions about Derber's mob ties.[9]

Not long after, the FBI summoned Derber for questioning. He winced under the harsh fluorescent lights as he entered the Miami interrogation room. The agents bombarded him with relentless questions. Who financed his ship? Who supplied the gambling equipment? What was his relationship with Lansky?

Derber reminded them he was a British subject and flatly refused to answer any questions. Any inquiries should be submitted in writing, and he would prepare answers as directed by counsel.[18] The agents exchanged frustrated glances, knowing they'd get nothing more from him.

Back on the *Empress* that evening, in the dim light of his cabin office, Derber sifted through the pile of liens and returned checks scattered across his desk. The gambling revenue had bought him some time, but it wasn't nearly enough to save the *Empress*. Creditors were breathing down his neck. The mob was demanding their cut. The FBI was closing in. With pressure mounting from all sides, Derber knew he needed an escape.

Hoping to clear his mind, Derber invited Sari for dinner and drinks at the La Ronde Supper Club in the Fontainebleau Hotel. The opulence might take his mind off his debts, even if only briefly.

Arriving fashionably early, Derber was enveloped in the Fontainebleau's grandeur. Champagne-crystal chandeliers sparkled above veined marble columns trimmed in gold, and white marble flooring with a chorus line of black bowtie tiles. Rosewood and gilt walls surrounded a circular bar at the center, which emitted a soft, welcoming glow. Semicircular sofas and easy chairs sat stranded on rounded carpet islands amid eight-feet-tall Greek goddesses, gargoyles, marble Roman busts, potted palms and terracotta winged cherubs. The pièce de résistance was the white marble 'Staircase to Nowhere,' which curved around a cylindrical photomural of a fallen Roman temple.

Derber found Sari by the fishpond, which doubled as a whimsical wishing well. The chandelier's crystal light shimmered across her angular cheeks. She wore a form-fitting aqua dress and four-inch heels. Her copper hair, styled in an elegant Bardot updo, had soft tresses cascading over one shoulder. By the time he approached her, he had gathered himself enough to clear his throat. "You are a dream walking," he whispered.[19]

Derber offered his arm and guided Sari through La Ronde Supper Club's neon-lit, double-door entrance. The maître d' greeted his guests with a smile and led them into the supper room, a midnight blue dome topped with an enormous chrysanthemum chandelier. Murals of dreamlike palm trees swayed on the curved, dark indigo walls. Pristine white-linen tables ascended in tiers like a Greek amphitheater with showgirls

Fontainebleau Hotel lobby.

in plunging necklines reclining among cigar-smoking moguls. Sari and Derber were seated at a coveted ringside table near the namesake circular stage, where the house singer crooned a silky jazz ballad.

Over dinner and cocktails, Derber relayed tales of his global adventures, prospecting for diamond mines and navigating uncharted territories. With each account of perilous expeditions and narrow escapes, his eyes ignited. As Sari would later recount in her memoir, she could tell Derber "lived for danger; it was his high, his fix. The only time he felt alive was when he was locked in hand-to-hand combat with death."[20]

In Derber's eyes, she saw a reflection of her own restless spirit. Recovering from a failed marriage and separation from her children, she had also turned to danger – not just for adrenaline, but for a chance to rebuild something meaningful from the wreckage of her past.

As if sensing her thoughts, Derber drew closer and asked how she became involved in the Cuban refugee movement. Sari leaned back, her lips curving into a smile. She paused, her cigarette poised lover-style in her hand, wrist languid. She took a long, slow drag.

It was a wild story. One evening, while cruising through Miami, she spotted a man violently beating a prostitute. She couldn't just drive by and ignore it. She pulled over, jumped out of her car and yelled off the attacker. Sari comforted the woman and gently helped her to her feet.[1]

Several Cuban bystanders thanked her and invited her to a local refugee meeting. Intrigued, she decided to check it out. At the meeting, she met a passionate group of Cuban refugees, students and people of conscience. To her surprise, she was introduced to José Miró Cardona, the first Prime Minister of Cuba following Castro's revolution. Cardona had fled to Miami after resigning in protest at Castro's regime. He had neatly combed, dark hair graying at the temples, a dignified, trimmed moustache and thick-rimmed glasses. He now led the exile movement under the Cuban Revolutionary Council, which had been selected by the US government to lead Cuba after Castro was deposed.

Cardona's speeches at the club painted heart-rending pictures of the immense suffering under Castro's rule – political prisoners tortured, families torn apart and a vibrant culture suffocated. Cardona's impassioned words resonated with Sari. The more she listened, the more she was called to the cause. The Cuban refugee movement offered her direction, a way to channel her empathy and strength into something meaningful.

As Sari described her involvement with the Cuban refugees, Derber nodded. The parallels between their plight and that of the Jewish refugees during World War II were striking. Both had taken to the sea in small boats, risking everything for a chance at a new life. The sight of desperate families crowded onto vessels, fleeing oppression, moved him deeply.

Derber despised communist totalitarianism. He had seen the brutal repression and economic stagnation that plagued the Soviet bloc – long lines outside empty grocery stores, security forces using batons to silence dissenters. Cuba could fall under the same tyranny, its rich culture and resilient people crushed by authoritarian rule.

Amid the lively band music and chatter, Derber and Sari's conversation turned to planning. Derber was an experienced navigator and seasoned captain. Sari was proficient in Spanish and had deep connections in the Cuban refugee movement.

As they sipped their cocktails, their eyes met over the rims of their glasses. Their discussion flowed between playful speculation and cautious sincerity, each trying to gauge the other's commitment. They both wondered if their dinner companion was a true believer or just playing spy, leaving them both wondering who was recruiting whom.

When the waiter asked for the dessert order, Sari changed the topic to the question of what makes a good life. Derber had pondered the question throughout his diverse careers as a war sailor, arms trader, gold and diamond prospector, corporate sleuth, private investor and aspiring cruise-ship magnate. Though the American Dream of unlimited abundance and perpetual reinvention was appealing, Derber found it incomplete. He envisioned a New American Dream encompassing love, purpose and adventure.

Sari grasped Derber's hand and led him through the back doors of La Ronde, past the pool, and onto the moonlit Miami Beach. She skipped ahead across the sand, swinging her arms as if playing an imaginary game. Derber watched, captivated by her playful spirit. "May I ask what you're doing?" he asked, his curiosity piqued.

"Catching moonbeams," Sari replied with a mischievous grin.

"Is it a difficult game, or can any number of people play?"

"It is very difficult. I mean, I'm the only person I know who does it well," she answered.

In one graceful motion, Sari slipped off her shoes and dress and dove headlong into the churning ocean. Derber could only murmur to himself, "How extraordinary."[21]

Lying weightless beneath the glistening stars, Sari drifted and rocked, buoyed by the gentle swells. Time was suspended, and all her worries dissolved into the dark expanse of the sea. The cool water chilled her skin, calming her mind and bringing peace.

With a renewed spirit, she emerged from the water, bounding the last few steps. She slipped back into her dress, which darkened where it met her body. As she adjusted her strap, her eyes met Derber's and she had an epiphany.

The debonair exterior was all a façade. The true nature of the British naval officer became clear. In a flash of insight, she recognized him – he was the modern-day incarnation of the Scarlet Pimpernel, the chivalrous hero from the British novel who rescued aristocrats from the guillotine's clutches during France's Reign of Terror. Just as the Pimpernel concealed his daring nature behind the affected air of a dandyish playboy, so too was Derber hiding his true identity. Sari's gaze pierced the veil. She saw the supreme swashbuckler, escape artist and master of disguise hiding beneath the tailored veneer. She recited the hymn:

> They seek him here
> They seek him there
> The Frenchies seek him everywhere
> Is he in heaven or is he in hell?
> That damned elusive Pimpernel

Assuming the role of Marguerite, Sari boldly declared Derber was none other than the Scarlet Pimpernel himself, and she demanded her rightful place in the brotherhood.

Derber grinned at Sari's formidable deductive powers. No one else had seen beyond his poised exterior to uncover the cunning and noble swordsman beneath. Without hesitation, he inducted her into the League of the Scarlet Pimpernel.

With the moonlight glistening off the waves, they laughed at their newfound understanding. What they craved was more than a midnight swim; they yearned to plunge, hand in hand, into the firewater together. Drawing closer, they embraced, their hearts full of love and devoid of fear.

6. THE FREEDOM FERRY

*New York, Miami, Mexico City and
Havana, 1962–63*

On June 20, 1962, a thousand miles away from Miami, distinguished attorney James B. Donovan welcomed a delegation to his Brooklyn law office. Among the visitors were Congressman Robert W. Kean and five representatives from the Cuban Families Committee for the Liberation of Prisoners of War. The organization represented members of the brigade that led the ill-fated Bay of Pigs invasion and were now languishing in Cuban prison.

The Cuban Families Committee (CFC) approached Donovan on Attorney General Robert Kennedy's recommendation. Early in his career, fresh out of Harvard Law, Donovan had worked with the Office of Scientific Research and Development, the agency that developed the atom bomb and radar. After the war, he served as general counsel of the Office of Strategic Services (the precursor to the CIA) and later as the assistant prosecutor at the Nuremberg trials. Most recently, he'd negotiated with the Soviets to secure the release of a US spy plane pilot shot down over the Soviet Union in exchange for the top Russian spy in America. Donovan's deep ties to the intelligence community allowed him to operate outside of normal diplomatic channels, earning him the title as "the most successful American practitioner of meta-diplomacy."[1]

Congressman Kean explained the purpose of their visit. "We came to see you because a highly placed government official, whose name we cannot yet disclose, suggested that you act as a general counsel for the Cuban Families Committee of the Bay of Pigs prisoners." The congressman cut to the chase and asked Donovan if he could convince Castro to release the Bay of Pigs prisoners. He underscored the urgency of the situation. The prisoners were being held on the remote Isle of Pines, with the entire facility wired with explosives that would detonate if the United States attempted another invasion of Cuba. Donovan was the prisoners' last hope. "Obviously, Mr Donovan, word has gotten around that you specialize in releasing people from bondage," the congressman explained.[2]

The mission went beyond simply bringing the prisoners home. The CFC also sought to free their friends and families to ensure they would be safe from retribution once the prisoners were freed.

Before Donovan would commit, he needed assurances from the White House that he wouldn't be violating the Logan Act, which prohibited foreign diplomacy by private citizens. He met with the CIA and RFK, who reassured him of the mission's legality. RFK's only caution was that Donovan would be operating independently of the White House, effectively serving as an envoy without portfolio.

With a gleam in his eye, Donovan signed on as CFC's pro bono general counsel. Operation Mercy was born. Although his mission was supposed to be independent of the White House, he coordinated regularly with RFK and the CIA. In one pre-briefing, the agency instructed Donovan to poison Castro during his visit by gifting him a wetsuit laced with tuberculosis. Donovan declined, saying, "I'm in the business of negotiation, not assassination."[3] Donovan held fast that diplomacy was the only viable approach.

Over several days of intense negotiations, Donovan and Castro worked out the ransom payment for the prisoners, although tensions occasionally flared. At one point, Castro withdrew from a tentative agreement, leading Donovan to insist that the prisoner release was the only viable option. "You can't shoot them," Donovan explained. "If you want to get rid of them, if you're going to sell them, you have to sell them to me. There's no world market for prisoners."[4]

Through their ongoing discussions, Donovan and Castro developed a deep mutual admiration. Seeing the potential for a broader accord, Castro asked Donovan how Cuba and the US could improve relations. With a wry smile, Donovan asked Castro, "Do you know how porcupines make love?" After a puzzled look from Castro, Donovan replied, "Very carefully."[5]

In December 1962, after six months of negotiations, Donovan and Castro secured an agreement to release all the Bay of Pigs prisoners, as well as several thousand of their relatives and friends. In exchange, Cuba would receive a $53 million ransom in medicine and food.

To maintain independence from the White House, Donovan enlisted the Red Cross to transport the prisoners and the ransom. Using a charity also allowed the White House to bypass the Trading

Castro and Donovan.

with the Enemy Act and let pharmaceutical companies donating to the ransom to receive a generous tax deduction. The Red Cross's criteria for the ship were clear: they needed vessels with ample passenger space, proximity to the Caribbean and private ownership to maintain plausible separation from the White House.

Meanwhile, back aboard the *Empress*, Derber sat in his office, surrounded by lawsuit papers and overdue payment notices. Seeking a distraction, he picked up the *Miami Herald*. The front-page headline detailed the devastating effects of Florida's coldest winter in a century. There was an update on JFK's trip to the Bahamas. However, a small article at the bottom caught his eye: "Red Cross to Help Ransom Captives."[6] It described the charity's efforts to transport the Bay of Pigs prisoners and their search for a suitable private ship.

His eyes shifted to the portrait of the *Empress* on his desk, and a faint smile appeared. He grabbed his office phone and dictated a telegram to be sent directly to President Kennedy:

TELEGRAM TO THE PRESIDENT from the Empress of Bahamas Steamship Co. Collins Ave and Lincoln Road, Miami Beach dtd 12/14/62 – offers to James Donovan and Red Cross the Empress of Bahamas to transport prisoners released from Cuba.[7]

Derber's telegram landed on the desk of National Security Advisor McGeorge 'Mac' Bundy, who immediately grasped its importance. He forwarded it to Robert F. Kennedy, who was secretly coordinating Operation Mercy from the White House.

Bundy's involvement highlighted the operation's critical national security implications. It also reflected his role as a shadow secretary of state, bypassing the formal authority of Secretary of State Dean Rusk. As the youngest dean in the history of Harvard's College of Arts and Sciences, Bundy brought a razor-sharp intellect to his roles in the NSA and the State Department. Despite his elevated position in government, he retained the trademark clear-plastic-framed glasses and modest suits of his academic roots, giving him the appearance of a professor in a hurry to reshape the global order.

Under Bundy's order, the Red Cross accepted Derber's offer to send the *Empress* to retrieve the Bay of Pigs prisoners.[8] What Bundy could not have known was that this seemingly straightforward decision would soon turn Derber into his sworn nemesis.

When the telegram confirming the assignment arrived, Derber exhaled in relief. The news could not have come sooner; HADAG's patience was wearing thin.[9] The overdue payments and mafia connections had strained their trust to breaking point. Derber understood that he had to act swiftly before they lost confidence altogether and recalled the *Empress*.

Wasting no time, he began assembling his team from the best in the business. The Empress Lines Ltd spokesman proudly declared, "These men were selected because they are some of the top maritime people in the profession. They are very appreciative of the fact that they have been called upon and are able to participate in such an important adventure as this is."[10]

Just as the mission was gathering pace, it faced an insurmountable obstacle. Castro unexpectedly changed his mind and demanded that the prisoners be returned by plane instead of ship.[11] The *Empress* was taken off of Operation Mercy. Soon after, Derber received a telegram from HADAG. His stomach tightened. They were canceling the charter and recalling the *Empress*.[12]

Derber's hand tightened around the telegram. His gamble on the *Empress* cost him everything: his entire savings of $400,000 and the Tennessee lumber property he co-owned with Adiel.[13] HADAG filed a lawsuit for damages.[14] The once-promising venture left Derber financially ruined.

HADAG returned the *Empress* from Miami to Hamburg, dumping the slot machines along the way. The *Empress of Bahamas*, known for its New Year's Eve fireworks and games "every day, all the way," reverted to the *Wappen von Hamburg*, shuttling German vacationers across the North Sea.[15]

Meanwhile, the Red Cross transported the Bay of Pigs prisoners back to the US on Pan-Am DC-6 airplanes. Several thousand friends and family members followed on ships.[16] The *Empress*, however, was not among them.

On December 29, 1962, President Kennedy welcomed the Bay of Pigs prisoners home with a celebratory speech at the Miami Orange Bowl. First Lady Jackie Kennedy opened the event in fluent Spanish, expressing hopes that her son would someday grow up to be "a man at least half as brave as the members of Brigade 2506." The President accepted the brigade's yellow and blue flag. "I can assure you," Kennedy promised, "that this flag will be returned to this brigade in a free Havana."

The Cubans in the crowd cheered, but many kissed their teeth and shook their heads. The President offered no hope for the those still trapped on the island, unable to flee to America. Nearly a quarter of a million Cubans had US visa waivers that were now useless because of Kennedy's travel embargo. The US government had encouraged them to apply for the waivers while, at the same time, blocking all travel. To make their situation even more dire, once someone applied for a US visa waiver, their ration book would be seized and they'd lose their job. The visa waivers, meant as a ticket to freedom, had become a cruel punishment.

After Kennedy's speech, the Cuban Families Committee approached Derber with a desperate plea. Although the prisoners had been safely returned, hundreds of thousands of Cubans still remained trapped on the island, desperate to flee. The committee asked if he could help transport those still seeking a way out.

The Freedom Ferry

The humanitarian mission called to him. This was an opportunity to help repair the world and give oppressed people a chance at freedom, much like the rescue efforts during the war.

He also did the numbers. With each passenger paying a few hundred dollars, the venture could not only resolve his financial troubles but also bring him a windfall. It was a rare chance to make a real difference while securing a life-changing fortune. Without hesitation, Derber agreed.[17]

Eager to set his plan in motion, he penned a letter to Robert Hurwitch, the Deputy Coordinator of Cuban Affairs in the State Department, seeking permission to launch his Cuba ferry service:

Dear Mr Hurwitch,
I have been Advised by [US judge] Mr Barrett Prettyman to write directly to you giving full details of our proposed scheduled run between Key West and Havana, Cuba …

We have been approached by various Cuban committees in Miami (church, civic, refugee and others) with the idea in mind of inducing us to operate the MS *ORANGE SUN* for the purpose of bringing to Florida those families and loved ones who have already been issued waivers from this country.

We propose to operate this vessel either daily, two or three times a week, or on any other schedule which may be practical and suitable between Key West and Havana. The Cuban committees, at this time, claim that the families here are paying an excess of $200 per person to bring relatives in to this country via Mexico and they are willing able and anxious to pay an additional amount besides the $25 forwarded to Cuba. This additional amount would not exceed $25 per person depending upon the number of persons brought out of Cuba each month. We would like to set up our offices in Miami whereby the families would pay this amount and we would, in turn, get approval from the Cuban and for each individual to leave Cuba.

We would also like to have approximately a 48 hour advance manifest and visa approved by the Immigration Department in Miami so as to eliminate any complications.

We are able to put this vessel into operation immediately pending the approval by the Cuban end and I would appreciate your assistance in this matter. I, therefore, await your prompt reply.

Sincerely,
Empress Lines Ltd
Harold Derber, President[18]

The letter included a copy of his INS application for permission to enter Cuba.[19]

Eventually, Derber's letter reached the State Department, which imposed two conditions for the ferry: the US had to approve the passenger list, and immigration and health officials had to clear the passengers in Cuba. The letter ended with a stern warning: "... any person's aiding and abetting [illegal] entry or attempted [illegal] entry will be subject to the provisions and penalties of the Immigration and Naturalization Act and in particular chapter 8 thereof."[20]

Despite appearing to grant conditional approval, the State Department's response was a sham. The US had no intention of sending inspectors to Cuba. By imposing these impossible conditions, the State Department had essentially blocked US visa holders from entering the country and threatened criminal prosecution for anyone attempting to help.

The White House's incoherent Cuban immigration policy was a product of the government's conflicting priorities. The CIA and Defense and State departments generally advocated for a restrictive approach to bar subversive agents, criminals and 'undesirables.' At the same time, the CIA was covertly helping Cuban counterrevolutionaries leave the island to prepare for another invasion. Meanwhile, the INS, the Department of Health and local Florida politicians were worried about the burden on social services.

President Kennedy favored a more open Cuban immigration policy, influenced by his own family's immigrant roots and the Bay of Pigs failure. He also sought to assert moral superiority over the Soviet Union and avoid building a Berlin Wall in the Caribbean.

While the Kennedy administration remained locked in policy indecision, the plight of Cubans worsened by the day. Harrowing tales of oppression and deprivation flooded in, underscoring the urgent need for action. Derber's ferry service offered a beacon of hope, but action was needed to avert a tragedy.

To launch a ferry, Derber needed an ally in the Cuban government. He partnered with the influential Captain Víctor Manuel Pina

Captain Víctor Pina (left), Cuba's Director of Civil Aviation and Derber's main ally in the Cuban government.

The Wireless Operator

Cardoso, director of the Cuban Civil Aviation Administration.[21, 22] The origin of their relationship remains shrouded in mystery. They may have been introduced through pro-Castro groups in Miami or intermediaries on the *Empress*. Regardless of its origins, Derber's relationship with Captain Pina would evolve into a strategic partnership with far-reaching consequences.

As a stalwart of the communist old guard, Pina wielded considerable influence within the Castro regime. He had been an early supporter of the Soviet-backed Popular Socialist Party and a crypto-communist under Batista. Following the revolution, Pina created Cuba's Ministry of the Interior and co-founded Cuba's intelligence service, Dirección General de Inteligencia (DGI), alongside Ernesto 'Che' Guevara and others.[21, 23, 24]

Pina's influence extended to the highest levels of government; he served as a trusted advisor to Fidel's brother, Major Raúl Castro. He cultivated strong ties with the Soviet Union and, as the architect of the Revolutionary Air Force, was the first Cuban military member to visit the USSR post-revolution. There, he secured MiGs for the fledgling air force. In sum, Pina was a living embodiment of the revolution.[25]

His motivations for supporting Derber's ferry were likely multifaceted. The ferry service could generate much-needed revenue for the cash-strapped Cuban government. It would also provide transportation to export dissidents and undesirables to the US. The venture also held significant propaganda value by exposing the absurdity of Kennedy's travel embargo.

Captain Pina and Derber arranged to meet in June 1963 at the Cuban Embassy in Mexico City, a notorious hotbed for spies and provocateurs. Derber arrived at the embassy, a white colonial building with tightly closed dark shutters. Stepping inside, the dimly lit lobby was filled with the scent of cigar smoke and old leather.

Pina, dressed in a green Cuban Air Force uniform, greeted Derber in the foyer. His hair was graying and he sported a trimmed moustache. The men retired to the office of the Cuban Consul, Eusebio Azcue Lopez. Azcue had a voluminous head of white hair, along with a matching bushy white moustache. As a CIA informant, Aczue alerted the agency's Miami office, JMWAVE, of Derber's arrival.[26] For extra measure, a CIA microphone was concealed in the leg of Azcue's coffee table.

Over hours of discussion, Pina and Derber negotiated an agreement for Derber's company to become the exclusive provider of transportation out of Cuba, with three trips scheduled per week, each carrying a thousand passengers. They shook hands

Signature page of exclusive agreement between Empress Lines Ltd and the Cuban government to provide transportation of Cuban passengers to the US.

to seal the deal, marking a new chapter in Cuban migration and a life-changing business opportunity for Derber. The men made plans to meet in the Bahamas to plan the next steps.

When Derber's plane landed in Nassau, he eagerly descended the staircase onto the sunlit tarmac. His expression fell when American INS officers appeared at the bottom, their eyes concealed behind dark sunglasses. They pulled Derber aside and informed him, in no uncertain terms, that traveling to Cuba would result in his US visa being voided, permanently barring him from returning to America.[27]

The news was devastating. Without access to the US, his mission – and his future with Sari – was suddenly in jeopardy. Before he could get his bearings, Nassau police officers clamped him on the shoulder and escorted him to an interrogation room at the back of the airport. They demanded answers about his business dealings, contacts and the real purpose of the ferry service. Calm and composed as always, Derber assured them the ferry was legal.

After nearly an hour of interrogation, Derber emerged and made his way to the airport restaurant, where Captain Pina was already waiting. Pina wore a business suit, while his officers wore military uniforms, subtly conveying that he operated beyond typical hierarchies.

They embraced and settled into their seats. Over the clatter of cutlery, Derber slid a folder across the table. Inside were the names of a thousand Cubans with US visa waivers. The Cuban government should decide which ones would make the journey to America.

Pina's gaze flicked to the sheets, then back to Derber. He paused, allowing Derber to understand the significance of his upcoming words. Derber needed to expand his ambitions. There were 73,000 Cuban refugees ready to be transported right then. The ferry service was a priority at the highest echelons of the

Cuban government. Pina insisted Derber visit Cuba in person to discuss the matters further.

Traveling to Cuba would require him to relinquish his US visa and abandon any plans of returning to America. Pina was adamant, however. He had a twin-engine Ilyushin-14 aircraft waiting on the tarmac, ready to take him to Havana to meet with Prime Minister Castro.[27, 28]

Derber met Pina's gaze. The invitation was an extraordinary opportunity – a chance to win the Cuban government's support and push back against the State Department's resistance.

For a moment, silence hung between them as Derber weighed the cost. Accepting meant giving up his future with Sari in America. Refusing could compromise the mission and endanger thousands of refugees. He could save them – but only by sacrificing the life he'd dreamed of with the one person he truly loved.

It was an impossible choice. He asked himself what Sari would want him to do.

Derber excused himself and stepped into the bustling airport hall. He strode to the US immigration counter and asked the clerk to type a letter, saying as follows: "As of this date, I relinquish my status as a resident of the United States." After a brief hesitation, Derber signed the letter and returned the pen, along with his US visa.[29, 30] America, his adopted home country, was now part of his past.

Bidding farewell to America was only the beginning of his troubles. Without a US visa, he needed a new country to call home. The Bahamas, with its British ties and turquoise waters, was a natural choice. Yet it wasn't clear whether Sari would give up her life in America to join him or if he'd have to embark on a new life alone.

Derber stepped aboard the Cubana de Aviación plane with Captain Pina, bound for Havana. He could only pray that his gambit would be worth it.

No records exist of Derber's first meeting with Castro, but it would not be their last. Castro's interest in the ferry project grew as he recognized its strategic importance for circumventing the U.S. embargo, expelling dissidents, and securing a propaganda victory against the United States.

On his return flight to the Bahamas, Derber anticipated settling into his new home country and commencing work on the ferry project. As the plane sat on the landing strip, he pictured his new life in Nassau: mornings with coffee on a balcony overlooking Cable Beach, and evenings under palm trees as the sea breeze carried the scent of hibiscus. But the unease grew as the minutes passed and the plane door remained shut. Finally, a Bahamian immigration officer boarded the plane and delivered a devastating message: the Bahamian government had deemed Derber "an undesirable immigrant" and he was forbidden to set foot on the island.[27, 31-34]

Derber flushed with rage. The decision was a blatant affront to his rights as a British subject. He had been denied entry to a British colony without due process or even the courtesy of a written explanation. Frustration boiling over, he declared himself sovereign, renouncing his loyalty to Britain, America and the Jews. He was now wireless, and everything was permitted.

Fuming, Derber returned to Havana, determined to plan his next move. While he regrouped, news of his ferry venture made national headlines and evening news broadcasts back in the US.

To earn public support for his cause, Derber turned to Jack Nageley, a fiery Miami lawyer and fellow World War II veteran who shared Derber's love of a good fight. Nageley didn't hesitate; he took to the airwaves, rallying public support for Derber's cause.

The Miami WTVJ newscaster asked Nageley what happened: "Mr. Nageley, why can't Harold Derber get back to Nassau?"

Sari and Nageley giving an interview.

"I have been advised by the Bahamian officials that the United States government has lodged a complaint against Mr Derber, and for this reason, he was permitted to land on Nassau soil, but he was not permitted to step foot on it," Nageley replied.

"What sort of complaint?"

"Well, I tried to pinpoint the officials at the time, and they would not give me a specific reason. There can be no doubt that the reason is that he has the exclusive contract from the Cuban government to bring these refugees out of Cuba. I feel he is unfairly treated because he is not permitted to land on British soil, which is the equivalent of deportation without any court authority or any orderly process of law."

...

"The latest reports say the *Orange Sun* won't sail for at least another week. Do you think it ever will sail to Cuba?"

"I think it will sail. I definitely do. We have ironed out all of the difficulties that presently exist. We have no way of anticipating what additional requirements the government will impose, but there has to be an end to everything, and we are going to satisfy each particular. We are going to proceed lawfully, and we are going to do it. There is only one way we can be stopped; that is from a command from the United States government to say, 'No,' and that's it."

"And yet they won't say that directly," the reporter observed rhetorically.

"That's correct because the government must follow the laws just as its citizens must."[35]

Nageley added, "The fiasco being perpetrated is worse than the Bay of Pigs invasion."[36]

Meanwhile, the Red Cross delivered the final voyage of the friends and families of the Bay of Pigs prisoners on the SS *Maximus*. When the ship docked in Fort Lauderdale Port, the passengers erupted in cheers: "Yankee si! Russia no!" "Viva Red Cross!" "Viva Kennedy!" and "Viva United States!"

The crowd's shouts grew louder, becoming a unified chant. "Ferry! Ferry!" they cried out. "Ferry! Ferry!" The chant echoed through the port, gaining strength with each repetition. They were pleading for Derber's ferry.[37]

Reporters asked a woman what the passengers were chanting. "There are rumors that [the ferry] will be done so political prisoners can be exchanged and so parents can join children already in the United States," the woman explained. Another woman added, "The people desperately want to keep things going, but the government has said nothing about any ferry service."[38]

Some of the refugees shared stories of the lives they had left behind, describing the harsh oppression and deprivation they had endured. In hushed tones, they also spoke of secret missile bases

SS Maximus, *the last Red Cross ship out of Cuba. The passengers are chanting for Derber's ferry.*

being installed on the island, adding an undercurrent of urgency and fear to their pleas.

When asked if the Red Cross supported the private ferry, a representative deflected: "The Red Cross is a humane organization dedicated to alleviating human suffering ... As far as we are concerned, this operation has been concluded."[39, 40] A US immigration director concurred, "We have no plans for any more ships of refugees. The job is completed."[37] The voyage of the *Maximus* marked the last escape from Cuba to the US – possibly forever.

That night, the television broadcast the heart-wrenching family reunions. Fathers rushed into the arms of their families, who embraced them tightly and showered them with kisses, tears streaming. One young boy leaned his head back and let out a piercing wail as he collapsed into his father's arms. Beneath the relief, however, there was sorrow. The tears were not only for those reunited, but for those still left behind, unable to escape.

While pacing his Havana hotel room, Derber received word that the US had officially declared the transportation mission complete. Yet hundreds of thousands of Cubans remained stranded on the island, their hopes for freedom fading with each passing day. Abandoned by the State Department's bureaucratic indifference, their plight had become desperate. Waiting for appeals or diplomatic resolutions would only prolong their suffering. It was clear – the time for playing by their rules was over. Through Nageley, Derber relayed a message to Sari: proceed with the plan.

7. WE WILL NOT BE STOPPED BY MILITARY FORCE

Miami and the Caribbean, 1963

Sari headed to the Senate Hotel, a well-known hotspot for Cuban militants. Across the lobby, her contact lingered in the corner, staring at her with a fixed gaze. The man was Lieutenant Colonel Irenaldo García Báez, the hotel's owner and former chief of military intelligence for the Cuban dictator Fulgencio Batista. Notorious in Cuban Miami as one of the regime's most brutal torturers, Báez had committed a mass execution of Castro's rebels, leaving a trail of blood that still haunted many.[1] When Castro took power, the new government sentenced Báez to 42 death sentences, but he escaped revolutionary justice by fleeing to Miami with his family, where he was admitted to the country without any paperwork. He used to work for one of the most sinister police forces in the hemisphere. Now he worked for Derber.

With the police nowhere in sight, Sari began arranging a stack of flyers on the table. As soon as the pamphlets hit the table, a surge of people flowed in: a teenage girl, an elderly man with haunted eyes, children without parents, grandmothers without grandchildren, husbands without wives.

Each was drawn by the flyer's promise. Translated from Spanish, it read, "The steamship company of Empress Lines

Senate Hotel.

Limited of the Bahamas announces the establishment of the passenger service by ship from Havana to Key West and packages containing medicines, food, or clothing from Miami to Havana."[2] Sari and Báez were selling the most exclusive commodity in Miami, unobtainable anywhere else: one-way tickets out of Cuba. The price was $50, half for transportation and half for harbor costs in Havana – a small price to pay to rescue a loved one.

Ticket buyers packed the lobby and spilled onto the street, the crowd growing louder and more restless by the minute. Suddenly, uniformed officers pushed through the crush, making straight for the makeshift ticket desk. Without hesitation, they ordered Sari and Báez to shut it down. They cuffed Báez for not having a license to sell tickets, while Sari played the naïve "good-looking secretary" and escaped arrest.[3,4] Though the police moved in swiftly, they were too late; Empress Lines had sold 1,500 tickets.[5]

When word of the new ferry service reached the State Department, officials were quick to clarify that they had not

We Will Not Be Stopped by Military Force

Flyer promoting the Havana–Key West ferry.

formally approved the operation. However, they reluctantly acknowledged that, under current regulations, it was not technically illegal either.[6]

WTVJ News caught up with Sari, unmissable in her tall beehive hairdo and striking cat eyeliner. The reporter pressed her with questions: "What happens to this money? Who has it? Where's it going? Will the people be able to get it back?" With calm confidence, Sari replied, "We have had very few requests for a refund because the Cuban people believe justly in our project, and they are confident that we are going to fulfil our guarantee of bringing their families in."[7]

They asked Derber's lawyer, Nageley. "Now, is this a money-making venture for you and Mr Derber, or what's your interest?" the reporter asked. Nageley replied, "In so far as I'm concerned it is not a money-making venture because I have as of yet to make the first quarter."

"What about after the first one hundred thousandth passenger comes over here? Won't you be making some money out of it?"

"I hope we do," Nageley replied with a chuckle.[8]

Alarmed by Empress Lines' progress, Gordon Chase, the Special Assistant for National Security Affairs, briefed Bundy:

> For the past couple weeks, State had been having a running battle with Empress Lines, a Bahamian steamship agency which hopes to transport 650 Cuban refugees to Miami each week. Empress Lines, which is run by a shady British national by the name of Mr Derber has already sold about 1,000 tickets to Cuban exiles who want to bring relatives and friends to Miami ... Empress Lines had received the approval (reportedly, on an exclusive basis) of the Cuban Government for its proposed service ... State does not want regular passenger service between Cuba and Miami ... A complicating factor is that Empress Lines has not been cooperative and has continued to forge ahead with its plan in the face of State's objections ...
>
> While State will undoubtedly be able to withstand Empress Lines' pressure, the story could hit the national press with an unfortunate slant – i.e. the US government is keeping poor Cuban people out of the US. While this line will have little impact on many Americans, it is clear that it will appeal to others.
>
> If the story breaks, tentative press guidelines are (1) that we certainly have great sympathy for the oppressed Cubans who want to leave Cuba, (2) that we have demonstrated our feelings by permitting a large number of refugees to come into the country already, (3) that a further influx of refugees will create problems for us, and (4) that we are now in the midst of reviewing the whole subject.[9]

The National Security Advisor's involvement highlighted the ferry's security threat. And Congress also raised alarms. One Florida

Republican reported, "Apparently a deal has been made with Castro so far as [Empress Lines Ltd] is concerned, to open up the shipping lanes between Key West and Havana. I made a protest about this, and I hope it is not accomplished."[10]

With Congress taking notice, the freedom ferry rose to the top of Kennedy's agenda. The President's advisor prepped him for questions about the ferry for his next press conference. He suggested the President could claim the ferry violated the trade embargo, even though the ban didn't apply to Derber, a British national. Kennedy's advisor admitted, "There is an outside possibility that, the promoters, who are skillful, determined and apparently unscrupulous, could avoid technical violations of the Treasury regulation."[11]

Undeterred by the police raid, Sari kept selling tickets through the Rescate Democrático Revolucionario, aka the Cuban Rescue Committee. Privately, Derber charged affluent passengers $1,000 per ticket, twenty times the advertised $50 price.[12]

Public opinion was divided. One letter to the *Miami Herald* wrote, "[Derber's] action dramatically calls attention to the hoax played on suffering human beings and their families by some unknown bureaucrats in our Department of State, who told tens of thousands of Cubans that they would be able to enter the United States with visa waiver letter and then shut off the means of travel." The letter was less understanding of Derber's profiteering, however, writing, "As for Mr. Derber making a fast buck or two, at the expense of these people, it is reprehensible, but at least, he is calling attention to a breach of faith by our State Department."[13] One detractor wrote, "I say enough is enough and this latest plan is just a racket and smacks of an organized Castro plot. Our reply should be a loud, 'No'." Another reader wrote, "The United States Department of State has given no reason to oppose the proposed journey of Cuban refugees via ferry from Havana to Key West ... We should welcome those refugees ... Let's at least help those Cubans who can escape to rebuild their lives in this country."

Continuing the media offensive, Nageley told WTVJ News: "We are committed to the idea that there is no difference between this and the Donovan deal except one thing. We are not paying 50 million dollars for ransom." Derber's second lawyer, Charles Ashmann, summarized the contrast: "[Derber] went down there and accomplished the same thing Donovan had done, only he wasn't sent down there by anyone. Somehow he got the Cuban government to release these refugees."[14]

The comparison between Donovan and Derber was telling. Most Cubans transported in Operation Mercy had no US visas, background checks or health screenings. Many of the supposed family members of the prisoners were criminals, spies or unwell. US corporations paid the Castro government millions in ransom, funded by American taxpayers through corporate tax deductions for the charitable supplies.

Derber's approach was arguably more legally and politically sound. His passengers paid for their tickets and had valid visa waivers. He provided the passenger manifest and followed all immigration and customs regulations. Unlike Donovan's operation, Derber's venture did not involve outsized payments to the Castro government.

While Derber faced prosecution, Donovan was lauded as a national hero and the greatest negotiator of a generation. The CIA would later award Donovan the Defense Intelligence Medal, the Agency's highest honor, for his work on Operation Mercy and other diplomatic achievements. Meanwhile, the government labeled Derber unscrupulous, shady, dubious, of questionable character, an internationalist, and "a threat to the security of the United States."

Donovan was a Harvard Law School graduate with high-powered connections in the White House. In contrast, Derber was a foreign-born maverick with a middle school education and no powerful sponsors. If Donovan was the meta-diplomat who operated above protocols, Derber was the anti-diplomat who barreled through them.

Facing the State Department's opposition, Nageley and Derber prepared for a fight. Nageley continued, "My client is so dedicated to this proposition that he has advised me that he will not be stopped by military force and the only way he will be stopped is if the British or American government shoot [sic] the vessel out of the water."[15]

One memo to Bundy reported, "A British national of questionable reputation, Harold Derber, and his American attorney, Jack Nageley, have actively sought to exploit Cuban exiles' desire to have relatives and friends still in Cuba join them." The memo cautioned that the US government may be confronted with accusations of building a Berlin Wall in the Caribbean if it tried to stop Derber.[16]

The State Department was cornered politically: blocking the ferry would appear oppressive while permitting it risked a humanitarian crisis.

It laid down stringent conditions for ticket sales: passenger lists required approval, clearance by US officials in Cuba was mandatory, and collecting the $25 harbor fee in the US was prohibited. However, the persistent demand for passenger inspections in Cuba, which the US had no intention of performing, exposed the deception behind their tactics.

The State Department was attempting to stop the ferry with impossible bureaucratic requirements while avoiding taking a public position. In an August 1963 memo, Chase wrote to Bundy, "There have been indications over the past few weeks that we may get increasing pressures from Empress Lines ... and possibly from the Cuban Government itself to resume further large-scale immigration from Cuba." Chase feared a widespread backlash.

"The public position should be of some interest to the White House since a closed-door policy on Cuban immigration could cause some level of public heat."[17]

Despite the US government's duplicity, Derber met their demands. Cuba consented to US inspectors and dropped their fee. Nageley announced in the press, "It will be a few days before we can comply with these regulations, but we shall do so. Cuban Transportation Director Víctor Pina has assured us his government will waive the $25 fee."[18]

Charging ahead, Derber attempted to charter his first vessel for the ferry, the Panama-flagged *Orange Sun*.[34] Báez announced, "The first boatload of 650 people will arrive in Key West Monday. We plan another trip on July 8 and the 15th using the ship Orange Sun. After that, we will use the 1000-passenger ship Orion."[19] However, the Panamanian government objected to their flag being used for the ferry, citing their prohibition on trade with Cuba. The Panama-flagged *Orion* was also not an option for the same reason. "This vessel is registered under the Panamanian flag," their lawyers protested, "and if placed in service to Cuba it would lose its status of registration and be subjected to severe penalties."[20]

Following the State Department's instructions, Derber submitted a passenger list of 600 names. However, State redirected him to the Swiss Embassy in Cuba, which referred him to the Cuban government.[21] They were sending him in circles.

Furious, Derber told the *Miami Herald*, "We will sail regardless ... Let them impound my ship, and we will fight the [US government] through the courts." He would sail "whether we have State Department approval of the passenger list or not."[22] The once-reserved wireless student had found the voice of a wartime captain.

The next challenge was to secure a boat and a flag. The flag had to come from a nation that maintained diplomatic ties with

Cuba and wouldn't easily bow to US demands. The UK wasn't an option, as it would likely cave to American pressure. One of the British Indies might work, but Derber was banned from the Bahamas and likely all the British colonies.

After some thought, Jamaica emerged as the perfect solution. With its recent independence from the British Crown, Jamaica would be less susceptible to pressure from the UK. The country also had no navy to physically stop the ferry. Conveniently, the timing coincided with Jamaican Independence Day. Derber and Sari could enjoy the festive celebrations while scouting for their new ship.

With plans to secure a ferry boat in Jamaica, Derber boarded a Cubana de Aviación flight from Havana to Kingston, with a scheduled layover in Grand Cayman.

From the airplane window, the Cayman Islands appeared as tiny green jewels scattered across the shimmering blue expanse of the Caribbean. When the plane began its descent onto Owen Roberts Field, dozens of vehicles and hundreds of figures came into view near the runway. The gathering was too large and too chaotic to be a response to an accident. Something wasn't right.

When the plane touched down, hundreds of people were standing on the runway shoulder, parked cars lining the edge.[23-25] As the aircraft rolled to a stop, leaders in the crowd pointed toward it, riling up the mob. In a sudden surge, people overpowered the airport police and stormed the runway. Cars barreled onto the tarmac, forming a blockade that trapped Derber's plane – along with his connecting flight to Jamaica. A breakaway group charged straight toward the aircraft.

The pilot's voice cracked over the intercom, informing the passengers that he had no choice but to return to Havana. The plane taxied to the departure strip and the engines roared back to life. As the plane climbed, Derber's connecting flight to

Jamaica shrank into the distance. The cars and trucks drove off in a cloud of dust.

This was no ordinary protest; it was a clear message that the State Department could reach him anywhere. But Derber hadn't come this far to be thwarted by a mob, no matter who was behind it.

US newspapers claimed the Caymanian crowd spoiled Derber's plan because they were fed up with subversive Cuban agents using their island as a layover to Latin America. Nageley, however, was not convinced: "I have little doubt that the demonstration was directed against Derber."[26]

Captain Pina recognized the CIA's handiwork. The Cuban foreign ministry issued a communiqué from him, saying the Havana–Cayman route had operated without difficulty "until yesterday when a crowd financed by the government of the United States and directed by elements of the CIA demonstrated in the Grand Cayman Airport." The Cuban government will carry out "the pertinent negotiations with the government of Great Britain to re-establish these flights which the government of the United States is trying to block."[27, 28]

The Cayman mob incident was now the third time Derber had been thwarted in the Caribbean, following his ban from travel to Cuba and his exclusion from the Bahamas. Throughout, American and British officials consistently denied any involvement. Two of the most powerful governments on the planet feared Derber's ferry to such an extent that they would undertake an international suppression operation and publicly deny it.[24]

Back in Cuba, the political tension escalated. Captain Pina, determined to increase the pressure on the US, handed Derber more political ammunition. Cuba agreed to release 85,000 political prisoners on the condition that the US admit 380,000 refugees.[29] By obstructing the ferry, the US would now be responsible for preventing the release of anti-Castro freedom fighters.

Nageley relayed the message to the press: "I have been advised by Mr Derber that the Cuban government will release all of its political prisoners on the condition that those Cubans who now have visa waivers are permitted to go to the United States."[30] "We shall operate, starting this weekend, on the assumption we are violating no United States law. Extensive researching indicates none is being violated."[31] He even volunteered to appear before the Senate Internal Security Committee to explain how and when Derber could get the political prisoners out of Cuba "at no cost whatsoever to the United States government."[32] The latter comment was a veiled critique of the $50 million ransom Donovan paid to free the Bay of Pigs prisoners.

When they arrived in Kingston, Derber and Sari were enveloped in the festive celebrations of Jamaican Independence Day. Black, yellow and green crosses fluttered from car antennae and adorned the twirling dresses of little girls. Junkanoo dancers paraded through the streets, swaying to the rhythm of the kettle drums. Jamaican Air Force planes, decorated in the national colors, roared overhead.

Hand in hand, Derber and Sari navigated through the celebrations, laughing and spinning among the street dancers. They held each other close, savoring every precious moment, knowing they had no future together unless she joined him abroad. Every step, every twirl, was a silent plea for more time. Soon, the music would fade, and they would have to face the impossible decision. But for now, they would lose themselves in the festivities, uncertain of what lay ahead.

As the night wound down, the couple retreated to the Jamaica Reef Hotel in Port Antonio, a luxurious retreat once owned by Errol Flynn. This secluded spot would become their headquarters for the ferry operation. They decided to start small: a single test run with a modest boat and a handful of passengers, just enough to prove the legality of their venture. This cautious approach also improved their chances of obtaining the necessary ship and flag. With a successful first voyage, they could pave the way for a full-scale ferry service, ultimately transporting thousands.

Derber chartered a 61-foot, 30-passenger air-sea rescue boat called the *Nana*. The *Nana*'s owner was a fellow Brit named Peter Whitehead, who had purchased the ship the week before.[33-35] Whitehead relished the cause. He gave Derber a line of credit to buy provisions and even refused an offer for the boat from the United States Embassy, which sought to edge out Derber's charter.[36] Whitehead kept the uncashed check from the Embassy as a souvenir, but it was another ominous sign that the US government would seek to obstruct Derber in Jamaica just as it had in the Bahamas and the Caymans.

Soon after Derber's purchase, the Port Antonio harbormaster – a Scotsman named Captain Alan Cameron Tough – came to inspect the *Nana*. In another lifetime, Captain Tough and Derber could have been close mates. Like Derber, Tough served in the British Merchant Navy during the Battle of the Atlantic and stayed on after the war. He was a fellow northerner and a skilled navigator, having chaired the navigation department at Lews Castle College in the West Isles of Scotland until the school dismissed him following a state inquiry.[37] Tough fled to Jamaica during the investigation and started a second career overseeing operations at Port Antonio.

Rather than grading nautical students' papers, Captain Tough found himself that afternoon reviewing the safety of Derber's ship, despite having no background in vessel inspections. After a cursory look over, Tough detained the *Nana* for multiple safety violations, even though she had passed a safety inspection only the previous week. The safety issues included the inability to launch lifeboats and the lack of a 'load-line,' a mark on the hull that shows how deep a vessel sinks when fully loaded.[38]

Tough ordered the boat be detained until "it meets the requirements of the International Conventions governing the safety of life at sea."[35] The Jamaican customs officer was more direct: "I am under instructions not to allow this vessel to sail."[35]

Nageley was indignant that the US was again pressuring Jamaican henchmen to ground Derber's mission: "If they don't let the ship leave Wednesday, I'll do something similar to what Hiroshima was to World War II."[39]

When it became clear that the boat detention might not be enough to stop Derber, the Jamaican authorities threatened the *Nana* crew with fines and seizure of their seaman's papers, prompting the entire crew to resign. Undeterred, Derber assembled a new crew from an abandoned British freighter.[38]

With his new team ready, Derber announced in the press, "We are sailing under the British flag, and Britain has not broken off diplomatic relations with Cuba. Our ship has been cleared from Kingston, and should the American Navy try to intercept us, we will radio for help to British warships cruising in the area. If necessary, we will even ask for the assistance of the Cuban navy."[40]

Nageley joined the cry, telling a reporter:

We've been hindered, harassed and given a lot of hogwash ever since our plans to evacuate Cuban refugees were announced. But the government will have to blow us out of the water to keep us from Havana – and maybe we don't stop then. Let's get one thing straight. If it's within human power to do so, we're going to get those people out of Cuba. We've met every condition the government has laid down. Don't sell tickets without a license, they said. We stopped. Give us a passenger list, they said. We gave them one, with all 1,197 names on it. Don't use the *Orange Sun* – we're not.

We want to fight Communism too. The Cuban underground will never fight with their families in Cuba, they want to get out. These people are anti-communists, they've signed pledges they are. If they fled in little boats by themselves, they maybe get shot. If they get away, they get into the US. But when we take them out – with the consent of the Cuban government, safely – then that's wrong.

He added, "We are simply helping anti-Communist Cubans to bring their families to the United States ... we are not giving aid or comfort to Communist Cuba."[41] The reporter asked Nageley who was bankrolling their project, suspecting a foreign power was at work. "An anti-communist source. I'm not at liberty to say," Nageley replied, hinting at larger forces behind Derber's project.[42]

While this unfolded, the Swiss Embassy, acting as the US representative in Cuba, scrambled to decide their next move. The cable from Berne to Havana read: "Until [Swiss Ambassador] Stadelhofer has been able to speak with Fidel Castro, we wish to avoid him finding himself in an embarrassing situation with Cuban authorities."[43]

At 3.40am on August 17, with Jamaican police spotlights trained on her, the *Nana* set sail from Port Antonio in defiance of the detention order. She was headed to Havana to pick up the refugees for the test run. A Jamaican police boat followed in pursuit.

Nageley updated WTVJ News: "My client ... took advantage of the fact that the Jamaican government does not have a navy and sailed out last night unadvised at about two or three o'clock in the morning." He confirmed, "The vessel should be in the vicinity of Cuba at this moment and should arrive in Havana, Cuba, tomorrow."[44] The Freedom Ferry was underway.

The *Nana* cut through the waves, pulling further from the pursuing police ship with every surge. One by one, the crew loosened their grips on rails and rigging. Sari squeezed Derber's hand, her eyes alight. "We're going to make it," she murmured.[45]

But just as they reached open water, there was the thunderous roar of aircraft overhead. Two Cessna Skywagons circled above, their green-and-yellow markings of the Jamaica Defense Force unmistakable against the morning sky.[41, 46]

As the planes drew nearer, the *Nana*'s engine began to choke, sputtering before the sound of rushing water rose from below decks. Panic gripped the crew as water flooded the engine room, forcing the boat to slow. Within minutes, the Jamaican patrol boats closed the distance and boxed them in, forcing the *Nana* back toward the coast. The Jamaican government had thwarted their daring attempt to reach Cuba before it could even begin.

As the *Nana* docked, dozens of rifle-wielding customs officers swarmed aboard. They quickly detained the Jamaican crew, allowing only the foreign passengers to walk free. With the *Nana* seized at Port Antonio under allegations of safety violations, the promise of freedom faded into a quiet surrender.[41, 47]

Trying to understand how the *Nana* could have escaped detention, the agency sent four "burly CIA officers" to interrogate Whitehead.[48] "I refuse to answer questions," he told them. "I am British, and you represent foreign power"'[49]

The Havana newspaper *Noticia de Hoy* attributed the intervention to the CIA: "The company 'Empress Line' of the United States announced yesterday according to the UPI that the North American Central Intelligence Agency (CIA) interposed its 'good offices' so that Jamaican authorities prevented the inauguration of a ferry line between Jamaica, United States and Cuba, to transport by sea the worms that want to go north." The article continued: "The American government acts in the case with its characteristic hypocrisy. He apparently washes his hands when he secretly pressures for his dictates to be carried out."[50]

The State Department denied any involvement in the Jamaican authorities' interception of Derber and the detention of his ship. "Any action by Jamaica to enforce its own law was clearly its own decision," said the State Department press office.[51] However, behind the scenes, the US was orchestrating the entire operation. The chargé d'affaires of the US Embassy in Jamaica "disclosed in strict confidence that his instructions from Washington were to try to get Derber and the 'Nana' detained in Jamaica for as long as possible, though not at all costs ..."[52] Presumably, the last qualification was a euphemism to not use physical force. The Embassy passed the orders to Jamaica, which was happy to comply. The White House press office briefed President Kennedy: "Our efforts to block this scheme have been to date successful ... We instructed our Embassy in Kingston to take appropriate steps with the Jamaican authorities to prevent the departure of the vessel."[53]

Gordon Chase briefed the White House that "Prime Minister Bustamante [of Jamaica] has not hesitated to place his country openly and unequivically [sic] on the side of the West and the United States in the present struggle with the Sino-Soviet bloc." He continued, "In response to our request the GOJ [Government of Jamaica] exerted its best efforts to obstruct and delay departure of the NANA, a boat which British citizen Harold Derber planned to transport refugees from Cuba to the U.S."[54]

It was remarkable that a small, 30-passenger ferry in the Caribbean was on the President's agenda, situated in the global conflict between the West and Sino-Soviet communism. But the *Nana* was more than a ferry; she was a vanguard ship. From the US government's perspective, if the *Nana* was not stopped, she could bring an unprecedented wave of communist spies and unwanted migrants to America.

While crewman Miguel Such worked to repair the *Nana*, Derber and Sari savored a sun-drenched afternoon on Port Antonio's wharf. Around them, porters hoisted crates of bananas and sacks of sugar, while children's laughter mingled with the dockworkers' shouts.

The tranquility was shattered when Captain Tough arrived, demanding to board the *Nana* and inspect the ship for safety violations. Derber scoffed and flashed the clearance documents. Tough barely glanced at them, and dismissed them as forgeries. Derber, jaw tight, demanded identification. Tough shot back: "I don't have to tell you who I am or show you anything; it is none of your business." Standing firm, Derber questioned whether Tough even had the authority to inspect a private, non-commercial ship. Tough waved a piece of paper and said, "This is my authority for going on board." Derber yelled that Kennedy had sent them. But Tough wasn't fazed. With a curt nod to Police Superintendent Harold Gayle, they both climbed aboard.

Tough surveyed the *Nana*'s deck, a sinister smile spreading. Without warning, he began tearing apart the life jackets, sending tufts of fabric flying. Derber and Such rushed to stop him, but the Jamaican officers held them back.

Then Tough turned his attention to Sari, calling her "a low-down white bitch." Enraged, Derber lunged at Tough, but the police officers restrained him. He struggled against their hold as Sari urged him to let it go, insisting it wasn't worth it.

With Derber and Such held back, Captain Tough descended into the hold, his boots clanging on the metal. Derber taunted him, asking how he planned to inspect the boat without tools. Tough smirked. Gripping a screwdriver like a knife, he began boring into the bilge. He then went on a rampage, throwing the gas pump into the bilge water and knocking over the drums, soda and beer bottles. Derber grimaced with every crash.

After completing the first part of his inspection, Tough exited the hold and walked to the skylight-hatch entrance to the engine room. Seeing their chance, Derber and Such broke free from the police and threw themselves over the hatch, attempting to keep it closed. Gayle and two other police officers rushed over to pull open the hatch. Gayle's force shattered the skylight glass, sending a shower of jagged shards into the engine room. The officers pulled Derber and Such away.

Derber stood with his fists clenched as Tough descended through the shattered skylight into the engine room, glass crunching underfoot. Soon, the clang of metal echoed from below as Tough hammered away at the engine with a wrench. Fed up with the onlookers, Tough ordered Derber and Such to be arrested. In seconds, additional plainclothes police stormed the boat and seized them.[55, 56]

At Port Antonio police station, officers confiscated Derber's British passport, claiming it was British property.[57] They then charged him and Such with assaulting and obstructing His Majesty's Officers.[58] Raging, Derber vowed to sue the Jamaican government for a million dollars for damage to his boat.

Thrown into a dank cell, Derber lay on a cold metal cot bolted to the wall. He seethed at the injustice he'd suffered at the hands of the Jamaican police, vowing they would pay. But they were just pawns; the real force behind them was the US government. And the State Department wasn't just a bureaucracy – it was something far darker. The ominous presence could cross oceans and slip into whatever host it needed to do its bidding: a Nassau customs officer breaking his oath, a Caymanian girl storming a runway, a Jamaican harbormaster crashing through glass, a Swiss diplomat lost in bureaucratic red tape, a presidential advisor spouting gibberish. It was like a *dybbuk* from Yiddish folklore, a vengeful spirit clinging to the living, never seeking redemption. He'd have to find another way to banish the spirit.

Word of Derber's imprisonment in Jamaica reached America. Nageley described the incident in an interview with a WTVJ News reporter.

"The Jamaican police of Port Antonio, who have not confiscated the vessel, went aboard the vessel again without authority of law and about thirty of the police swarmed aboard. Mr Derber attempted to go aboard to see what they were doing and to ascertain the extent of the damage that they had caused aboard the vessel, and he was summarily arrested and placed in jail."

"Can't you bail him out?" the television reporter asked.

"I have been advised that he has [sic] not going to be admitted to bail. I have further advised him to retain local counsel because the same constitutional rights that prevail in the United States also prevail under the United Kingdom laws," Nageley replied.

"Well now with the present ship tied up, impounded at Port Antonio, what's your next move?"

"Well, we've already made plans for another vessel, and I'm advised the vessel is underway. We are not going to disclose its name, its size, its origin, or its registry. But I am convinced that such a vessel is either prepared to move now or already underway."

"Well now you've already taken on Washington, the British government, the Bahamian government, and now the Jamaicans. Are you going to run out of governments to fight soon?" the reporter asked.

"I'm going to run out of patience, I'll tell you," Nageley replied.

"Well, do you think you can last out with all of these governments resisting your movement?"

"There will have to come a time when the US government is going to say whether or not they are for or against these people who are anti-communist, and whether or not they are going to permit them to cross the Cuban wall."[59]

Nageley added, "We're going to find out whether the State Department really wants to fight communism or whether it will refuse to let these people in the country."[60]

Furious at Derber's arrest, several dozen activists from the Cuban Rescue Committee protested at Miami's Torch of Friendship monument, a symbolic gateway for immigrants. Irate protestors carried a large sign that read, "We want to save our families." Children wore badges that read, translated from the Spanish, "We fight to bring our family from communist Cuba." Another group of protesters occupied Bayfront Park, demanding the Jamaican government release the *Nana*.[61]

Buoyed by the protests, Derber announced, "News of the freedom fighters' action proves our cause genuine ... Nobody seems to realize that for each day we are delayed people in Cuba and their relatives are suffering heartache and anguish."[58]

After three days in jail, Derber and Such were released on £150 bail. At trial, Captain Tough alleged Derber kicked him. Derber countered, saying it was impossible for two reasons. Firstly, it was beneath his dignity. Secondly, he broke both of his feet in the war. The court eventually convicted Derber and Such of assaulting Gayle but not Tough, fining them £15 each or two months in prison. Derber agreed to pay the fine and immediately announced his intention to appeal.[56, 62-64]

Chase shared the welcome update with Bundy: "Through a variety of devices we have been able to delay Derber up to now without issuing a public statement that we will not permit any further flow of refugees from Cuba."[65] State also notified the Interdepartmental Coordinating Committee of Cuban Affairs (ICCCA) and the Joint Chiefs of Staff.[66] Derber and Sari's activities were now being reported to the highest level of the US military.

Realizing that they had delayed Derber but not stopped him, the State Department began devising contingency plans in case he reached Florida's waters. Chase wrote, "Our plan is to seize the boat and let the Cubans into the US. However, there are reports that Derber may stay outside the 3-mile limit and send the refugees in, in row boats. Assuming Derber does this, State and the lawyers are trying to come up with a way to get at Derber so he won't be able to do it again."

Chase was referring to the three-mile limit from the United States coast that marked the end of United States legal territory. If Derber stayed at least that distance from the coast he'd be in international waters and beyond the US government's reach.

Then came the summons that would change everything. Days after his arrival in Kingston, Derber received an invitation to meet with Fidel Castro.[67] The invitation promised discussions that could shape the fate of hundreds of thousands of Cubans.

The details of Fidel Castro and Harold Derber's meeting are still a mystery, leaving room for speculation. They likely discussed the political impact of transporting Cuban refugees and how to navigate the complex diplomatic landscape. Castro's main concern was probably the legal status of visa waivers, which was crucial for making the operation legitimate and safe for passengers. He may have also seen the ferry service as a propaganda tool, aiming to cast his regime positively while criticizing the US blockade. Meanwhile, Derber likely sought guarantees of safe passage and logistical support, aligning with his goal of establishing regular shipping between Cuba and the US. Whatever they discussed, the outcome would significantly affect Derber's mission.

Following the meeting, Fidel extended his hospitality to Derber and Sari, offering accommodation at the Hotel Habana Libre, formerly the Havana Hilton. Only three years earlier, Castro and his revolutionary forces had marched into the hotel lobby to mark their takeover of the capital and the nation.

With the importance of their secret meeting still fresh, they returned to Port Royal in Jamaica, ready to set their plan in motion.[68] One following dawn, Derber and Sari stepped off the Morgan Club's pier and boarded the *Nana*. Sari left a note for the Club's owner, Sir Anthony Jenkinson, to remit the bill to her lawyer in Miami.

The *Nana* had 400 gallons of water, food, two lifeboats, a ship-to-shore radio, six crew members and 490 gallons of diesel fuel, enough to reach Havana. At dawn, she slipped from Port Royal in violation of her detention order and sailed for the Isle of Pines, Cuba, for repairs. En route, the crew noticed storm clouds gathering on the horizon.[69]

Warnings about the gathering tropical storm began spreading throughout the Caribbean. Meteorologists tracked its development with growing dread, forecasting it would become one of the deadliest hurricanes in Atlantic history. Residents scrambled to board up homes and secure their belongings as the sky darkened to a menacing gray. The ocean began to churn with rising waves, crashing against the shores, while palm trees bent under the increasing gales. Local radio stations urged people to seek shelter and brace for the devastation of what had now been named Hurricane Flora.

The crew of the *Nana* worked feverishly to complete the repairs and outrun the approaching storm. Meanwhile, Derber took a flight back to Havana to minimize delays. As his plane climbed, it was buffeted by the intensifying winds.

With a Cuban warship escorting her, the *Nana* departed from the Isle of Pines. However, it was too late. The *Nana* sailed headfirst into the wrath of Hurricane Flora. Battered by towering waves and howling winds, the *Nana* sprang three leaks and the starboard engine cut out. Water gushed in from all sides and the ship was overwhelmed. All eight crew members leapt onto the escort boat, one grabbing the ship's registration papers.[70]

Hurricane Flora killed several thousand people and destroyed several thousand homes across the Caribbean. Derber, Sari and the *Nana*'s crew were lucky to have escaped with their lives. The *Nana* was not as fortunate.

The White House and British Embassy exchanged frantic cables trying to determine if reports of the *Nana*'s sinking were true. The US press added to the confusion. The editorial page of the *Miami Herald* wrote, "There was a false report several days ago that the vessel which Derber is using had sunk off Cuba. We regret that the report proved untrue." The editorial continued, "We recall that Harold Derber, mainspring of the enterprise, said he held a contract with Fidel Castro's Communist regime to provide the service. Thus, he is acting for the Red dictator, who will be the only beneficiary of such stunts as yesterday's attempt to make a test case in Key West."[71]

With the *Nana* at the bottom of the Florida straits, Derber needed to find a new boat for the test run. Captain Pina obliged. He met Derber at the Havana Yacht Club and gave him the *Nelson II*, which closely resembled the *Nana*.[72, 73]

To pass off the *Nelson II* as the *Nana*, workers painted the hull white and wrote 'Nana' on the stern. Derber recovered the original *Nana*'s papers and contacted the British Embassy to register two ships – the *Nana* and the *Nelson II*. Decorated with a new name, a fresh coat of paint, updated registration papers and the Union Jack in place of the Cuban Lone Star, the new *Nana* was a beautiful tribute to her namesake.

The State Department launched a final effort to pressure the Cuban government via the Swiss Embassy. The message was straightforward: "[Swiss Ambassador] Stadelhofer should make a strong oral protest to the Cuban government ... This oral protest should be followed by a written protest, for which the language will be furnished by the Department of State."[74] With no leverage left, the US was reduced to relying on diplomatic gestures passed through neutral channels, hoping it would be enough to make a difference.

With a boat, a flag and a crew at his side, Derber was prepared for the voyage. The US had made its move; now it was his turn.

8. THE EXILE RUNNER

Cuba and Florida, 1963–64

On October 22, 1963, six Cuban families gathered at Port Mariel under the cover of night. Among them were eleven men, ten women and two small children, one a wide-eyed three-year-old girl. Under the stern watch of a Cuban intelligence agent, they silently boarded the *Nana*. After a subtle nod from the agent, the ship pushed off toward Florida, flanked by Cuban naval escorts.[1-3]

The Nana *transporting Cuban refugees from Havana to Florida. Derber and Sari can be seen on the starboard side of the pilot cabin.*

At 9 a.m., Coast Guard patrol planes locked onto the *Nana* off Key West. The pilot strained to make out her name through the morning haze, but her silhouette matched the description. Cutters and an amphibious plane closed in.

Without warning, a patrol boat roared through the waves, aiming straight for the *Nana*. With a sharp twist of the wheel, Derber swerved, barely avoiding a collision. Passengers screamed, clutching the railing as the boat tilted, cold spray hitting their faces.

Derber's heart pounded as the two vessels sped side by side toward US waters. With the Coast Guard cutter closing in, Derber pushed the throttle to its limit. The engine roared, waves crashing against the hull as the passengers held on. The cutter edged closer, its wake churning the water. The three-mile limit was just ahead – if they could make it that far.

Just as it seemed the cutter would overtake them, the *Nana* shot across the boundary into US waters. A collective gasp swept through the deck. They had made it.

Nana *being pursued by the Coast Guard while coming into Key West.*

Dozens of men in dark suits and military uniforms, arms crossed, waited for them on the Key West pier.[4] When the vessel docked, officials stormed the boat. They formed a human barrier around Derber and Sari while directing the passengers to disembark.[5]

The refugees took their first steps onto American soil, some clasping their hands in prayer, others hugging their loved ones. The three-year-old girl, in a Sunday dress and bobby socks, leapt onto the pier and into her new life.

Derber watched the scene unfold from the boat. What had begun as a daring business venture had become something more meaningful – a symbol of hope. It was worth everything he had sacrificed.

While the refugees were free, his own liberty still hung in the balance. Derber introduced himself to the officers as the ship's master and Sari as the purser. Sari, calm and composed, presented the ship's manifest and crew passports. One officer went through Derber's suitcase and grabbed the *Nana*'s registration papers, not realizing they were for the original *Nana*.

Without a US visa, Derber wasn't legally able to step off the boat and enter the country. As a seaman, he was allowed to be in US waters, but if he stepped onto the pier, he could be arrested for entering the country illegally.

He explained to the officers that he planned to continue to Mexico with Sari, but the Coast Guard had other ideas – one junior guardsman ordered Derber off the boat. And with that simple command he had given Derber legal permission to enter the country without a visa. It's unclear if this was a brilliant gambit on Derber's part or a fortuitous accident, but either way, Derber stepped off the pier and back onto American soil.

Officers immediately separated him from Sari and ushered him into a waiting car with pitch-black windows. As they drove

Passengers disembarking from the Nana.

to Miami, the officers bombarded him with questions. Who were his contacts in Cuba? How had the passengers been chosen? Was he working for Cuba? Derber answered the questions calmly.

Hours later, he found himself in a fluorescent-lit interrogation room in Miami.[6] The questioning dragged on through the night. Derber explained that he was a shipowner contracted to bring Cuban refugees to Florida. The passengers had valid US visa waivers, and he was merely helping them escape communist oppression. When the officers pressed him about his businesses, Derber insisted on speaking with his lawyer and refused to answer further without legal counsel.

Meanwhile, officers interrogated Sari in a separate facility. The questioning stretched until dawn as they pressed her about her involvement in the operation and whether she had entered Cuba without permission from the US government. Sari remained composed, explaining that she had traveled to Cuba as part of the ship's crew and was unaware that, as a crewmember, she required special permission to enter the country.[7,8]

Remarkably, the officials didn't press charges against Sari, neither for traveling to Cuba illegally nor transporting the Cuban refugees. Whether it was due to her US citizenship, her striking looks or perhaps her covert operations in Havana, Sari managed to escape any legal repercussions.

After her grueling questioning, Sari stood before a WTVJ reporter, unfazed. He was fascinated by her work in Cuba. What was it like? Did she meet any Russians? Did she look forward to going back? "Not necessarily, no. Well, I have no reason unless it was in the line of work," Sari replied matter of factly.[9]

After Sari's exchange with the reporter, attention turned to the fate of the *Nana* passengers. Following short interviews, immigration officials approved their refugee status and released them to start their new lives in America. Most of the passengers refused to speak with reporters, fearing they'd be sent back to Cuba. However, one brave passenger spoke out about the dire conditions in his home country: "Now Cuba really is hungry. There are days when a Cuban eats nothing. People faint waiting in line for food." He continued: "Havana is full of waiting lines. There are hours-long lines in front of grocery stores, meat markets, restaurants, everywhere. Often for nothing, since there is nothing to be bought. Often there are disorders. There is an armed militiaman at every Havana corner."[10]

After questioning, authorities held Derber in the immigration detention center in Tampa.[11] The heavy metal doors groaned shut behind him.

Derber faced both criminal and immigration charges,[12, 13] although the specific allegations were unclear. When Nageley asked for details, the Assistant US Attorney simply replied, "Take my word for it, he is a security risk."[11] Nageley argued Derber was being held to silence him from speaking to the press,[14] to which Derber wryly added, "I could tell too many stories."[15]

With the legal battle escalating, Derber's lawyer, Charles Ashmann, told a TV news reporter that "no formal charges have been brought against him [Derber]. It would appear that the only thing he's guilty of is successfully bringing twenty-three Cubans who wanted to free themselves from Castro to the United States."[16]

Dark-suited agents escorted Derber into the Tampa federal courthouse. Wearing black, round sunglasses and handcuffed to a chain around his waist, he strode into the courtroom with its vaulted ceilings and gleaming brass fixtures.

The judge called the hearing to order. Derber whistled softly and tapped his pen against the defense table as he scored his first legal victory. The judge ruled that Derber had entered the county legally due to the command from the Coast Guard officer.[17] Further, the INS couldn't deport him until the criminal case was decided.[18]

Derber entering the courtroom.

In the trial, the government painted Derber as a dire national security threat. "His trips into Cuba, out of Cuba, the arrangements to get these refugee Cubans out of Cuba, indicates to me that we are faced with a security risk which we want to thrash out," they argued.[19] They insisted the national security case was too sensitive to be discussed in a public courtroom. In secret, the FBI was investigating his connection to mob boss Santo Trafficante.[20]

Derber in the Tampa Federal Court building with Sari.

When the initial hearing ended, Sari rushed into Derber's arms. As they held each other, she whispered quiet reassurances. Only she understood Derber's torment of enduring the court's slow, grinding pace. In the busy courtroom, their embrace spoke volumes about a bond few could grasp. But the moment was fleeting; officers quickly pulled Derber away, leading him back to his cell.[11]

The reporters thronged around Sari when she stepped out of the courtroom. They all wanted to interview the stunning 'Captain's Girl' in her full-sleeve gold dress, black high heels, cat eyeliner and scarlet hair in a foot-high beehive. "This whole business stinks," she told reporters. "The charges against him are ridiculous."[21] Sari set the record straight: "The whole thing started when he offered the *Empress of Bahamas* steamship to help bring back the Cuban Bay of Pigs veterans last year. He was turned down. But several exile leaders asked if anything could be done about bringing other relatives, who had been granted visas from both Cuba and America." She continued: "Harold wrote time and again to the State Department in Washington and asked if he could do this. He even flew up to talk to them. They wouldn't say either way he could or he couldn't. In June, he met Cuban government officials in Mexico and came back with a contract."

"What was the journey from Cuba like?" one reporter asked.

"The voyage took nine hours. We were escorted in by a destroyer escort. Coast Guard planes kept coming in to look at us. It is not true we refused to let the Coast Guard people on board. We stopped twice and they never made an effort."

"What's at stake in this trial for Mr. Derber?"

"Harold knows he could be deported because of this," she continued. "If so, he says he'll go back to England. Well, I'll go with him ... We're very close."[22]

Overwhelmed, Sari broke away from the reporters, her heels clicking against the courthouse steps. The cigarette trembled in her

Derber and Sari in a tender moment.

hand as she exhaled a plume of smoke. Joining Derber in England had once seemed certain, but now she was unsure. When she first partnered with him, she envisioned a life of unbridled adventure, not one mired in endless legal battles. If she were to fight in court, it would be to regain custody of her children who were living with her ex-husband's parents back in Bradenton. Even if, against all odds, she won that fight, uprooting her children to England seemed impossible. Every path led to heartbreak.

The next day, Derber stood before the court. A faint smile crossed his lips as the judge announced the charges: reckless operation of a ship, refusal to let customs officials board and failure to give 24-hour notice of arrival at port.[23, 24] He caught Sari's gaze in the gallery and gave her a quick wink. Despite the government's bluster, all three charges were misdemeanors. Amazingly, they didn't charge him with transporting the Cuban refugees. Their threats had been hollow. Derber had endured orchestrated mobs, police brutality, unjust imprisonment and exile, all for a non-existent crime. Soon afterwards, even the misdemeanor charges were dropped by the judge as baseless. Derber had called the government's bluff and won.

Meanwhile, hundreds of miles away in Washington, the White House scrambled to contain the fallout of the unraveling case. Kennedy's press office prepared the President with carefully crafted talking points for the media: "We will continue to welcome those Cubans who find their way directly to this country ... But we will not allow the establishment of schemes such as the one attempted by Mr Derber in disregard of our laws and policies."[25] Remarkably, the President's briefing overlooked the glaring fact that none of the criminal charges had stuck.

But the government had an ace up its sleeve. *Nana* crewman Robert Bacilio Dawson offered crucial information: Derber had swapped the original *Nana* with a different vessel. The discovery had crucial legal implications: Derber had submitted false registration documents upon his arrival in Key West. Seizing the opportunity, the government charged Derber with the felony offense of presenting false registration papers.

Furious with the charge, Derber filed a federal class action lawsuit against President Kennedy. The suit, representing several hundred Cubans, claimed Kennedy broke his promise from his Orange Bowl speech to reunite Cuban families in America. Derber argued the plaintiffs applied for visa waivers based on Kennedy's speech, leading the Cuban government to seize their ration books and fire them. The judge joked that the political system would collapse if politicians were held accountable for broken promises. After the lawsuit, the Internal Revenue Service hit Derber with a lien for back taxes dating back to 1957, most likely in retaliation.[26-29]

While still facing the criminal charge, Derber's lawyer posted the $5,000 bond. In a surprising oversight, a US Marshal accidentally

Derber leaving the federal courthouse.

freed Derber from jail, unaware the additional INS hold was still in effect. "It was a slip up," the marshal later admitted. "We should have honored the detainer and didn't." With his usual composure, Derber strolled into the Miami sunlight, knowing his freedom would last only until the authorities discovered their blunder.

The mistake didn't go unnoticed for long. As soon as the blunder came to light, the Miami-Dade Police Department launched a citywide manhunt. Detectives fanned out across South Beach and Little Havana, slipping into alleyways, questioning locals in hurried Spanglish, flashing photographs of the well-dressed man with a pencil mustache and unmistakable British accent. They scoured the marinas along Biscayne Bay, questioning yacht owners and dock workers, desperate for a lead. All of Miami held its breath, waiting to see if the manhunt would end in Derber's dramatic capture or another of his brilliant escapes.

Hours later, Sari's phone rang. She broke into tears when the British voice on the other end casually asked if she had any dinner plans. When they met outside the restaurant, Sari and Derber fell into each other's arms, holding each other for a long moment before stepping inside to avoid Derber being detected. Joined by Sari's twin sister and their roommate, they slid into the soft velvet booths, the warm aromas of the restaurant offered a fleeting escape from his time in confinement. Every moment of the evening felt precious, their glasses raised in quiet celebration of friendship and freedom, both earned and accidental.

Whispering their final goodbyes, Derber and Sari held each other close as if to hold back time. Their eyes met in a quiet understanding. With a final nod, he stepped back, returning to his uncertain future.

The next morning, when the police arrived at Derber's Miami flat, he welcomed them with his usual charm, insisting he was no fugitive and would appear in court as planned. But for that one night, surrounded by love and laughter, he'd glimpsed a life that felt achingly close – a reminder of all that was at stake in the coming trial.[30-32]

Later that day, the court convened. Derber stood and pleaded not guilty. His attorney informed the court that Derber would be the sole witness for the defense. In contrast, the prosecution had prepared eleven witnesses, including three key members of Derber's own crew, all poised to deliver devastating testimony.

Derber's attorney asked the court to reduce his $10,000 bond, citing his client's plans to remain in the country and marry Sari. The prosecution countered, arguing, "After two years as a permanent resident here Derber gave up his status in order that he could go to Cuba. He has no respect for this country or its laws." The attorney continued, "He appears to be an internationalist who is not tied to this country."[33] The judge agreed, saying, "As a Britisher he doesn't have the ties here that would induce him to stay around as others might."[34] Ultimately, the judge denied the request to lower the bond, viewing Derber as the picture-book definition of a flight risk.

Despite the court's concern, Derber's escape routes were closing fast. He had already been barred from the Bahamas, the Cayman Islands and Jamaica,[35] and it was only a matter of time before the rest of the British colonies followed suit.

While Derber awaited his fate, President Kennedy visited Miami to address the Inter-American Press Association. Per protocol, the FBI's Miami Office provided the Secret Service with a list of subjects in the Miami area deemed potential security risks to the President. They identified five subjects who posed possible threats: three Cuban exile militants, two of whom were members of the CIA murder squad Operation 40; an American communist activist; and Harold Derber.[36] It was unclear how Derber could have endangered the President from his Miami jail cell, but his inclusion on the list underscored his perceived level of danger. After his Miami visit, the president went on to Dallas.

On that fateful day, November 22, 1963, a big scream echoed through the jail's corridors. Derber heard the news: President John F. Kennedy had been assassinated.[37]

As the nation plunged into mourning, the government's prosecution of Derber pressed ahead. His unyielding political adversary, the State Department, showed no signs of relenting.

The government hoped the bombshell testimony from Crewman Dawson would turn the tide. Speaking with a strong Jamaican patois, Dawson revealed that the first *Nana* sank and Derber replaced it with a boat provided by the Castro government: "The *Nana* sprang a leak and 20 miles out of Havana the eight Cubans abandoned the ship taking the *Nana*'s papers with them ... The Nana was sinking and I saw her sink. She went down nose first in deep water." He recalled Derber telling him "he'd get another boat from a man named Captain Pina who said was a good friend of Raul Castro." Dawson added, "I was present when some men painted its blue hull white and painted the name *Nana* on the stern."[38] The jury members turned to each other in surprise as the government prosecutor grinned.

Bolstering Dawson's testimony, a customs agent next testified that the original *Nana* and the vessel in Key West had different dimensions. A Coast Guard marine inspection officer testified that pictures of the *Nana* taken in Jamaica didn't resemble the second vessel. The original *Nana* was also a sea-air rescue vehicle with a keel, but the second vessel had no keel.[39]

The courtroom fell silent as Derber took the stand. Seeking to dispel any doubts about Derber's loyalty, Nageley asked about his political allegiances. "Are you a communist?" he asked. "No, sir," Derber replied. He also denied being a subversive or a foreign agent.

On the cross examination, Derber demolished the prosecution's case from the witness stand. He readily acknowledged that the original *Nana* sank in a storm, and the Cuban government provided the replacement ship.[40] The prosecutor demanded why Derber hadn't disclosed the switch. "I was not asked," Derber replied. "I asked to see my attorney and was not allowed to do so ... I told them I would not talk until I could see my attorney ... I had not been charged at the time." He denied presenting false registration papers. "I never gave any registration papers to anyone," he testified. "I handed over cargo and passenger lists but that was all." Why did he sign the papers? "I did not want them to take them," Derber said. The officials removed the documents from the vessel without his permission. "I signed them but did not swear to them. I did not reveal anything one way or another ... I had nothing to hide."[41]

Tense quiet filled the Tampa courtroom as the jury deliberated Derber's fate. Four agonizing hours later, the jury filed back in. Their faces were inscrutable. The foreman's voice sliced through the silence: they were deadlocked. The judge, with no other choice, declared a mistrial.[40, 42] Derber grinned slyly and caressed his moustache. He shouted to the judge across the courtroom, "I want my boat back."[43]

Although Derber's case ended in a hung jury, it revealed the impossibility of prosecuting those who transported Cubans. The government's threats had been empty all along. In response, the White House quickly acted to close the loophole Derber had exploited by turning the inspection guidelines into regulations. The new rules required refugees to be inspected by US immigration and health officials in Cuba before they could leave.[44] But since no such officials were present in Cuba, these inspections were impossible, effectively trapping the refugees on the island indefinitely.

Despite beating his criminal charges, Derber still faced expulsion. Throughout the deportation proceedings, Derber remained mute in protest. Engaging in any form of communication would have legitimized the sham of a trial. He was silent when asked to state his name, express his preference for legal counsel or even acknowledge whether he understood the purpose of the trial.

Derber sat calmly as the government leveled its charges. "The security of the United States is threatened by the applicant [Derber]. The applicant has defied our government and has worked closely with the communist government of Cuba," the brief said. "His entry is prejudicial to our best interests and to permit him to continue his performance engenders the welfare and safety of the United States. He is excludable on this ground."[45] Without a hint of a reaction, Derber slipped on his sunglasses and began whistling as the judge issued a sealed court order for his deportation.

Upon arriving at Miami International Airport, Derber emerged from the black INS car and was engulfed by a throng of shouting, jostling reporters. The INS officers formed a protective barrier around him, guiding him through the chaotic crowd. "Will you return to the Western Hemisphere, Mr Derber?"

"I can't say exactly," Derber replied. "Maybe Mexico, Cuba, the West Indies."

"And what are your next plans?" another reporter pressed.

He took a breath and answered, "There are thousands of Cubans desperate to leave the country ... You haven't heard the last of me."[46]

Just then, Sari broke through the crowd of reporters and threw herself into Derber's arms. The camera flashes caught the glint of her heart charm bracelet as she held him tightly.

After several long moments, the officers urged them to move, and Derber pulled back and brushed a stray tear from Sari's flushed cheek. His gaze lingered until he turned to make his way to the departure gate. Sari covered her face, struggling to contain the overwhelming sorrow of all they had lost.

Derber had expected this day. He had made provisions to make sure that someone would care for Sari after his deportation. Months earlier, he had introduced Sari to an exceptional, decent man. He was a gaming sales rep who placed pinball machines on the *Empress*. The man loved Sari. He vowed to protect her and provide the life Derber could no longer offer. For good measure, Derber had mob enforcer Sam Benton look after her safety.

Sari spoke to the reporters through her trembling tears. "It's been a long fight," she said. "But he did beat them in the end, didn't he?" Indeed he had. Derber's defiance had exposed the contradiction at the heart of the government's Cuban immigration policy – a flaw others would soon challenge, emboldened by what he had started.

The reporters approached Nageley for comment. "I hate to see him go," Nageley said, his voice filled with conviction. "He's a real sharp guy. I got to know and like him very much. He's going to be another shipping magnate like Aristotle Onassis."

Climbing the stairs to board his plane, Derber glanced back at the departure gate window, where Sari stood waving. He waved back, turned and climbed the stairs onto the British Airways flight to London.[46]

LIFE IN MIAMI was never the same for Sari. She took a steady job at the Fontainebleau transportation desk while continuing to manage some of Derber's Miami-related affairs. Over time, though, their connection quietly faded, and eventually they lost touch. Reclaiming her birth name, Sarah, she moved to Chicago with her new partner. With his loving support, she successfully regained custody of her three young children and dedicated herself to creating a peaceful and fulfilling life for her family.

In her older years, whenever her children and grandchildren mentioned Harold Derber's name, Sarah would recite the hymn of the Scarlet Pimpernel, her eyes misty with memories of

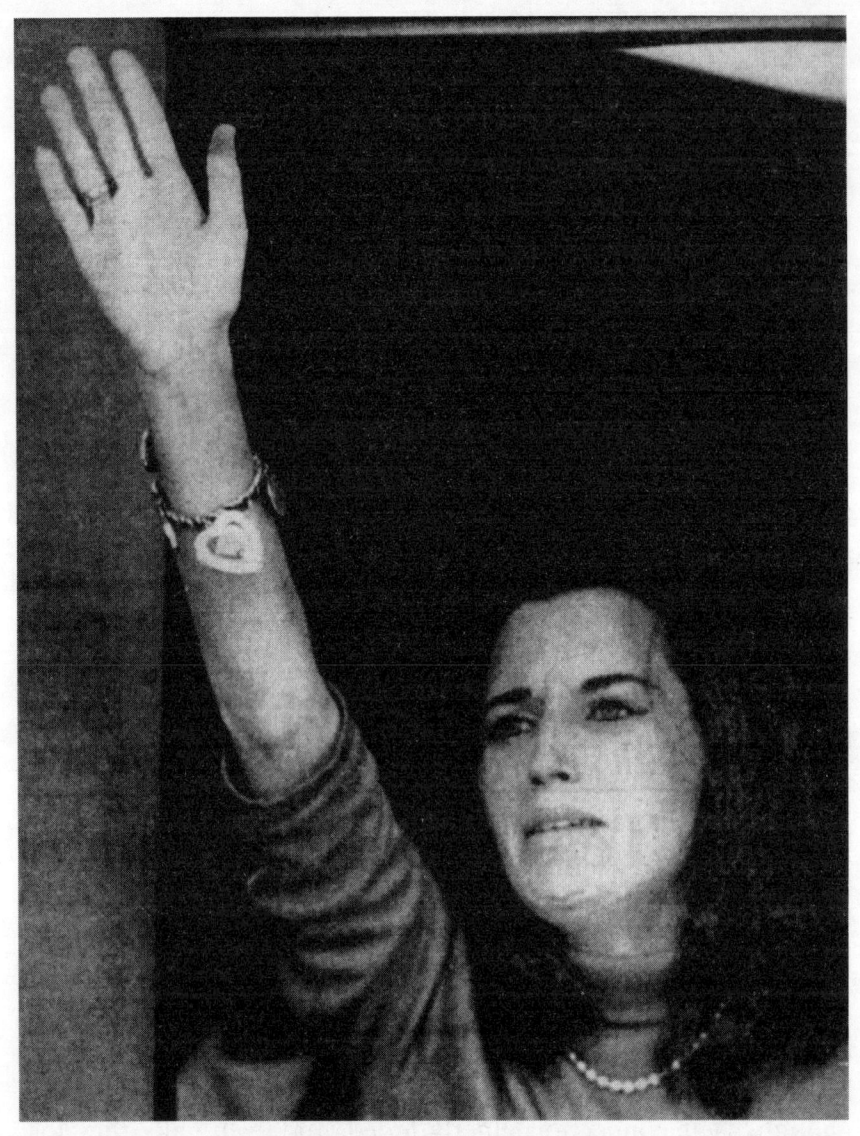

Sari bids Derber farewell.

their daring escapades and their night together on Miami Beach. Safely tucked away in the pages of her memoirs, she preserved the yellowed newspaper clippings chronicling their remarkable adventures, from the Sea-Going Twins on the *Calypso Liner* to smuggling refugees into Key West. And in the back of the album, she left several pages blank for what happened next.

9. LOVE AND HATE AND HUMANITARIAN SOLUTIONS

England, Mexico and Cuba, 1964–65

Thick fog over London Airport forced Derber's plane to divert to Shannon, Ireland. As they descended, the emerald patchwork of County Clare came into view, a brief moment of calm before the storm.

The moment he stepped into the arrival hall, he was swarmed by reporters hurling questions. He recounted his harrowing adventure in America. Three destroyers, a weather ship and a cutter had chased him into Key West, where the Americans imprisoned him without providing legal counsel. He was persecuted and exiled for aiding the victims of communism, but he had no intention of backing down.

"It is my intention to go back and fight the American authorities to get my boat back and to start again where I left off, for I have a license from the Cuban government to take passengers from Cuba to America," he announced. "I feel that I am doing a job of work which was meant for me to do. I am now looking forward to resuming that work."[1] Excusing himself, he waded through the reporters to catch his connecting flight to London.

At London Airport, Derber sat down for an interview with ITV News. Dressed in a three-piece suit and a smart tie, he maintained a calm demeanor as he answered the probing questions.

The Wireless Operator

Derber arriving in London Airport, escorted by agents.

"Was the Cuban government paying you?" the reporter asked.

"No, they paid me nothing. It was strictly on a business deal where I got money for carrying the passengers," Derber replied.

"But you must have known you were probably playing with fire, bringing Cubans into America?" the reporter continued.

"Yes, I was playing with fire, but on the other hand, it was 100 percent legal."[2] Playing with fire, entirely legally, was a perfect summary of Derber's life philosophy.

While in London, Derber visited his brother Jack, a former RAF serviceman who now ran a schmatta store selling used clothing. Over tea, they caught up on Jack's service in the war and Derber's travels. But as the afternoon waned, the inevitable weighed on them that it was time for Derber to confront the past and visit his parents.

Arriving at Manchester station, Derber headed to his parents' modest semi-detached house in suburban Prestwich. It had been twenty years since he last saw them, leaving as a young man with his kit bag slung over his shoulder.

With his exploits in Cuba and expulsion from the US splashed across the *Manchester Evening News*, it's unclear if his parents embraced him as a humanitarian crusader or shunned him as a subversive agitator. Maybe they discussed his meeting with Castro, his narrow escape from Jamaican warplanes and his defiance of the State Department. Or perhaps they chatted about Manchester United's FA Cup run, the latest gossip at the synagogue and their lovely new shoe stall at the Royal Exchange. Whatever their reunion entailed, Derber likely knew it had been a mistake to come back to England and he could never return.

Leaving his parents' home, Derber made his way to his temporary residence at 7 Hartley Avenue, a well-maintained two-story red-brick Tudor house. He pushed aside the overdue notices and court summons cluttering his desk to make room for his drink.

Derber was drowning in debt and his US bank accounts were frozen,[3,4] but he had a way out. Fortunately, British law had a convenient loophole: the UK courts didn't recognize the claims against him because he couldn't appear in US court to defend himself, making the debts unenforceable in England.

Free from his financial and legal entanglements, Derber returned to his mission – the freedom ferry. The business opportunity was still vast, and the plight of the Cuban people was more urgent than ever. He penned a letter to his trusted ally, Captain Pina, sharing his bold plans to relaunch the ferry:

> You are probably aware of most of my activities and predicaments during the past few months, however as you know me I am just begining [sic] my activities, as you know I never give up and if unsuccessful at first I keep on trying until I succeed. I will definitely complete all I set out to do even though I have suffered heavy losses up until now, though I have faith and will regain my position.[5]

Though the project had drained his life savings, exiled him from his adopted country, and severed the love of his life, his determination had only hardened.

Just two months after his expulsion as a national security threat, he wrote to the US government of his plans to relaunch the ferry: "Please be advised that 'EMPRESS LINES LIMITED' will be operating a vessel between Havana, Cuba and Key West, Florida...Our contemplated voyage will depart Havana on March 16th, 1964."[6,7]

State pushed back, stating they wouldn't send health inspectors to Havana. Furious at their refusal, Derber responded with another letter, arguing that their policy was unconstitutional:

Dear Sir,

Received your cable of March 7th 1964 and noted all its contents, however I am at a loss to comprehend your statements. How can the U.S.A. government request or demand companies or individuals to abide by laws and regulations when the government authorities itself constantly disregards its own constitution, laws and regulations acting in an illegal manner.

You have instituted a requirement of pre-examination of Cuban nationals holding United States visa waivers, prior to departure from Cuba, but refuse to pre-examine these people. This in its self [sic] seems and no doubt is NONE CONSTITUTIONAL [sic].

You have issued visa waivers to Cuban nationals which are only valid for direct transportation between Cuba and the U.S.A., but you prohibit direct transportation, which basically terms the visa waivers nothing more than a farce. This will compel an action based on the ESTRADA v AHERNS court decision,[8] which you are fully aware that the U.S. courts have ruled against the U.S. Immigration and Naturalization Service.

The immigration authorities have imposed a 23,000 dollar fine without any legal basis against the vessel NANA, again acting without regards to law and legal rights....

The issuance of the visa waivers has and still is causing extreme hardship to all the recipients. Once a visa waiver is received the holder then applies for an exit permit. On application for this exit visa the applicant surrenders his or her employment and rations. These people are now existing rather than living merely because they renounce communism and evidently were falsely promised a haven within the U.S.A. These people over 300,000 are virtually being persecuted because of an American unfulfilled promise. Is this the action of a so-called peace loving [sic] free country that has and still promises to stand by a people who fight the spread of communism or just

American propaganda using the lives and freedoms of a none communistic [sic] peace loving people.

The U.S.A. government, having checked the applicants prior to issuing these visa waivers were satisfied as each stated and declared they were against communism, therefore wished to leave their homeland. Having once issued these visa waivers the U.S. government I am sure wishes to fulfill its promise, however not to disrupt its policy I again request a form of transhipment [sic] be permitted with the use of the visa waiver.

The political prisoners at present held in Cuban jails would also be released without paying fantastic sums of American dollars, as performed with great elation by Mr. Donovan for the release of a mere 1,175 approximately, prisoners. It is definitely possible to free large numbers of these prisoners, but again U.S.A, policy and attitude is causing these people to be detained.

I have ordered a temporary postponement of EMPRESS LINES LIMITED March 16th 1964 voyage, in order to await your reply and intelligently discuss and satisfy this question without having to resort to court action as Estrada v Aherns.

Thanking you for your prompt attention.

Very truly yours

Harold Derber[9]

Despite the US government's opposition, Derber pressed ahead. He notified the Swiss Embassy in Havana and the *Miami Herald* of his plan to transport 500 passengers from Havana.[10] "I'm not telling when the 500 will arrive but I've got a big healthy surprise coming up."[11]

Derber's bold plan to relaunch the ferry hit the American airwaves. "Remember Harold Derber?" the WTVJ broadcaster asked the audience. "He's the Britisher expelled by United States

Love and Hate and Humanitarian Solutions

authorities to England for operating that unauthorized ferry shuttle for Cuban refugees from Havana to Key West ... This time Derber plans to play it a little more cozy than before. He intends to sail from Cuba, under a British flag, letting his passengers off in small boats outside the three mile limit."[12, 13]

Eager to rekindle their past exploits, Derber wrote to Nageley with a touch of affection, "We'll have a drink together in the islands next month." Nageley replied to reporters, "This may be a neat trick, considering he's banned from Nassau and Jamaica as well. Oh well, you know Harold. He's liable to try anything," Nageley replied.[14, 15]

Reporters asked Nageley how Derber secured the ships. "I don't know where he got the boats," Nageley replied. "He might have dickered with Castro for them or with a British shipping line taking cargo to Cuba."[16] They also asked his old flame, Sari, whether Derber would go through with it. "He went before. I don't see why he won't this time," she replied.

As Derber prepared to relaunch the ferry, Castro grew increasingly puzzled by the US government's failure to enforce the new immigration checks implemented after the *Nana* affair. According to the new regulation, refugees arriving without health inspections in Cuba should have been denied entry, yet they were being admitted without restriction. Castro turned to the Swiss Ambassador, seeking an explanation.

> The Cuban Prime Minister casually asked me about the legal effectiveness of the American 'Visa Waivers'. I referred to the additional conditions introduced by the State Department at the end of the previous year (after the 'Test Case' with the 'Nana'), which had been published in the Cuban press. He then inquired about what would happen to people who secretly leave Cuba on ships. My response: As far as I remember, these cases would not fall under the mentioned regulation. He countered whether this

was logical. My reply: Love and hate, as well as humanitarian solutions, could not be logically explained.[17]

Ambassador Stadelhofer was right – the policy defied logic. Cubans were entering the US without the immigration and health checks the State Department insisted were essential. If exploited, this loophole had the potential to unleash a wave of a quarter of a million Cuban immigrants onto Miami shores.

The State Department moved swiftly, recognizing the growing danger posed by Derber. Chase notified Bundy: "For some time now, Harold Derber, a British national, has been attempting to set up a ferry service between Havana and Miami. We foiled one attempt last year and actually put him in jail for three months. However, Derber is at it again and, as usual, we are trying to put as many roadblocks in his way as possible. We don't know yet whether or not we have been successful in discouraging him."[18, 19]

Leaving no doubt about the threat's severity, Chase alerted United States Atlantic Command (CINCLANT), the unified combat command of the Department of Defense, to be alert for two of Derber's ships departing from Havana.[20] It was becoming clear that stopping Derber would require a show of force.

Undeterred, Derber launched a new plan to establish a ferry service from Havana to Spain via Mexico City. He sought assistance from the British Embassy in Mexico: "We are presently interested to commence a new and regular line operating between ports in Mexico and ports in Cuba and then onto points in Spain."[21] Derber followed up with a telephone call to the British Commercial Counsellor in Mexico, who recounted, "Although Mr. Derber was less aggressive than I had expected and indeed showed a good sense of humor, he is clearly a very sharp customer ... His main purpose was to ask about the possibilities of starting up a service between Cuba, Spain and Mexico ..."

The Counsellor was reluctant to help, noting that given "the present delicate political situation in the Caribbean, a service of this kind would inevitably have repercussions which extended far beyond Mexico."[22] The Head of the Americas Department in the Foreign Office gave the Commercial Counsellor the context: "I do not think you need to go to any great trouble on his behalf ... I am not sure if you know that Derber was deported from the United States a few months ago ... He has also, through his Member of Parliament, given the Colonial Office a lot of work of late."[22] In response to Derber's request, the British Ambassador in Mexico commented in an internal memorandum, "Mr. Derber is a man of straw who believes there is money to be made out of transporting would-be refugees from Cuba to other countries ... He is something of a barrack-room lawyer and we must be careful not to give him grounds for complaint."[23]

In July 1964, Derber flew to Mexico City, where he announced his ferry service's resurrection on a larger scale. "I'm setting up business activity again ... I have five ships ready to sail."[24] He explained that "Fidel Castro doesn't want these people in Cuba anymore. He has led me to understand that once these people who do not sympathize with his regime are evacuated, he would also permit removal of most of the 80,000 political prisoners being held in Cuba."[25]

Derber traveled to Havana to resume planning for the ferry.[26] His key contact for coordinating the new service was Braulio Alfonso Martinez, who was also a DGI (Cuban intelligence) agent.[27,28] Derber and Martinez developed a close working relationship, with Martinez often inviting Derber into his personal life. One notable occasion was the lavish *quinceañera* party for Martinez's daughter in Havana, which Derber attended alongside his trusted associate, Captain Pina.

The Wireless Operator

Captain Pina and Derber (far right) in Havana.

Pina and Derber.

From Havana, Derber headed to Montreal, where he worked to establish a new boat line with the help of Martinez.[29] Backed by his old stock fraud associates, he secured funding for four ships: the *Salta, Arkadia, Cariba* and *Iripina*.[30-32]

While Derber gathered his fleet, President Castro dropped a bombshell announcement that sent shockwaves through Havana and Washington. Standing before a crowd at Havana's Plaza de la Revolución, the dictator declared that all Cubans were now free to leave for America, 'the Yankee paradise.' He would allow departures from the Port of Camarioca on the northern coast.[33] With a defiant gesture, he declared, "Now we shall see what the imperialists do or say."[34]

Castro's declaration sparked a frenzy. Hundreds of Cuban-Americans scrambled to find any seaworthy boat to reach the Port of Camarioca and retrieve their loved ones. This chaotic exodus became known as the Camarioca Boatlift.

Thousands of Cuban refugees flooded into Miami, none of whom had undergone the health and immigration inspections in Cuba required by law. The US government had no choice but to retract the flawed regulation, effectively opening America's doors to Cuban refugees.

When America repealed the flawed law, Castro declared himself triumphant: "Only a few months ago they lost the battle of Camarioca. Hundreds of little boats began to come to Cuba. They paid more attention to the revolution than to the laws of the United States. They lost the battle."[35]

With the pace of Cuban immigration increasing, the White House was forced to overhaul American immigration law entirely. One week later, standing before the Statue of Liberty, President Johnson signed the Immigration and Nationality Act of 1965. Alongside the Act, Johnson directed the government "to immediately make all the necessary arrangements to permit those in Cuba who seek freedom to make an orderly entry into the United States of America."

"I declare this afternoon to the people of Cuba that those who seek refuge here in America will find it," the President announced. He further called upon all states to "join with Florida now in extending the hand of helpfulness and humanity to our Cuban brothers."[36] Cuban refugees were now free to enter the US.

The legislation prioritized family reunification and abolished the national origins quota system, shifting immigration away from Western Europe and toward Asia and Latin America, reshaping America's demographic composition for generations to come.

Reflecting on his victory, Castro remarked, "It was the Camarioca solution that forced them to open the door. Why? Because [when] they closed it they began promoting illegal departures from Cuba – in little boats, rafts, by all means ... Everybody took to his boat and chaos was immediately created. The imperialist had no choice but to legally open the door."[37]

However, Castro's political victory soon gave way to heart-rending tragedy. When hurricane season arrived in November, hundreds of Cuban immigrants either perished or were stranded in the Florida straits.[38] The Camarioca Boatlift turned from a daring exodus into a humanitarian crisis.

In a bold move to stem the tragedy, the Cuban and American governments signed an agreement for the US to provide commercial air transport for Cuban refugees. Over the next several years, the Freedom Flights airlift brought 300,000 Cubans to the US, marking the largest airborne refugee operation in American history.

With the Freedom Flights underway, Derber's ferry scheme became obsolete. The irony cut deep: the US government was now praised for doing exactly what it had once imprisoned and exiled him for. With no mission left, his fleet vanished as quickly as it had appeared, and Derber slipped back into the shadows.

PART III

PART III

10. SHIPPING INTERESTS

Havana, Latin America and Miami, 1966–74

Sitting in his Havana hotel room, Harold Derber stared out the window: street vendors called out for buyers, a couple argued on the corner and small children chased a ball between rusted-out cars. The world outside moved on, but his time in Cuba was running out.

It wasn't even clear where he could go. He'd been banned from America, the Bahamas, the Caymans, Jamaica and likely all the Crown colonies. Returning to England was unthinkable; there was nothing left for him there.

Running out of options, Derber secured a six-month tourist visa to Mexico. But with few prospects for income, he returned to the only life he truly understood – the one outside the law. This wasn't a relapse; it was stepping back into the world he knew so well.

Over several weeks in the summer of 1967, he became a regular customer at Banco Internacional's central branch in Mexico City. Always the picture of a refined Englishman, he'd arrive in a crisp pinstripe suit to deposit his checks from respectable international banks. But one day, with the same polished smile and unshakable composure, he handed the teller a set of bad checks with no funds to cover them.

As the teller worked through the checks, Derber's eyes moved around the bank, scanning the guards' positions and mentally noting the layout. The wait stretched on, but eventually the manager stamped the papers and approved the transaction. The teller, oblivious to the deception, handed over 343,750 Mexican pesos ($27,500) in neatly bundled cash.

Derber turned and walked toward the exit with his distinctive springing gait. He pushed through the door and, within minutes, vanished into Mexico City without a trace.[1-3]

Mexican immigration officials pursued Derber throughout the country, eventually receiving a tip he was hiding in Cuernavaca, a known haven for organized crime. In August 1967, Mexico's Secretary of the Government, the department in charge of national security, dispatched five of their most seasoned agents to apprehend him. However, in an unexpected turn of events, the government abruptly rescinded the order without explanation.[4]

Undeterred, the Mexican Immigration Service continued their pursuit, eventually apprehending Derber in Mérida on the Yucatán Peninsula. Shackled and under heavy guard, he was transported back to Mexico City and held in an immigration detention facility, likely the dismal Estación Migratoria Las Agujas. There, he faced charges of writing fraudulent checks and overstaying his six-month tourist visa.[2,3]

Derber's fall from grace was devastating. Only a few years earlier, he had been a luxury cruise ship captain, his photo splashed across the *Miami Herald* with his glamorous lover by his side. Now, he was trapped in a Mexican cell, facing fraud charges and deportation.

Despite his dire situation, one sliver of hope remained. If his US deportation order had expired, he could try to sneak back into the country undetected, even without a valid US entry permit. He devised a bold plan. After his release, he'd book a flight with a layover in Miami and attempt to slip into the city.

If caught, he could feign ignorance, claiming it was just a stopover. If successful, he could restart his ventures and reclaim his former life.

After his release, Derber wasted no time. He booked a flight to London via Honduras and Miami. In September 1968, his Pan Am flight landed at Miami International Airport.[5] As he stepped off the plane into the bustling gate area, he was surrounded by Americans in floral shirts and Cuban men in neatly pressed guayaberas.

His pulse quickened as he approached immigration control and placed his frayed blue British passport on the counter. The officer flicked through the pages, stared at him, and then down at a binder, repeating the process.

The officer's face lit up as he slammed his finger on a name in the binder. The immigration official had found Derber in the INS and State Department 'look-out' books. He immediately called for backup and detained Derber for violating his deportation order.

Miami Police officers cuffed Derber and transported him to the Miami-Dade County jail, familiar to him from his stay there five years ago. In his first hearing, Derber learned that the INS would seek to deport him for a third time. Whereas last time he had stayed silent, this time he would push back.[6]

At the trial, Derber's lawyer contended that the original deportation hearing violated his client's rights by denying him legal counsel. Further, he was never criminally convicted. "He was cleared of all criminal charges against him in Miami," his lawyer argued, "but since he was deported, he is being looked upon as a leper around the world."[7] His attorney further argued Derber should be allowed to stay in the US for business reasons, specifically a lawsuit in Florida related to the *Empress* and one in Washington state over a commercial property dispute.[8]

Derber languished in jail while the judge deliberated. Meanwhile, Pan Am footed the bill for his incarceration, since they were responsible for ensuring passengers had proper visas. Derber wryly joked to his cellmates that the county was overcharging the airline for the 'Full American Plan.'[9]

After days of uncertainty, the judge finally made his decision and granted Derber a ten-day stay in America under 'transit status.'[10] Following the verdict, courtroom reporters asked Derber what he was doing in Mexico and Honduras. Derber grinned for the photographers and didn't answer.[9]

When his US transit visa expired, Derber headed to Vancouver, Canada, where he lined his pockets by trafficking in forged bond certificates.[11] Once the Royal Mounties caught up to him, he was banned from the country, so he fled to Honduras.

In Tegucigalpa, Honduras, Derber made ends meet captaining fishing boats, remaining in the country long enough to obtain a Honduran passport. Meanwhile, he frequently made excursions to Colombia, where, amid the shadowy docks and smoky cantina, he began plotting his next venture. A new US legal loophole had created the smuggling opportunity of a lifetime.

In October 1970, President Nixon signed the Controlled Substances Act (CSA), a comprehensive anti-drug bill that repealed most existing narcotics laws and implemented a unified system for regulating controlled substances. However, in a surprising oversight, the Act failed to reinstate provisions banning drug possession on the high seas, leaving a legal gap in maritime drug enforcement.[12,13] For the first time, possessing drugs in international waters was entirely lawful.

Although subtle, the loophole created by the CSA was wide enough for a cargo freighter loaded with drugs to glide through unnoticed. And Derber, ever attuned to the margins of law and opportunity, was among the first to recognize its potential. One freighter journey could secure a fortune that would alter the course of his life.

It was easy enough to justify. Trafficking arms was a necessity, oil a calculated gamble, and refugees a moral obligation. Drugs were simply the next step. And unlike arms, marijuana was harmless. He'd stay clear of transporting hard drugs like cocaine, heroin and quaaludes. This wasn't about ruining lives; it was about reclaiming his own.

The plan was straightforward. He could find marijuana suppliers in Mexico and Colombia and distributors from his US network. All he needed were the boats.

Scouting Colombia's ports, he spotted a bold solution. The fishing vessels anchored in the harbor were lightly guarded and, in some cases, abandoned for weeks at a time. The idea of simply taking what he needed grew more tempting with each passing day. If he was going to build a smuggling empire, he had to start somewhere.

In 1971, Derber brazenly stole four ships in Colombia, including the *Coral Rock* and *Lobster Farm*.[14] To maintain appearances, he deployed them as legitimate fishing vessels while quietly laying the groundwork for his smuggling operation. However, maintaining a fleet proved more difficult than stealing it. The crew he hired quickly grew restless, going unpaid for several months as Derber juggled mounting expenses and logistical challenges.

By April 1971, tensions reached a breaking point. Frustrated and desperate, two fishermen decided to take matters into their own hands. Seizing the *Coral Rock*, they made a bold dash for the Colombian island of San Andrés. As they approached the island, the fisherman radioed the naval station, their voices crackling with urgency: "San Andrés ... San Andrés ... this is the *Coral Rock* ... we have taken this ship. We are Colombian sailors, and we are heading to port to seek protection."[15] Upon docking in San Andrés, the fishermen handed the vessel to the authorities, hoping for payment.

The Wireless Operator

Determined to reclaim his vessels, Derber hijacked the ships in late 1972 and set a course back to Honduras. His triumph, however, was short-lived. Not far from their destination, Honduran police boats appeared on the horizon. They intercepted him and officers boarded the vessel, arresting him without resistance.

Investigators quickly discovered he was also wanted in Nicaragua and Mexico for writing bad checks. He insisted he was a British citizen despite having a Honduran passport.[16]

In his Honduran prison cell, Derber remained fixed on securing his release and amassing his fleet. He had to seize the loophole opportunity before it was too late. After his release in the spring of 1971, the Honduran government deported him and he relocated to Colombia. In Bogotá, he promptly renewed his British passport at the UK Consulate, listing his occupation as "captain."

Settling in Colombia, he applied for a residence permit. While he had previously left the religion section of his immigration documents blank, he now listed his faith as Lutheran. He wandered through the dilapidated harbors and marina hotels, making ends meet by repairing boats and captaining ships. Over time, Derber's exile in Latin America began to take a visible toll. His once-neatly styled wavy hair grew unruly, accompanied by shaggy sideburns. His pressed white dress shirts were exchanged for unbuttoned, worn-out blue ones that hung loose on his now gaunt frame. His once-polished shoes were caked with sand and white salt.

Despite his deteriorating appearance, Derber pressed forward with his plan. He set his sights on the *Mil Mar I*, a fishing ship docked at La Bodeguita pier.[17-20] One afternoon in March 1973, Derber invited the pier watchman for lunch and discreetly handed over 50,000 pesos. The watchman pocketed the money with a sly smile, promising he'd be conveniently away from his shift the following night.

From Derber's Colombian residence application.

Under the cover of darkness, Derber and his crew approached the pier. True to his word, the bribed watchman was nowhere in sight. The men exchanged glances. Once aboard, they would navigate the craft out of Cartagena harbor and head to Puerto Rico.

They boarded the vessel and Derber took the helm, clutching the steering wheel while the boat's powerful engines hummed to life. Suddenly, police sirens pierced the silence. Red and blue lights exploded across the deck. They had walked straight into a trap set by the watchman. Mexican military intelligence officers stormed the ship, bludgeoning Derber and two of his crew while two others escaped.

The police yanked the beaten men to their feet and snapped on handcuffs. The *Mil Mar I* bobbed in the harbor as the three men were taken away to Cárcel de San Diego prison in Cartagena.[21]

Lying battered on his cot, Derber vowed to seek revenge. Drawing on the same tenacity that had driven him to sue JFK and the Jamaican government after his arrests, in March 1973 he filed a 20 million peso lawsuit against the Colombian government, alleging the unlawful seizure of his ships.[16]

The Colombian authorities quickly moved Derber to Cárcel Nacional de Ternera, a decaying prison notorious for its brutal conditions. For eight grueling months, he endured the prison's oppressive heat, rampant disease, and constant threat of violence, sustained only by his fixation on the loophole. He knew time was running out before the government would close it and the opportunity would vanish forever.

Anticipating his deportation from Colombia upon his release, Derber began devising a plan to re-enter the United States. Returning would not only allow him to find ground distributors for his marijuana shipments, but also avoid additional fraud charges in Colombia. However, given his history of deportations and arrests, obtaining a US visa would be nearly impossible. He would need to strike a deal and only hope the price was worth it.

Derber was released from Ternera prison in August 1973. Several months later, he secretly fled to Miami as Colombian agents pursued him for the additional fraud charges.

In February 1974, Derber arrived at Miami airport, six years since his last attempt to enter the country. He approached the passport-control booth and handed over his UK passport and a seemingly impossible document: a valid 30-day B-1 business visa approved by the INS and State Department. The visa identified him as a "non-immigrant with business purposes" and his occupation as "shipping interests."[22] Remarkably, every trace of his trips to Cuba had been erased from his passport.[23] After a brief review, the officer gave a curt nod, stamped the passport and slid it back across the counter.

Derber walked through passport control, his gait lifting as if he were two stones lighter. Ten years ago, the US government had expelled him as a national security threat. Against insurmountable odds, he had fought his way back to America. And now that he was in, he could use perpetual visa renewals to secure his residence.[24]

Shipping Interests

How Derber managed to obtain a US visa remains a mystery. He had been deported as a national security risk, imprisoned in five countries, and expelled from several others. The answer likely lies in his visa application – a document the US government continues to withhold. His NSA file remains classified as well, protected under an exemption for intelligence sources.

Emerging from the modernized arrival hall, Derber took in the new Miami: roaring jumbo jets, skyward, billboards touting upscale Cuban restaurants, and muscle cars idling in the pick-up queue. Yet, the swaying palmettos and the familiar fragrance of bougainvillea reassured him: after ten long years, he was finally home.

At the Royalton Hotel, Derber settled into the plush chair of his luxury suite. He pulled out a worn Colombian 50 peso note from his wallet, tore the bill in two, and placed each half in a separate envelope.[25]

11. THE NIGHT TRAIN

The Atlantic, Cartagena, 1974–1976

The 110-foot rusty cargo freighter pitched in the Atlantic swells 50 miles off the Carolina coast. Its dented dark-green hull bore the words "Labrador, St. Johns, Nfld." Barely visible under a layer of green paint were raised letters spelling "Night Train."[1]

A converted fishing trawler pulled alongside the freighter. Both vessels rocked together in the dark waters. The trawler captain sent a coded sequence with his flashlight; a light on the freighter responded. Moments later, a ladder descended over the hull.

The trawler captain climbed the ladder and boarded the freighter. The lone crewman on the deck acknowledged him with a nod. Without a word, the captain produced a torn half of a Colombian 50 peso note from his pocket. The crewman searched his collection for his matching half. The two men held their torn notes together under a flashlight, and exchanged satisfied grins when the two halves matched.

The captain signaled his men, and they formed a human chain leading up to the freighter's deck. Over the next few hours, under cover of darkness, with both boats bobbing in the ocean, they transferred hundreds of black plastic-wrapped bales from the freighter's hull to the fishing trawler. When the cargo was secured, the trawler slipped off toward the coastal lights of North

Carolina. The *Night Train* sailor remained on the deck, waiting in darkness for the next boat.

While the *Night Train* crossed the Atlantic, a radar operator at the National Drug Interdiction Program stared at his screen, baffled. He had never seen a pattern like this one. "It looks like half a star exploding on the screen," he muttered.[2] The bizarre pattern returned the following night and the night after that. "You'd see the smaller blips streaking out toward the shore. Boom! First one 'star' would 'explode,' then boom, another. Three or four each night." Eventually, he and his fellow operators deciphered the perplexing pattern. It was a mid-ocean rendezvous between a massive ship and half a dozen speedboats.

The federal agencies were up against a smuggling tactic they had never seen before: position a massive drug-laden ship just beyond the twelve-mile limit of US territorial waters, and transfer the drugs mid-ocean to smaller, faster powerboats.[3] These 'pickup' boats would then race toward the coast, creating the unusual radar signatures of blips streaking away from the mothership in all directions.

On sight of the next star formation, the Coast Guard dispatched cutters to intercept the rendezvous, but they were outrun by the high-performance speedboats. "They'd zip into shore and that was it. It was damn near impossible to catch them," one Coast Guard officer said.[2] Over time, "Cigarettes or Magnums, usually driven by kids, got as conspicuous as a Commie flag over this building," one Miami customs official remarked. "Anyone who drives one was either a speed freak or a smuggler."[4]

By exploiting the mothership loophole, traffickers were operating beyond the reach of law enforcement, allowing them to move vastly larger quantities of drugs with negligible risk.[5] A single mothership could carry more marijuana than a hundred small boats, fueling drug smuggling on an unprecedented industrial scale.

Among drug agents and traffickers alike, one mothership's name in particular kept coming up in hushed conversations – the

Night Train.[6] This elusive mothership had become the stuff of legend, a ghost vessel responsible for trafficking staggering amounts of drugs with a near-mythical ability to remain invisible. While operating undetected, the *Night Train* made monthly trips, hauling 40 to 100 tons of marijuana per voyage, unloading from Florida to Canada.[7] Yet "nobody had ever laid eyes on it," a regional DEA director commented.[8]

The *Night Train* managed to avoid detection through advanced counter-surveillance. "These people have very sophisticated electronics equipment," one DEA agent noted. "Single sideband transceivers, long-range radios ... communications in code are maintained throughout the network."[9] The ship's elusiveness drove law enforcement mad. "[The *Night Train*] drove us crazy," one Coast Guard lieutenant commander complained. "We never knew what she was. She was one of those ships in the night. All we knew was her name and that she constantly off-loaded on us and we were just one step behind her."[10]

Both the vessel's owner and its flag remained maddeningly elusive. The answer, though, was closer than it seemed: the *Night Train* was owned by none other than Harold Derber of 7 Hartley Avenue, Manchester, England.[6, 11-13]

Harold Derber, a son of Manchester, had pioneered the drug mothership, forever revolutionizing the narcotics trade. His technological breakthrough brought drug trafficking into the modern era of industrial shipping. Upgrading from small yachts and trawlers to massive cargo freighters contributed to a fourfold surge of drug imports in the mid-1970s, helping turn a counterculture vice into a mainstay of American society.

The *New York Daily News* would later celebrate Derber for his radical invention:

> Someone in the marijuana smuggling racket should build a monument to Harold Derber. Cast in bronze, of course, and

The Wireless Operator

Rare sighting of the Night Train *ghost ship off the Florida Gold Coast.*

properly heroic, it would show Derber on a pedestal in Fort Lauderdale, pointing out to sea, in the general direction of the golden land of Colombia. For Harold Derber is already a legend ... He is remembered for a stroke of invention that was so simple it verged on genius. Harold Derber invented the mother ship.[14, 15]

Derber would have smiled coyly at the recognition, for he alone had the vision and skills to turn the mothership concept into a reality. While other ship owners were likely aware of the loophole, Derber seized his opportunity, drawing on decades of experience in maritime smuggling, evasion and counter-surveillance, deep criminal connections across Latin America and the US, and, most importantly, a passion for exploiting loopholes.

With growing demand in America and increasing supply from Colombia, the opportunity for expansion was unmatched. Derber oversaw a fleet of at least a dozen drug motherships, at times dispatching as many as seven ships in a single month.[16] His operation transported several hundred tons of weed to America annually, making him the country's largest marijuana trafficker.[17] If someone sparked a joint – whether in the bohemian enclaves of Greenwich Village, the ivy-covered halls of Cambridge, Massachusetts, or the sunny beaches of Miami – chances were high that his fleet had supplied the product.[15] True to his moral code, Derber only trafficked marijuana, steering clear of more lucrative but destructive drugs like cocaine and heroin.[18]

As Derber's operation expanded, agents across the Coast Guard, DEA, Customs and maritime police became incensed by their repeated failures to catch the elusive motherships. The US Customs director overseeing narcotics interdiction in Georgia and the Carolinas was especially determined. He was infuriated that they hadn't been able to go after the mothership that supplied the marijuana. He drafted a plan for Miami Customs to use long-range Navy reconnaissance planes to patrol the Atlantic for drug ships, declaring, "I'm going to get me one of those Mothers."[19]

The Customs Department forwarded the plan to the State Department, where it landed on the desk of Secretary Henry Kissinger, who also served as Chairman of the Cabinet Committee on International Narcotics Control. With Kissinger's approval, a covert DEA program called Operation Stopgap was launched.[19] This highly classified operation allowed the DEA to secretly use military resources for drug interdiction, circumventing the Posse Comitatus Act, which barred the use of military resources for civilian law enforcement.[20] Operation Stopgap was so secretive that Coast Guard officials denied its existence under oath, and the DEA later destroyed all records related to the operation.

Under Operation Stopgap, the DEA deployed advanced military technology to track the motherships, firing the opening shot in the War on Drugs. Navy aircraft and satellites scoured the skies, tracking freighters from Colombian waters to the Atlantic coast. Against Congressional restrictions, DEA agents embedded themselves in Colombia and other strategic locations, extending their operations deep into enemy territory.[21]

Multi-agency task forces launched coordinated surveillance operations at suspected drop-off sites along the coast. The objective was to follow the pickup boats back to the elusive motherships – and find the criminal mastermind behind them.

12. OPERATION ZEBRA

Florida and North Carolina, 1974

The bikini-clad woman and her two male friends rose from their tents at their camping site off Jewfish Creek in Key Largo. It was September 1974, a time of national turmoil over the Nixon pardon, but here, that unrest felt miles away. For the past few weeks, they had passed their time sunbathing on the shores, fishing for speckled trout, and watching the tides roll in and out. The picturesque view of lush mangroves and Old Rose Harbor was marred only by an abandoned shipping container.

One quiet morning, two vehicles rumbled into the clearing, sending birds scattering from the trees. A pickup truck and a van pulled up to the dilapidated container. Three middle-aged men stepped out and surveyed the area. When they were confident it was all clear, they unlocked the container and began heaving black plastic-wrapped bales from inside into the waiting vehicles.

The female camper grabbed her walkie-talkie and gave the signal. Within seconds, sirens filled the air and police cars barreled into the clearing. Patrol boats roared into shore, spraying water in all directions. A helicopter and plane pulled in overhead. The woman threw on her dark blue DEA jacket, her camping trip now over.

Officers poured out of their vehicles, guns drawn, shouting orders to place hands on heads. The three men froze, their faces paling. One man's eyes darted wildly, searching for an escape, while another's hands trembled uncontrollably. The third stood rigid, his jaw clenched.

Two of the men identified themselves: John D. Steele of Hallandale, Florida, and Charles V. Wilson of Miami. The third man, with wild hair, black eyes and a dark, weathered face, refused to speak. The police exchanged frustrated looks, completely unaware they had just apprehended Harold Derber. If they discovered his identity, Derber could face prison again – or worse, deportation. His whole life was at stake.

Some officers stayed with Derber while the others searched the area. They were stunned to find a ton of marijuana packed in the trucks. Another officer, his voice trembling, hollered the others over to the abandoned shipping container, where they found another two tons.[1]

The suspects were taken to the Miami-Dade station, where all three men were charged with marijuana possession with intent to distribute. Derber kept his expression neutral, his mind already working through his next steps.

When officers processed Steele, they discovered he was not just another criminal. Steele had once been the Republican mayor of Hallandale, Florida. Prior to that, he was a city attorney, councilman and two-time Congressional candidate. He was also an associate of fellow Hallandale resident Meyer Lansky.[2] Steele's political career had ended in disgrace when his role overseeing Hallandale's illegal 'bolita' gambling operation came to light.[3] Now he ran a wholesale seafood trucking business in North Carolina.

In his slow, gentlemanly southern drawl, Steele explained how he got caught up in this mess. "These things always seem to be happening to me," Steele explained. "I was just there to pick my truck up and when they started loading it, I just got in. I've never felt like such a jerk."[4] The officers exchanged doubtful glances and held Steele and Wilson on $50,000 bonds.

John D. Steele, former mayor of Hallandale, Florida.

Derber's fate now rested in the hands of his interrogators. He sat motionless under the harsh lights. Across the table, two detectives hurled questions, intent on breaking his composure. He gave his name as Harold Deb, born in England on 26 February 1924, instead of his true birthdate of 24 February 1926. He said he was a captain and provided the names of his parents, Joseph Deb and Kathrine Pierce, deliberately changing his mother's real maiden name, Pasersky. When asked for his address, he offered only "New York."[5] His steady gaze betrayed nothing.

Determined to uncover the identity of their elusive prisoner, the police sent Harold Deb's fingerprints to the FBI. Days later, when the report came back, the lead detective almost dropped the file. They weren't dealing with just anyone – they had Harold Derber in custody, the infamous exile runner. The detective read the file aloud: visa violations, marshal and immigration holds, reckless operation of a boat, failure to stop for immigration and customs officials, and multiple deportations dating back to 1957.[6]

Derber was quickly transported to his Miami-Dade jail cell and had his bond set at $100,000. His mind raced with questions. How had they uncovered his operation? Were they watching his ships and drop-off points? Did they know he had discovered the loophole? The three tons they busted him with were only the tip of the iceberg. If they got a lead on his massive operation, he'd be staring down a long, harsh sentence.

Weeks of incarceration bled into months, until the trial finally arrived. The court learned that Marine Patrol Officer Ted Akey had become suspicious of two lobster boats docked at Old Rose Harbor in Key Largo.[7] He had found marijuana seeds scattered by the dock, leading him to investigate further. Ignoring a 'No Trespassing' sign and a locked gate, Akey followed the trail to a fisherman's shed, where he discovered more marijuana traces.

Seizing the opportunity, the defense attorney argued the officers had no right to be on the property. They didn't have a search warrant, and hadn't even applied for one. The marine patrol defended the search, saying, "Marine Patrol Officers can go on property like that to look for marine violations such as dredge and fill. Had there been crawfish, we would have been able to go in there legally."[8] The crawfish argument left the defense attorney smirking.

Finally, the day arrived for the judge's ruling. The courtroom fell silent as the judge cleared his throat. In a stunning turn of events, he dismissed all charges due to the lack of a search warrant. Against all odds, Derber had slipped through the government's grasp once again.

Derber shook his lawyer's hand and slipped on his sunglasses. After glancing at the government prosecutors, he strode toward the exit. After four months in prison, he was free once again.

SOME TIME LATER, Derber visited a café near the courthouse to grab a coffee. No sooner had he settled into his seat than two men approached his table as if they had chanced upon him. Their worn jeans and flannel shirts stood out from the tailored suits and police uniforms. They were relaxed, but something about them wasn't right. He recognized one from the pickup crews, while the other was a stranger.[9]

Derber suspected the men were covert agents, and he was right. One of them was Officer Akey, the man who had first discovered the Key Largo drop site and was now working undercover.

The first agent introduced Akey by his alias, Kelly Summers. The name was odd, yet Derber didn't react. The two men slid into the seats across from him, and Derber studied their expressions, gauging their intentions.

Akey claimed he was interested in piloting a pickup boat. Derber scrutinized the supposed boatman. He had met many boatmen trying to make ends meet in a desperate economy. He had also encountered plenty of undercover agents.

Derber played along. He asked Akey how much he made a year. "$10,000," Akey replied.[10] Derber let the silence stretch, setting down his coffee with a slight smile. "I can make you ten times that," he said.

Akey nodded and reached into his pocket for a business card with his phone number, which he handed to Derber. The number was for a dedicated line in the marine patrol office. Derber glanced at the card, memorized the number and tucked it into his jacket.

Rising from his seat, Derber settled the bill and, with a spring in his step, strode out of the café, vanishing into the Miami crowd. Akey couldn't help but admire his composure. Derber struck him as "a good fellow" and "very reserved." Akey added Derber "was the kind of guy you'd make a movie about. He'd be the Errol Flynn."[10] The officers watched him vanish, aware they were only pawns in a much larger game.

Unable to penetrate Derber's network, the Coast Guard refocused on the pickup boats. In May 1975, their strategy paid off – they spotted a suspicious green and white Maltese Magnum powerboat racing in circles fourteen miles west of Grand Bahamas Island.[11] The guardsmen pulled up and discovered the boat was unmanned. They intercepted the vessel and towed it to West Palm Beach, where they turned it over to the DEA. The two men from Pompano Beach, known to have been aboard the boat two days earlier, were presumed dead.

The DEA's investigation of the abandoned speedboat yielded disturbing evidence. The agents found blood smeared all over the deck, cockpit and bow. They also found wetsuits and power tools with the price tags still attached. Authorities suspected the boat had been used to transport marijuana from a larger boat stationed offshore. They brought in Derber's associate, John D. Steele, and his son to question their connection to the speedboat.

Following Steele's questioning, the DEA received intelligence about a trawler trafficking marijuana through Pamlico Sound. Acting on this information, the DEA coordinated with the US Customs Agency and the State Bureau of Investigation to launch Operation Zebra. Their target: the *Lillian B*, a 112-foot Second World War submarine chaser converted into a fishing trawler.[12-14]

For four grueling months, agents surveilled the *Lillian B* and the docks as the trawler offloaded its mysterious cargo in the middle of the night. During most runs, the trawler was transporting fish through Pamlico Sound. But occasionally, she would pull into poorly lit docks and unload packages to men waiting onshore. They wielded flashlights and posted lookouts on the loading docks. The agents posted their teams to tail the lookouts.

On January 10, 1976, the agents' patience was finally rewarded. They observed the *Lillian B* pass through Ocracoke Inlet and pull into an isolated coastal inlet in Bear Creek, near

Mesic. The ship docked in front of a gray building with peeling paint, a fish processing plant registered to Mayo Seafood Co.

In complete darkness, men began transferring plastic-wrapped bales, aka 'square grouper,' into parked vehicles. They loaded about 10,000 pounds into a panel truck and 250 sacks into another truck and a house trailer.

The lead agent gave the signal and several patrol cars barreled down the small dirt road to the dock, kicking up a storm of dust. Other cars sealed off the highway and marine boats blocked the water escape routes. "We're federal agents, cease operations," an officer shouted through a loudspeaker.[14]

Dozens of agents from the State Bureau of Investigation, DEA, Customs, and Pamlico County Sheriff's Office descended on the scene. The smugglers scrambled to evade capture, scattering like crows fleeing a gun blast. Five men dove into the frigid creek and swam away. Four or five men slipped through the cordon and disappeared into the woods. Four were arrested on the spot.

Two of the men who swam away hid in the woods overnight, only to be caught at dawn. "They just lay there all night, afraid to move," said Pamlico County Sheriff Leland V. Brinson. "They were afraid they would get shot, I reckon. I don't know why they didn't freeze to death."[14]

Agents apprehend one of the smugglers at the Lillian B *bust.*

Agents unload 25 tons of marijuana from the Lillian B.

The agents arrested nine men, including John D. Steele, Steele's son and Ernest Hugh Mayo, the owner of Mayo Seafood Co. They charged the men with possessing a controlled substance for distribution and conspiracy to violate federal customs laws. Officers also seized the cabin cruiser, vehicles, two shotguns, a few M16 rifle clips and a sister ship called the *Clara*. The police found traces of blood in the house trailer and noticed a section of carpet was missing.

The scale of the seizure left even seasoned agents in shock. The amount of marijuana "boggles the mind," one State Bureau of Investigation director said.[15] Agents recovered 25 tons of marijuana from the *Lillian B* and the vehicles, making it the largest drug seizure in North Carolina history and probably the largest ever on the East Coast. Another 12 tons were seized at a nearby warehouse.[16] On the bridge they discovered "enough radio equipment to monitor every customs radio band from the Gulf coast up," one agent said.[15]

The sheer volume of the bust made it clear they were standing on the brink of something much larger. The State Attorney General observed, "I think this is really only the tip of the iceberg. We're convinced in the Department of Justice that more drugs are coming in on the coast of North Carolina than in any other place on the eastern coast and this is proving it." With a nod to the area's history, he added, "That's why Blackbeard frequented this area so much."[14]

Several months later, as the dust settled on the *Lillian B* case, Pamlico County Sheriff Leland Brinson would receive a call from Miami Homicide.[17] Detective James Carpenter relayed a tip that there was a body buried in a tree grove about 50 yards from the Mayo Seafood trailer where the *Lillian B* bust went down.

Following the lead, a customs agent searched the area and found a suspicious dirt mound not far from the trailer. Beneath the soil, he discovered a shallow grave containing a badly decomposed corpse wrapped in a bedsheet and plastic. Only a few ligaments held the head in place. Blood-stained orange fabric in the grave matched the carpet from the Mayo Seafood trailer.

Theories about the murder began to circulate among law enforcement. Officers reasoned the murder resulted from "a serious disagreement between ringleader elements in the smuggling operation." Sheriff Brinson speculated the victim was "probably buried by friends who were unable to notify authorities because it would reveal their smuggling operation."[18, 19]

To unravel the mystery, Sheriff Brinson sent the victim's badly decomposed fingerprints to agencies across the country, hoping to find a match. After an extensive search, there was a crucial break in the case: the victim was identified as Michael Watkins, a Miami mechanic originally from Camden, New Jersey. He had the misfortune of bearing a passing resemblance to Derber. The police called his killing an "honest mistake."[18, 20] No one was ever charged with Watkins's murder, and the motive for the killing remained unknown.[21]

While Watkins's grave remained hidden for months to come, the trial was already illuminating the shadowy outlines of the smuggling operation. In the North Caroline court hearing, one trafficker divulged that the *Lillian B* had collected the marijuana mid-ocean from a 110-foot cargo freighter known as the *Night*

Train. The ships met southeast of Cape Hatteras in the Outer Banks. Under cover of night, the crews spent two and a half hours transferring several hundred 50-pound bales of marijuana from the freighter to the *Lillian B*.[22, 23] Likewise, the other pickup boat *Clara* had retrieved her contraband from the *Night Train*.

The mention of the *Night Train* sent a ripple through the courtroom. The agents were all too familiar with the ship. What they needed was to get to the ship's owner. Unknown to them, he was already en route to Colombia, preparing to expand his fleet and cement his grip on the marijuana supply.

By 1974, Colombia's marijuana market was thriving. Its high-potency product dominated, as competition waned due to herbicide eradication efforts in Mexico and strict drug enforcement in Jamaica.[24] With limited competition and a high-quality crop, Colombia had risen to become the dominant exporter to the US market.[25]

But if Derber didn't secure a steady supply soon, someone else would. The key to that operation was Winces Velasco Peterson, a fellow Brit based in Colombia known for his endless stock of marijuana and uncompromising methods.[26, 27] Velasco's combination of business savvy and ruthless vengeance would eventually make him the trusted import-export broker for the notorious Pablo Escobar.[26, 28]

Working with Velasco promised Derber a steady flow of marijuana, yet the partnership required careful navigation. One misstep, and Derber's peaceful marijuana business could turn deadly.

Derber's plane touched down on Velasco's private airstrip fifteen miles away from his expansive villa in Barranquilla.[26] On the tarmac, Velasco greeted Derber with a firm handshake and a cut-glass British accent. Ironically, Velasco was in many respects more British than Derber, with his London-born mother, English secondary schooling and business studies at Oxford.[27]

Upon arriving at the villa, Velasco led Derber through the immaculate gardens, past sunbathing women and watchful armed guards. Once inside the lavish living room, they promptly turned to business. Velasco detailed the process to fulfill Derber's order: buyers would source crops from local Indian farmers, and workers would harvest, clean, pack and compress the product into bales at a central facility. From there, it would be transported to the secluded docks of La Guajira, where Derber's mothership awaited offshore.

The terms were agreed, and the two men sealed the deal with a handshake. Derber knew any betrayal of Velasco would bring his vengeance, shared British heritage or not.

With his Colombian supply and an armada of freighters, Derber constructed a smuggling network that stretched from Miami to Montreal.[29] Like a corporate executive, he divided operations between his lieutenants: he managed the international supply chain and mothership fleet, while Steele oversaw the ground transport and pickup boats.

Among their pickup captains, Tracy and Darrell Boyd – better known as the 'Smith Brothers' – were among the best in the business. With their dark, full beards, sun-weathered skin and mirrored aviators, they personified the outlaw romance of seventies drug-running, eventually becoming legends in Florida smuggling lore.

Despite the Boyd brothers' reliability, Steele's operation was not without setbacks. In one critical shipment, 1,200 pounds of marijuana vanished from the *Gina IV*, a 25-ton mothership.[29-33] Furious, Derber immediately called Steele to fix the problem. Trying to contain the fallout, Steele contacted Darrell Boyd, demanding repayment. "Let's get this twelve hundred pounds straightened out so we don't start going around shooting at each other," Steele warned, aware of how quickly tensions could spiral into violence.[34]

The missing load was an inside job that rattled the operation. The marijuana had been stolen by the crew of the *Red Machine*,

Tracey and John Darrell Boyd, the "Smith Brothers."

who posed as the legitimate pick-up crew during a rendezvous with the *Gina IV* near Orange Cay Island. Despite their failure to produce their half of the torn 50-peso note, the *Gina IV*'s captain handed over the 1,200-pound shipment, committing a reckless breach of protocol that enabled the audacious heist.

Trouble flared again when Derber discovered one of his North Carolina field managers had siphoned off $250,000. Steele uncovered that the manager had been handing out free bales of marijuana to customers, as if running a back-alley giveaway. Although the situation was serious, Derber chose to move on; he had a much larger issue to contend with in Colombia.

Derber's Colombian motherships reached the US by threading the Windward Passage, a narrow strait between Cuba and Haiti. Captains had to carefully navigate the twenty-mile-wide section of the passage that remained in international waters. Despite their efforts, many strayed into Cuban territory, where they were intercepted by patrol boats. The Cuban government was seizing the ships, confiscating their illicit cargo and arresting the crews, posing a growing problem for Derber and the Colombian cartels.

To arrive at a solution, in late 1975, the Cuban Ambassador to Colombia, Fernando Ravelo-Renedo, called an urgent meeting in Bogotá with the leaders of the fledgling Medellín Cartel. Ravelo-Renedo was not only a diplomat. He was also secretly head of Departmento de América, the branch of Cuba's intelligence service supporting the Marxist insurgencies across Latin America.

Though the meeting's purported aim was to negotiate the release of the seized Colombian ships, cargo and crews, the outcome was far more extraordinary. Ravelo-Renedo had excellent news. He informed his guests that the Cuban government would not only release the seized ships, cargo and crews, but also provide direct support for their enterprise. They would provide free passage through Cuban waters, access to Cuban ports, radar cover, repair and refueling services, a Cuban flag to disguise the ships' origins, and even gunboat escorts to their mothership rendezvous points.

Ravelo-Renedo only asked for two items in return. First, the drug traffickers pay an $800,000 docking fee. Second, on their return trip from North America, the Colombian vessels must transport arms from Cuba to the Marxist guerrillas in Latin America, including Colombia, Nicaragua, Guatemala, Honduras and El Salvador. The deal was agreed, sealing the first narco-terrorism alliance of the Western Hemisphere.[35, 36]

The guns-for-drugs pact was a strategic masterstroke for Cuba. The weapons exported the revolution across Latin America, while the drugs poisoned their American adversary. More importantly, the trade generated a steady stream of hard currency. The Cuban government pocketed $10 million per month, funding weapons shipments for insurgent groups across Latin America. The ripple effects of the deal reshaped the region's political landscape, fueling conflicts and revolutions that would echo for decades.

Through the trade arrangement, Derber returned to his role as an arms runner,[37] as he had done in World War II, the Arab–Israeli War and the Cold War. Back then, it was about a cause – or a profit. Now, it was about survival.

Over the next few months, Derber's role in the guns-for-drugs trade deepened.[38] He acquired weapons from private dealers, local gun shops and Miami pawnshops. He assured Steele the shipments were destined for the Colombian government, even though the true beneficiaries were Marxist guerrilla groups intent on toppling their governments. What had begun as the relatively harmless trade of marijuana had now evolved into something far darker, fueling violence and unrest throughout Latin America.

In the end, Derber's old nemesis – the State Department – hadn't prevailed after all. Despite branding him a national security threat and forcing him into exile, they had failed to stop him. He had released the third-world atomic bomb, and the shockwaves were only beginning. Next came the money.

13. VAST OPPORTUNITIES

Miami, New Jersey, 1974–76

Back in Miami, Derber reconnected with his old friend Adiel, resuming their friendship as if no time had passed. Over late-night drinks, they reminisced about their glamorous cruise ships and high-stakes escapades. It's unclear if Adiel knew about Derber's new, more dangerous exploits.

As he did every week, Derber visited his local Miami bank, his leather briefcase heavy with cash. He crossed the cool, air-conditioned bank lobby and nodded to the banker, who led him to the back room. After the customary exchange of pleasantries, Derber set the briefcase on the desk and popped it open, revealing neat stacks of bills. Calm and composed, he gave his standard instructions: purchase certificates of deposit and transfer the remaining funds to his Banco Nacional de Panamá account.[1]

The banker began counting the bills by hand. As he waited, Derber couldn't help but think that he needed a better system.

Back at his apartment, Derber called his longtime stockbroker, Robert E. Brennan, president of Mayflower Securities. Adiel had introduced Derber to Brennan years ago, and they remained in touch.[2] Derber had loaned Brennan's previous brokerage $100,000 and invested in one of its underwritings.[3]

Derber phoned Brennan, hoping the broker could help launder his growing piles of cash.

The timing of Derber's phone call was fortuitous. The SEC was about to revoke Mayflower's broker-dealer registration due to securities violations, and Brennan desperately needed a financial lifeline.[4] Derber graciously extended Brennan a $250,000 unsecured loan, which Brennan used to launch his new firm, First Jersey Securities. First Jersey absorbed Mayflower's assets and resumed operations in the same office.[3, 5]

Brennan was grateful for the support:

> I talked to Harold Derber and told him what my plight was, and really I wasn't even talking to him with the viewpoint of getting money from him. I was telling him as a friend that I was done in. You know I was just about done in – was going to have to close shop in a couple of days. Within two days he came up with a quarter of a million dollars out of the blue. Totally unsecured money, no strings attached. He was sent from God to help me and that's really the way I look at it to this day.[5]

According to Brennan, Derber had made the loan because he "enjoyed the relationship with a person he perceived to be young and aggressive on Wall Street and who he believed was going to be tremendously successful."[5] But Derber had another, more cunning plan for Brennan's brokerage – laundering his enormous drug fortune.

Derber may also have seen reflections of his own story in Brennan's. Brennan, raised in a cramped Newark flat with nine siblings, shared Derber's knack for turning ambition into fortune.

Robert Brennan in an advertisement for First Jersey Securities.

The SEC promptly launched an investigation, suspecting First Jersey was merely Mayflower with a new name. Undeterred, Brennan built First Jersey into an investment powerhouse. According to Brennan, he was providing everyday investors access to some of the most dynamic and innovative companies in America. In the view of regulators, it was a pump-and-dump scam. As one salesman explained, "Brennan incorporates companies, self-deals with them, and then takes them public or else he finds corporate shells, acquires insider stock, and then sells out."[6] A regulator summarized it more bluntly: "They've grabbed the patent on running up low-priced stocks."[6]

Brennan repaid Derber's favor with generous stock offers, explaining, "I do look out for Mr Derber and try to do the best that I can for a lot of reasons, including the fact that he helped me at a time when nobody else would come near me."[5] He felt enormous gratitude for Derber, describing him as "a man who I felt I owed one to after he came up with the money and saved my economic life."[7]

Derber served as one of the cornerstone investors for First Jersey, with Brennan noting, "[He was] one of the biggest customers we had early on."[6] But he was more than a large client, he was an investment powerhouse willing to take extraordinary risks. "Mr Derber is a very wealthy man," Brennan observed, "and I usually only call him when I want him to make a substantial purchase and he's willing to take high risks. Quite frankly he's the only customer I have in his category that I can call up. He's almost like a speculative institution."[5] "If I call up Mr Derber and I say invest $100,000, $200,000 into this venture, it's very speculative, but I think it's a good situation, he wouldn't bat an eyelash." "He'll ask me if that's all he should invest."[5]

Over time, Derber laundered vast sums through First Jersey, growing his drug profits many times over.[8] His fortune grew to at least $22 million, spread across banks in the US, South America and Canada, including some joint accounts with Adiel.[5, 9-12] The DEA estimated hundreds of millions of dollars passed through Derber's bank accounts.[3]

With the money flowing, Derber, Adiel and Brennan enjoyed high-end outings in New York and Florida. In Manhattan, they savored steak dinners at Delmonico's. In Miami, they indulged in culture and cuisine, attending an auction for the artist Erté, the father of Art Deco. Other nights, they would gather at Ray's apartment for drinks.[2] When not dining with his associates, Derber would hit Miami hotspots like the Forge and the Mutiny with his young girlfriend Sandra.[13]

Although his life seemed charmed and untouchable, it was about to come crashing down. His laundering operation had begun to attract dangerous attention, and soon enough the Gambino crime family came calling. After a series of quiet negotiations, Derber struck a deal to funnel their money through First Jersey.[12, 14]

Fueled by Derber's money laundering, First Jersey Securities grew into the largest non-exchange-listed brokerage in the country, eventually becoming one of the largest alleged securities frauds in American history. Derber's sizable investments through First Jersey soon raised red flags with the SEC. "There were suspicions that there was something big and suspicious going on," one SEC investigator said. "When they found out Derber was in marijuana, they figured that possibly there were organized crime connections."[9] In response, the SEC widened their investigation, adding drug money laundering to the growing allegations against First Jersey.

Brennan was indignant at the SEC's accusations, calling them "gutter-like and scurrilous."[2, 15] "It would bother me a lot if Harold Derber was involved in drugs and used me ... or my firm as a vehicle to continue in a lifestyle that I abhor."[5] He added, "Derber has nothing to do with First Jersey other than as a customer. It would be a very low blow to mention him in terms of the securities business. People have unbelievable imaginations when marijuana is involved."[6]

All Brennan knew of Derber was that he was a "very wealthy man" who made his fortune in shipping, and that "he was an apolitical British national who once had a for-profit enterprise smuggling refugees to South Florida."[16] Nothing suggested Derber was involved in crime. He came across as "a subdued, quiet, gentle type guy,"[9] "a gentleman with a British accent."[6]

Homing in on First Jersey's drug ties, the SEC asked the DEA for information on Derber – but the agency stonewalled. According to one SEC investigator, "The DEA kept diddling around and diddling around and diddling around."[9] Meanwhile, the DEA went behind the SEC's back, requesting a list of Derber's security holdings directly from the US Embassy in Panama, keeping the SEC in the dark. It took an intervention from Secretary Henry Kissinger himself to ensure the embassy shared the information with both agencies.[17]

Miami Homicide faced similar resistance from the DEA while investigating the murder of Derber's lookalike. Detective James Carpenter complained, "When I first started talking to them, they denied having any file on Derber ... They finally acknowledged who he was. They said they had done some checking and found a few things out. They said maybe he was a Russian agent. They said maybe he had been a spy in World War II."[9] Eventually, the DEA relented. "They finally acknowledged to me that he was moving many, many tons of grass ... They came up with the names I had already found out saying, 'Yeah, you're right'."

The *Miami Herald* also hit a wall with the DEA. The newspaper sought interviews with DEA agents involved in the Derber case but was turned down, even though the agency freely granted interviews for other investigations.

The DEA's reluctance to cooperate with the SEC, the State Department, Miami Homicide and the press only deepened suspicions of a larger conspiracy. Rumors swirled that Derber, one of the country's largest marijuana traffickers, was secretly working with the DEA. His ability to secure a US visa, despite being deported twice and imprisoned in five countries, began to make sense. All signs pointed to the shocking possibility that Harold Derber had struck a deal with the feds.[18]

Yet even with that protection, other government agencies were closing in. The SEC subpoenaed him to testify about First Jersey's drug money connections. Meanwhile, the Coast Guard, DEA, Customs and the Navy were combing the Atlantic for his elusive mothership fleet. Simultaneously, police in Miami and North Carolina were hot on the trail of his ground operations. In New York, the Justice Department probed his connections with the Gambino family,[14] while the CIA dug into his possible links with Russian and Cuban intelligence. Nearly every US agency was now on Derber's trail.

His only saving grace was the lack of agency coordination. One exasperated Florida investigator complained, "Every law enforcement agency in the US has information on Derber. If someone could only put it all in one file, and sort it out, we could probably still get convictions on a thousand crimes."[3] He added, "The FBI won't tell the DEA; Customs won't tell the SEC, and no one will tell the states. Everyone's tight-lipped to protect his own turf – and to avoid paperwork hassles. A lot of criminals are going free."[3]

But the government wasn't his only problem. The criminal factions were also circling. After the *Lillian B* bust, Derber's American partners had flipped and were giving up names to save themselves. Meanwhile, the Colombian and Cuban cartels were resorting to increased violence. The booming cocaine trade was turning drug smuggling from a civil business into a deadly enterprise. What was once a world of 'gentlemen smugglers' had become a lethal game.

To give himself more protection, Derber compiled a secret cache of files set to be delivered to the authorities in the event of his untimely death – a dead man's switch. The exact contents were unknown, but rumors swirled that they contained the names of informants or a complete business ledger.

One evening, Derber returned to his Miami apartment to find the door ajar. Twenty years of smuggling had taught him to trust his instincts. Someone had been here.

He nudged the door open. The rooms appeared untouched, everything in its place. The papers were safe. He checked a hidden compartment where he stashed $250,000 in cash. It was empty – all the money was gone.

When he called the police, he remained calm and reported only $10,000 stolen.[12] He couldn't risk them discovering the full extent of his operation.

The break-in forced a reckoning: how much longer could his protection last, and who was really behind it? Some still pointed to the DEA, but others suspected foreign powers. "I always suspected, with his connections and what he could get done, that Harold could have been an agent for some government," one source said.[19] Others pointed to his uncanny ability to slip out of legal trouble. "There was something fishy about the way he could always get out of jail in a hurry," another source commented. "He served only a short time in a Mexico prison after being charged in a civil matter, and less time in a Colombia jail after a check bounced," an associate said. His connections at the highest echelons of the Cuban government were evident. "That was obvious because when you went to see him in Mexico City he could get you whoever you wanted out of Cuba in just two days," another recalled.

Theories about Derber's intelligence connections ranged from the plausible to the outlandish. The financial publication *Barron's* commented, "A dapper and mysterious man, said by some to have been a CIA agent and by others everything from a Russian spy to a member of the Mafia, Harold Derber was, at the very least, an opportunist. At various times he had run guns, Cubans, and marijuana for profit."[3]

Uncertainty about his origins only added to the enigma. He was allegedly born in Russia, and his family moved to England just before the war. Newspapers mistakenly reported his real surname as "Tuchverdarber"[3] or "Tuchverderver."[14] He claimed to have served as a captain in the Royal Navy during the war, although the UK government had no record of any military service.

Of all the allegations, the most shocking came from classified US intelligence documents seen by the *Atlanta Constitution* claiming that Derber was the KGB station chief for Miami.[20] If Derber was indeed 'Moscow's Man in Miami,' it would mean he was overseeing a high-stakes Russian spy operation on American soil at the height of the Cold War. With no Soviet embassy in the city, Derber would have been running an illegal station without diplomatic immunity from espionage charges.

This revelation raised the disturbing possibility that Derber's drug empire was not merely a personal profit scheme, but part of a broader clandestine mission to funnel drugs to Americans and arms to Marxist insurgents, all potentially under the unwitting protection of the DEA. At the same time, rumors swirled that he was a double agent, playing both sides against each other.[21] But with the government authorities and criminal factions closing in, Derber's possible intelligence connections could only protect him for so long.

Knowing his time was running out, Derber picked up his fountain pen and wrote to his mother in England for the first time in years: "I own seven ships and one beautiful 75-ft yatch [sic] besides many other properties. But best of all, I have large cash assets."[3] He listed all his possessions and offered to create tax-free trusts for the family, making them beneficiaries of his numbered accounts.[3] He asked if his family wished to inherit his belongings, including his ship, *The Forwarder*. It was a gesture meant to bridge the years of separation, a reminder of when he was just a teenage radio operator sending home nearly every shilling to support them during the war.

When the reply finally came, Derber stared at the letter for a long moment. His family wanted nothing to do with his estate or him. They had turned away, just as he had done to them so many years ago.

LATE ON THE EVENING of March 22, 1976, Derber pulled his green Porsche into a spot in front of his luxury Miami condominium on Millionaire's Row.[14, 19, 22, 23] He was scheduled to appear in New York the next day to testify at the SEC probe into First Jersey.

As he approached his building's entrance, two figures stepped out from the shadows: a lanky man adjusting his wire-frame glasses and a short, burly man smoking a cigar.

Five sharp cracks rang out, each bullet jolting through Derber's back. Gasping, he stumbled toward the entrance. Searing pain tore through his right shoulder and he collapsed.

The thin man stepped forward, his shadow looming over Derber. Two muzzle flashes lit the night in a brief, intense brilliance before the world plunged into darkness. All was quiet except for the soft rattle of bullet casings. The autopsy would later show that the bullet lodged in his skull was engraved with his initials.[12, 24] The two hitmen vanished in an olive-green Ford while Derber lay dead on the pavement, crowned by a wreath of blood-soaked palm leaves.

Derber's murder.

EPILOGUE

Bahamas, 1977

Nearly a year after Derber's murder, the Coast Guard finally captured the *Night Train* off Abaco Island in the Bahamas. It marked the first success of Operation Stopgap, the secret DEA initiative to use military resources to combat narcotics trafficking.[1]

The mission began in the fall of 1977 when an undercover DEA agent met a distributor at a Holiday Inn in Fort Lauderdale, who revealed that he had a freighter loaded with marijuana and was offering $50,000 to smuggle it ashore. He was looking for men interested in helping unload the boat mid-ocean. Over a series of follow-up meetings, the arrangement was agreed.

In December 1977, the government assembled a crew of civilians and undercover agents, all posing as drug traffickers, and supplied them with a fishing boat named the *Catchalot II*. Among them was Officer Akey, who had previously busted Derber in Key Largo.[2] To ensure the legality of the mission, the Coast Guard secured authorization from Secretary of State Henry Kissinger.[3]

With preparations complete, the *Catchalot II* and her dungaree-clad undercover crew arrived at the designated rendezvous point with the *Night Train* in the Florida Keys, south of Marathon. However, the ghost ship was nowhere to be seen. After nearly a day of waiting, a Piper Navajo buzzed the boat and dropped two gallon-sized plastic water bottles into the ocean. Inside was a handwritten letter with instructions and coordinates to find "mother." At the bottom was written: "Destroy these notes."[4]

At the revised rendezvous point, the *Catchalot II* found a rusty freighter with a dent in her bow. "What a tub this is!" one agent whispered to his colleague. Another agent noticed the ship's true name under a coat of paint. "My God," he said. "It's the Night Train."

"It was really a sight," one agent said. "For months, we'd heard about a ship called the Night Train that was supposed to be dropping off marijuana along the coast, and all of a sudden here it was."[5] The agents relayed the news to the senior DEA officers in the command station, who burst into cheers. After years of pursuit, they had finally found the mythical ghost ship.

The *Catchalot II* and *Night Train* exchanged the radio handshake and codewords on a prearranged frequency. Then an

Plane dropping water bottles containing the coordinates for the Night Train rendezvous.

The Night Train *seen from the* Catchalot *during the bust.*

undercover DEA agent activated a covert radio beacon on a separate frequency to relay the freighter's position to the Coast Guard endurance cutter *Dauntless*, lying in wait nearby. The Coast Guard was not taking any chances; the *Dauntless* was renowned as the nation's premier drugbuster. The ship turned on its direction finder and raced toward the *Catchalot*'s signal.

While the *Dauntless* sped toward the location, the undercover agents unloaded 150 plastic-wrapped bales of marijuana from the *Night Train*. "We took on about 6,000 pounds of the parcels, and then backed off, agreeing to wait until dark to finish," one DEA agent recalled. "When it got dark, the captain of the Night Train began to radio for us to come alongside and pick up the cargo," one DEA agent said. "We pretended we were having radio trouble – we'd flip it on and off in the middle of sentences, and swear at it like crazy."

The *Dauntless* surfaced over the horizon and the *Night Train* captain yelled, 'Shark! Shark!' over the citizen band radio.[6]

Undercover customs agent on the Catchalot, *alongside the* Night Train. *He's signaling to watch for aircraft.*

The *Night Train* fled, while documents and packages flew overboard. When the *Dauntless* closed on the freighter, the *Night Train* tried to ram the Coast Guard ship and continue to escape. The guardsmen on the *Dauntless* fired a .50-caliber machine gun and 3-inch non-explosive training rounds across her bow, but the *Night Train* refused to surrender. The Coast Guard officers then aimed their gun at the pilot's house, threatening the crew's lives. "That got their attention," said the *Dauntless* captain. The *Night Train* yielded, and the *Dauntless*'s armed guardsmen stormed the ship.

Inside the cargo hull, authorities uncovered a staggering 54 tons of marijuana – the largest marijuana seizure in American history at the time, and still one of the largest ever recorded.[4,5,7-12] In the year following the *Night Train*'s capture, over two hundred motherships were ferrying narcotics to America, exploiting Derber's invention. His killers remain a mystery.

Epilogue

Marijuana seizure from the Night Train.

ACKNOWLEDGEMENTS

From the bottom of my heart, I wish to thank the families for their courage and candor in sharing their recollections. I'm deeply grateful to Sarah Cohen's son, Michael Gottlieb, and grandchildren, Todd Thorn and Meggan Shields. They entrusted me with Sarah's memoirs and generously provided their precious and sometimes difficult memories. Their openness was invaluable in depicting the many facets of Sarah's remarkable personality.

Thank you to Víctor Pina Tabío, son of Captain Víctor Pina. Víctor's portrait of his father and his perspective on Cuban politics were invaluable. I'm also deeply grateful to Víctor for sharing the mail correspondence between my cousin and his father. I like to think that Captain Pina and Derber would have smiled knowing their families were still discussing their exploits sixty years later. Let me extend a warm thanks to Ellie Adiel, widow of Rehavam 'Ray' Adiel. Her recollections helped me obtain a fuller picture of Ray and his unique friendship with my cousin.

Henry Sommer was the first to introduce me to our mutual cousin, Harold Derber. I'm indebted to Harry for the introduction and the multiple rounds of copy editing, particularly on the courtroom scenes. I'd also like to thank my cousin Linder Derber Specht, who generously shared her childhood reminiscences and the family folklore of Harold Derber. I also wish to thank the relatives of Harold Derber who chose to stay anonymous. I fully respect and understand their decision.

Thank you to my sister, Becky Tuch, who provided relentless encouragement and incisive feedback. I'm lucky to have a writer as a sister, particularly one as supportive and thoughtful as Becky.

My developmental editors, Eli Bortz and John Knight, were relentless in their emphasis on character development. Their efforts helped ensure that Harold Derber's life did not eclipse the man.

Thank you to my beta readers Ben Birnbaum, Nick Rees Gardner, Erica Ball, Hadley Moore, Warren Maxwell, Anders Køie, Edith Wiegell Køie, Kunal Vyas, Simon McCoy, Joanne O'Shea, Alex Standish and Alexander Smith. Their feedback on the earlier drafts was priceless. I'm also grateful to the Elliot Park Dog Walking Crew for their early morning encouragement.

I would like to thank the numerous professors, archival researchers, authors, curators and journalists who helped with the research and provided feedback on the manuscript. It is important to stress that any errors or omissions are my lapses alone.

Let me thank Professor Jorge Dominguez of Harvard University, Lina Britto from Northwestern University, Senior Lecturer Anita van Dissel from Leiden University, and Brian Latell, Professor at Florida International University and former CIA National Intelligence Officer for Latin America.

I'm particularly indebted to Martin Sugarman of the Association of Jewish Ex-Servicemen and Women (AJEX), who provided extensive insight into the life of British merchant mariners during World War II. Let me extend profound thanks to Alexandra Cropper from the Manchester Jewish Museum, Erwin van Delden and Jan Bossenbroek of the National Maritime Museum (Het Scheepvaartmuseum), Welmoed Bons of the Netherlands Institute of Military History, Ole Jørgen S. Abrahamsen of the Norwegian War Sailor Register (Krigsseilerregisteret), Julio Batista from the Bay of Pigs Museum, and Juan Antonio Villanueva from the Cuban Heritage Collection at the University of Miami.

Thank you to the author and former *Atlanta Constitution* journalist Robert Coram, author and former *Barron's* journalist Kathryn Welling, and former *Miami Herald* journalist William Amlong.

Acknowledgements

I'm grateful to Lou Kramer from the Wolfson Archives at Miami Dade College, Connie Beach-Sims at the National Archives and Records Administration, and Stacey Chandler at the John F. Kennedy Presidential Library.

I've been fortunate to work with an amazingly talented and dedicated team of archival researchers. Thank you to Marj Linder in the US; Steven Smith, Mark Nicholls, Erol Gross, and Kirsty Hooper in the UK; Rose Lerer Cohen in Jerusalem; and Sergio Gomez and Edna Muñoz in Bogotá.

Let me also thank the members of law enforcement: former Agent William McNally from US Customs and Sergeant Nikoli Trifonov from the Miami Police Department Cold Case Unit. I'm enormously grateful to Sergeant Trifonov for his help and patience in accessing Derber's murder investigation file.

I'm indebted to former Marine Patrol Agent Ted Akey who generously shared his reminiscences of the undercover operation to bring down Derber and capture the *Night Train*. His photos of the *Night Train* seizure helped bring the daring mission to life.

Thank you to my agent, Linda Langton. With her roots in Manchester and her current life in New York, our partnership was destined to be. Thank you to Connor Stait and the team at Icon Books for taking a chance on this first-time author. I'm also grateful to Connor and Steve Burdett for their expert editing.

And, as ever, to my love, Mette. "She wasn't doing a thing that I could see, except standing there leaning on the balcony railing, holding the universe together."—J.D. Salinger

LIST OF ILLUSTRATIONS

PART I
1. Escape from Manchester
1. Manchester Jewish Lads' Brigade squad. North West Film Archive, Manchester Metropolitan University. — 4
2. Manchester Jews' School class. Manchester Jewish Museum Archive. — 7
3. Victoria Memorial Jewish Hospital. Manchester Central Library Archive. — 17
4. SS *van Ostade*. Jos Telleman, www.arendnet.com — 23
5. SS *van Ostade* crew list (excerpt). National Archives in Washington, DC. — 23

2. War
6. MS *Cypria*. www.warsailors.com — 31
7. HX convoy. National Archives of Canada. — 33
8. MT *Havprins*. www.warsailors.com — 37

3. Questionable Ventures
9. Brazil visa. National Archives of Brazil. — 45
10. Ray Adiel. Eleanor Adiel. — 49

PART II
4. The Three-Mile Limit
11. *Calypso Liner* advertisement. *Miami Herald*. — 56
12. Calypso Twins. *Miami News*. — 58
13. *Calypso Liner* brochure. Author's personal collection. — 59

5. The New American Dream
14. *Empress of Bahamas* advertisement.
    Miami Hurricane.   65
15. Fontainebleau Hotel lobby brochure.
    Author's personal collection.   72

6. The Freedom Ferry
16. Castro and Donovan. Donovan family.   79
17. Captain Víctor Pina. Pina Tabío.   85
18. Exclusive agreement. FOIA USCIS Derber.   87
19. Nageley interview. Wolfson Archive.   91
20. SS *Maximus*. Wolfson Archive.   93

7. We Will Not Be Stopped by Military Force
21. Senate Hotel postcard. Author's personal collection.   96
22. Ferry flyer. Swiss Federal Archives.   97

8. The Exile Runner
23. *Nana*. Florida Keys History Center, Monroe County Public Library.   119
24. Passengers traveling. Wolfson Archive.   120
25. Passengers disembarking. Author's personal collection.   122
26. Derber in glasses. Wolfson Archive.   124
27. Derber and Sari. Associated Press.   125
28. Derber and Sari in tender moment. Wolfson Archive.   127
29. Derber leaving courthouse. Swiss Federal Archives.   129
30. Sari farewell. *Miami News*.   136

9. Love and Hate and Humanitarian Solutions
31. Derber arriving in London Airport. ANL/Shutterstock.   138
32. Quinceañera party. Víctor Pina Tabío.   146
33. Pina and Derber. Ibid.   146

List of Illustrations

PART III

10. Shipping Interests

34. Residence application. General Archive of the Nation, Bogotá. — 157

11. The Night Train

35. *Night Train.* Messick. — 164

12. Operation Zebra

36. John D. Steele. *Fort Lauderdale News.* — 169
37. Smuggler apprehended. *High Times.* — 173
38. *Lillian B* unloading. *News and Record* — 174
39. Smith Brothers. Darrell Boyd. — 178

13. Vast Opportunities

40. Brennan advertisement. *US News & World Report.* — 183
41. Derber's murder. Wolfson Archive. — 191

Epilogue

42. Plane. Ted Akey. — 194
43. *Night Train.* Ibid. — 195
44. Undercover agent. Ibid. — 196
45. Seizure. *Fort Lauderdale News.* — 197

ABBREVIATIONS

BdU	Befehlshaber der Unterseeboote (U-boat Supreme Command)
BMN	British Merchant Navy
BNP	Banco Nacional de Panamá
CFC	Cuban Families Committee
CIA	Central Intelligence Agency
CINCLANT	Commander in Chief, US Atlantic Command
DEA	Drug Enforcement Administration
DGI	Dirección General de Inteligencia (Cuban Intelligence)
FBI	Federal Bureau of Investigation
HX	Halifax
ICCCA	Interdepartmental Coordinating Committee of Cuban Affairs
INS	Immigration and Naturalization Service
JFK	John F. Kennedy
JLB	Jewish Lads' Brigade
JMWAVE	CIA Miami Station
KGB	Komitet Gosudarstvennoy Bezopasnosti (Soviet Intelligence Agency)
M-19	19th of April Movement (Colombian guerrilla group)
MJS	Manchester Jews' School
Nfld	New Foundland
NSA	National Security Agency
ON	Onward North

ONS	Onward North Slow
PMG	Postmaster General
RAF	Royal Air Force
RFK	Robert F. Kennedy
SC	Slow Convoy
SEC	Securities and Exchange Commission
USSR	Union of Soviet Socialist Republics
WAC	Western Approaches Command

BIBLIOGRAPHY

Archives

AJHS	American Jewish Historical Society Archives
MML	Archives Centre at the Maritime Museum, Liverpool
FRUS	Foreign Relations of the United States, Office of the Historian
GAN	General Archive of the Nation (Archivo General de la Nación, Bogotá, Colombia)
GL-LRS	Guildhall Library, Lloyd's Register of Shipping
IWM	Imperial War Museum Archive
IMMH	International Maritime Museum Hamburg Archive
ISA	Israel State Archives (לארשי תנידמ ןויכרא, Arkhiyon Medinat Yisra'el)
JFK	John F. Kennedy Presidential Archive
LBJ	Lyndon B. Johnson Presidential Archive
WLF	Lynn and Louis Wolfson II Florida Moving Image Archives, Miami Dade College
MCL	Manchester Central Library Archive
MJA	Manchester Jewish Museum Archive
NAA	National Archives at Atlanta
NACP	National Archives at College Park, Maryland
NAFW	National Archives at Fort Worth, Texas
NAUK	National Archives at Kew, Surrey, UK
NADC	National Archives at Washington, D.C.
NAB	National Archives of Brazil (Arquivo Nacional)
NAC	National Archives of Canada

NAN National Archives of Norway (Riksarkivet)
NIMH Netherlands Institute of Military History Archive (Nederlands Instituut voor Militaire Historie)
NWF North West Film Archive, Manchester Metropolitan University
NCNH Norwegian Center for War Sailor History (Norsk senter for krigsseilerhistorie)
SFA Swiss Federal Archives (Schweizerisches Bundesarchiv)
UOMA University of Oxford, Bodleian Library, Marconi Archives
USJR University of Sheffield, Jack Rosenthal Drama Scripts Collection
UWRU University of Warwick, Radio Officers' Union, 1938–67 Collection

Digital Collections

Arnold Hague Database (AHD)
Convoyweb.org
Cuban Information Archive
Maritime History Database, Norway (Sjøhistorie)
Mary Ferrell Foundation Digital Archive
University of Texas at Austin, Latin American Network Information Center
War Sailor Register (Krigsseilerregisteret)
Warsailors.com

Interviews and Correspondence

Anonymous relatives of Harold Derber
Anonymous childhood acquaintances of Harold Derber
Anonymous trafficker associates

Bibliography

Eleanor Adiel, widow of Ray Adiel
Ted Akey, Florida Marine Patrol Agent
Darrell Boyd
Robert Brennan
Kevin Foley, DEA Special Agent
Michael Gottlieb, son of Sarah Cohen
Víctor Pina Tabío, son of Capitan Víctor Pina
Todd Thorn, grandson of Sarah Cohen
Laurence Vaughan-Williams, ex-husband of Sybil Derber

Government Correspondence

MI5 Security Service. Letter to Author Regarding Harold Derber. April 9, 2024
Ministry of Interior, State of Israel. Response to the Immigration Authority Query. September 4, 2024.

Memoir

Cohen, Sarah E. *Unpublished Memoir*. In possession of Todd Thorn.

Freedom of Information Act Files

Federal Bureau of Investigation, Records related to Sarah Elizabeth Cohen. FOIA Request #: 1607104-002. Released May 1, 2024.
National Security Agency, Records related to Harold Derber. FOIA Request #: 119061. Denied August 9, 2024 under exemption Section 1.4(c): 'intelligence activities (including covert action), intelligence sources or methods, or cryptology.'
US Citizenship and Immigration Services, Records related to Harold Derber. FOIA Request #: NRC2023325302. Released November 24, 2023.

US Citizenship and Immigration Services, Records related to Sarah Elizabeth Cohen. FOIA Request #: PPO2024000166. Released June 28, 2024.

US Department of State, Records related to Harold Derber. FOIA Request #: F-2024-00917. Released October 25, 2024.

US Drug Enforcement Agency, Records related to Charles Wilson. FOIA Request #: 24-00006-F. Denied January 24, 2024 under exemption § 552 (b)(7)(e) 'techniques and procedures.'

US Drug Enforcement Agency, Records related to Harold Derber. FOIA Request #: 23-01112-F. Denied January 24, 2024 under exemption § 552 (b)(7)(e) 'techniques and procedures.'

US Drug Enforcement Agency, Records related to Lillian B. FOIA Request #: 24-00944-F. Records destroyed.

US Drug Enforcement Agency, Records related to the Night Train. FOIA Request #: 24-00943-F. No responsive records.

US Drug Enforcement Agency, Records related to Operation Stopgap. FOIA Request #: 24-01126-F. Records destroyed.

Periodicals

Atlanta Constitution, Atlanta Journal, Atlantic, Barron's, Bild-Zeitung, Boston Herald, Bradenton Herald, Charlotte News, Charlotte Observer, Chicago Tribune, Coventry Evening Telegraph, Daily Gleaner, Daily Herald, Daily News, Daily Press, Daily Telegram, El Informador, El Mundo, El País, El Tiempo, El Universal, Esquire, Evening Bulletin, Evening Telegram, Evening Telegraph, Florida Today, Fort Lauderdale News, Guam Daily News, Guardian, Hamburger-Abendblatt, High Times, Irish Weekly and Ulster Examiner, Jewish Chronicle, Leader-Post, London Gazette, Los Angeles Times, Manchester Evening News, Miami Herald, Miami Hurricane, Miami News, Nation, Naval History Magazine, New York Times, News and Observer, News and Record, Noticias de Hoy, Orlando Sentinel, Palm Beach Post, Pamlico County News,

Bibliography

Pensacola News Journal, Philadelphia Inquirer, Port Angeles Evening News, Prensa Latina, Providence Sunday Journal, Reader's Digest, Record, San Pedro News-Pilot, SEC Digest, Sentinel, Signal, Stars and Stripes (Pacific Ed.), Stornoway Gazette and West Coast Advertiser, Tallahassee Democrat, Tampa Tribune, U.S. News & World Report, Washington Post, Western Manufacturing, Wilmington Morning Star, Winston-Salem Journal.

Television Broadcasts

"Attorney Chuck Ashmann (MSOF) Applying for Writ of Habeas Corpus to Get Britisher Harold Derber Out of Trouble With U. S. Immigration Officials; (Cuban Shuttle). 34 Ft." In *TVN0792 – WTVJ Newsfilm Reel # R6B, Can 2751, Clip 9*, Wolfson Archive, October 27, 1963.

"Attorney Jack Nageley (MSOF) on Plan to Transport Cubans from Havana to Key West. 63 ft." In *TVN0772 – WTVJ Newsfilm Reel # Q40A, Can 2685, Clip 5*, Wolfson Archive, July 26, 1963.

"Attorney Jack Nagely [sic] (MSOF) on Arrest of Empress Lines Owner Harold Derber by Jamaican Police. 60 ft. (Cuban Shuttle)." In *TVN0777 – WTVJ Newsfilm Reel # R1B, Can 2700, Clip 12*, Wolfson Archive, August 20, 1963.

"Attorney Jack Nagely [sic] (MSOF) with Ed Fleming on Problems Involved in Planning for Refugee Shuttle between Cuba and Key West. 93 ft." In *TVN0765 – WTVJ Newsfilm Reel # Q38B, Can 2667, Clip 1*, Wolfson Archive, July 1, 1963.

"Attorney Jack Nagely [sic] (MSOF) with Jere Pierce on Empress Lines Ltd. Cuba to Florida Shuttle. 102 ft." In *TVN0775 – WTVJ Newsfilm Reel # Q40D, Can 2692, Clip 9*, Wolfson Archive, August 7, 1963.

"Cuban Refugees Protest US Opposition to Refugee Shuttle Between Havana and Key West; Torch of Friendship. 18 ft."

In *TVN0777 – WTVJ Newsfilm Reel # R1B, Can 2699, Clip 13*, Wolfson Archive, August 18, 1963.

"Cuban Refugees Shuttle Ship "Nana" Loaded at Jamaica; Attorney Jack Nagely, Miami (MSOF) Why Ship Was Stopped by Jamaican Officials. 81 ft." In *TVN0777 – WTVJ Newsfilm Reel # R1B, Can 2699, Clip 9*, Wolfson Archive, August 17, 1963.

"Man Deported from USA for Smuggling Cuban Refugees to Florida: Harold Derber Interview." *ITN TV Interview*. Editorial #: 1714627064. Object Name: fs210164012_0. Getty Images Archive. January 21, 1964.

"Murder, Harold Derber; Gangland Style; Shots Body; 15 Ft." In *TVN2084 – WTVJ Newsfilm Reel, Can 7773, Clip 1*, Wolfson Archive, March 23, 1976.

"Ocean Liner, Wappen von Hamburg is Readied for Possible Use in Transporting Cuban Prisoners Back to Miami." In *TVN0724 – WTVJ Newsfilm Reel # Q20A, Can 2516, Clip 10*, Wolfson Archive, December 21, 1962.

"Sari Cohen, Empress Lines Limited (MSOF) on Havana-Key West Service and Monies Collected from Cubans for Tickets Aboard Ship Orange Star. 18 ft." In *TVN0763 – WTVJ Newsfilm Reel # Q37C, Can 2663, Clip 4*, Wolfson Archive, June 25, 1963.

"Sari Cohn, [sic] Secretary to Jack Nagely [sic] on Trip from Cuba with Harold Derber (Cuban Shuttle); (SOF). 64 ft." In *TVN0772 – WTVJ Newsfilm Reel # R6B, Can 2750, Clip 15*, Wolfson Archive, October 25, 1963.

"Ship Maximus Arrives Port Everglades with 1204 Cubans Aboard; Ralph Renick (MSOF) into; Joe Abreall (MSOF) with Baptist Missionaries Kicked out of Cuba, Lucille Kerrigan and Ruby Miller; Immigration Director Edward Ahrens (MSOF) Manolo Reyes (MSOF) in Spanish; Paul Moore (MSOF) Last trip for Red Cross; Pickets at Ship. 308 ft." In *TVN0765 –*

WTVJ Newsfilm Reel # Q38B, Can 2668, Clip 5, Wolfson Archive, July 3, 1963.

Movies and Videos

The 1938 Jewish Lad Brigade Camp. Film Number: 3226, North West Film Archive, Manchester Metropolitan University. 1938.

"גדעונים: במורשתם נלך." Association for Commemorating the Martyrs of the Communications and ICT Corps, 2016, https://www.youtube.com/watch?v=fPr2g_51icw.

Co-Operative Wholesale Society Limited. *Manchester Took It Too*. C.W.S. Publicity Department Film Production Unit. Film number: 176. North West Film Archive. Manchester Metropolitan University. 1940/1941.

Parker, Alan. "The Evacuees." UK: BBC, March 5, 1975.

Vikene, Gunnar. "War Sailor." Norway: Netflix, October 22, 2022.

Letters

Derber, Harold. Letter to Braulio Martinez. June 26, 1965.

———. Letter to Braulio Martinez December 27, 1965.

———. Letter to Víctor Pina. March 14, 1964.

———. Letter to Víctor Pina. December 27, 1965.

Police and Autopsy Reports

City of Miami Police Department. Harold Derber Murder Investigation File. Case #: 615994. 1977.

Office of the Medical Examiner. Metropolitan Dade County. Autopsy Report on Harold Derber. Case No. 758A. March 23, 1976.

State of North Carolina, General Court of Justice, Superior Court Division. James Alexander Watson Warrant. File #: 77 Cr 273. January 20, 1978.

Archives

Foreign Relations of the United States, Office of the Historian

Foreign Relations of the United States, 1961–1963, American Republics; Cuba 1961–1962; Cuban Missile Crisis and Aftermath, Volumes X/XI/XII, Microfiche Supplement. Edited by Edward C. Keefer, Louis J. Smith and Charles S. Sampson. Washington, DC: United States Government Publishing Office, 2021.

General Archives of the Nation, Bogotá

Objeto; Harold Derber Ciudadano Britanico. Prontuario de Harold Derber. Document: RG 46.238. Departamento Administrativo de Seguridad, División de Extranjería. General Archive of the Nation. March 8, 1971.

Garcia, Carlos Arturo Castro. Memo from Director General of Security to Head of the Division of Foreign Affairs. Prontuario de Harold Derber. Document: TD 139.300. Departamento Administrativo de Seguridad, División de Extranjería. General Archive of the Nation. April 26, 1973.

Israel State Archives

Israel Immigration Lists, Israel State Archives. 1948.

John F. Kennedy Presidential Library

National Security Files, Box 056, "Cuban Refugees, Ferry Service, 7/63-11/63". ID: JFKNSF-056-010. JFK Library

Bibliography

Transcript of Donovan's Oral Report to Miskovsky, Reel 4, NSA Cuba Collection. Papers of Robert F. Kennedy. Attorney General Papers, 13-14. "6-5: Cuba: Cuban Crisis, 1962: Cuban Prisoner Exchange (James B. Donovan)" ID: RFKAG-217-002. JFK Library.

Briefing Paper for the President's Press Conference. Subject: Ferry Boat Service Between Havana and Key West. President's Office Files, "31 October 1963: Background materials". ID: JFKPOF-061-006-p0159, Box 061. JFK Library, October 31, 1963.

EMBTEL 56. Situation Report as of Noon EST on MARVIC. Telegram from Jamaican Embassy to Secretary of State, National Security Files, Box 123, "Jamaica: General: 1963: June-November". ID: JFKNSF-123-004-p0050. JFK Library, August 15, 1963.

Bundy, McGeorge. *Memorandum for the Attorney General.* National Security Files, Box 402, "Chronological File: General, December 1962". ID: JFKNSF-402-003-p0091. JFK Library, December 15, 1962.

Lyndon B. Johnson Presidential Library

Country Files, National Security File, Box 30, "Cuba – Refugees, 10/63–7/65". LBJ Library.

Country Files, National Security File, Box 58, "Jamaica, Volume 1, 11/63–6/68 [2 of 3]". LBJ Library.

National Archives at Atlanta

The United States vs. Harold Derber. Miami Criminal Dockets, Case Numbers 63-500 – 63-599. RG: 21. NAID: 472367143. National Archives at Atlanta, December 9, 1963.

The United States vs. Harold Derber. Miami Criminal Dockets, Case Numbers 63-600 – 63-714. RG: 21. NAID: 472367361. National Archives at Atlanta, January 29, 1964.

National Archives at College Park, Maryland

POL – Political Affairs & Relations, Relations Cuba/US Movement – Orange Sun Lines. RG: 59. NAID: 2059876. National Archives at College Park.

Political Affairs & Rel. Relations – United States (Orange Sun – Harold Derber). RG: 59. NAID: 77414843. National Archives at College Park.

Political Relations – U.S.A. Harold Derber. RG: 59. NAID: 77414844. National Archives at College Park.

Subject Files, 1961–1972, Proposed Havana-Key West Ferry Service. RG: 59. NAID: 1254233. National Archives at College Park. Obtained through Freedom of Information Act request. Released July 1, 2024.

National Archives at Washington, D.C.

Passenger and Crew Lists of Vessels and Airplanes Arriving at Honolulu, Hawaii, September 21, 1957 – October 19, 1957. RG: 85. NAID: 169474915. National Archives at Washington, DC, 1957.

Passenger and Crew Lists of Vessels Arriving at and Departing from Ogdensburg, New York, May 27, 1948–November 28, 1972. RG: 85. NAID: 4477230. National Archives at Washington, DC, 1957.

Passenger and Crew Manifests of Airplanes Arriving at New York, New York, December 1, 1957–November 3, 1969. RG: 85. NAID: 2848504. National Archives at Washington, DC, 1961.

Roll 32: Old INS Roll 17: August 27, 1956 – September 20, 1956. RG: 85. NAID: 366526046. National Archives at Washington, DC, 1956.

S.S. Van Ostade Crew List. Crew Lists of Vessels Arriving at Boston, Massachusetts, 1917–1943; Record Group Title: Records of the Immigration and Naturalization Service, 1787–2004; RG: 85. NAID: 4477487. National Archives at Washington, DC, 1943.

National Archives of Brazil

Brazil, Rio de Janeiro, Immigration Cards, 1900–1965. Folder: 004816347, Image: 00015. National Archives of Brazil, March 27, 1957.

National Archives, UK

1939 Register Booklet. County: Lancashire. Enumeration District: NCOV. Borough, Urban or Rural District: Blackpool County ... Reference: RG 101/4254H/14. National Archives; Kew, Surrey, UK, 1939.

Activities of Cuban Aircraft and US Objection to Re-Opening of Air Routes to Cuba. Reference: CO 1031/4859. National Archives; Kew, Surrey, UK, 1963.

Convoy Number HX 259 from Halifax (later New York) to UK. Sailing on 30 9 1943 and ... Reference: ADM 199/2190/62. National Archives; Kew, Surrey, UK, 1943-1944.

Home Office: Aliens Department: Internees Index, 1939-1947. Reference: HO 396/93/286. National Archives; Kew, Surrey, UK, 1939.

Intelligence Reports on the Political Situation Bahamas. Reference: CO 1031/4762. National Archives; Kew, Surrey, UK, 1963.

Intelligence Reports: Cayman Islands. Reference: CO 1031/4768. National Archives; Kew, Surrey, UK, 1963.

Medal Listing of Derber, Harold. Discharge Number: S38484. Date of Birth: 24 February 1926. Reference: BT 395/1/24515. National Archives; Kew, Surrey, UK, 1946-2002.

Refugee Problems and Derber Case. Reference: FO 371/174120. The National Archives; Kew, Surrey, UK, 1964.

Refugees from Cuba: Security of UK Territory in Bahamas. Reference: FO 371/168228. National Archives; Kew, Surrey, UK, 1963.

Refugees from Cuba: Security of UK Territory in Bahamas. Reference: FO 371/168229. National Archives; Kew, Surrey, UK, 1963.

Refugees from Cuba: Security of UK Territory in Bahamas. Reference: FO 371/168231. National Archives; Kew, Surrey, UK, 1963.

Ship Name: Cypria. Gross Tonnage: 4366. Reference: BT 389/35/179. National Archives; Kew, Surrey, UK, 1939–1946.

Ship Name: Havprins Former Ship Name: Havsborg Gross Tonnage: 8066. Reference: BT 389/37/87. National Archives; Kew, Surrey, UK, 1939–1946.

War Office: Soldiers' Documents from Pension Claims, First World War (Microfilm Copies and Medical Cards). Piece: 4289a, Reference: WO 364. National Archives; Kew, Surrey, UK, 1920.

National Archives of Norway

New York/London, AV/RA-S-4523/1/E/Ee/L0009: Cypria 1944. National Archives of Norway.

London-kort Harold Derber. Det Norske Innskudds- og Trekkontor i Oslo, AV/RA-S-2081/F/Fe/Feb/L0007: Cotty, J. - Despotides, S., 1940-1961, s. 2173. National Archives of Norway.

London-kort Hyman Tuchverderber. Det Norske Innskudds- og Trekkontor i Oslo, RA/S-2081/F/Fe/Feb/L0027: Thompson, Alex – Wardle, P., 1940-1961, s. 985. National Archives of Norway.

New York-kort Hyman Tuchverderber. Notraship – Diverse Arkivmateriale, RA/S-2156/F/Fa/L0041: New York Kort: Tom-Va. National Archives of Norway.

Swiss Federal Archives

Projet Nageley / Derber, 1963. File Reference: E2200.36-09#1976/154#68*. File Reference: B.72.0.2. Delivery: 1976/00154 Schweizerische Vertretung, Washington (US-Washington, D.C.) (1933–1972), Swiss Federal Archives.

USA: Transport Maritimes, "EMPRESS LINES Ltd" (Dossiers). Reference: E2200.176-03#1989/77#1150*. File Reference: B.521. Delivery: 1989/00077 Schweizerische Vertretung, Havanna (CU-Havanna) (1957–1979). Swiss Federal Archives.

Miscellaneous Archives

Manchester Jews' School, Cheetham, Admission Register, 18 Sep 1916–29 Aug 1949, Identier: GB127.M66/126/2/2/6, Manchester Central Library Archive.

Radio Officers Marconi Examination Results, 1909–1983. Reference: D/ROE/1-121. Vols. 79 and 85. Access number: MMM.2000.31.1-121. Archives Centre at the Maritime Museum, Liverpool. September, 2007.

Hyman Tuchverderber Service Record on S.S. Van Ostade. Inventory Number 2817, Archive 159 Londense Collectie Koopvaardij, The Hague. Netherlands Institute for Military History Archive, 1943.

Wireless War. Physical description: PRD. 323 51-4010. Catalog number: Art.IWM PST 4039. Imperial War Museum. 1943.

CIA Reports

AMTRUNK Operation – Interim Working Draft, Dated 14 February 1977, with Attachments. Record: 104-10103-10097. CIA, February 14, 1977.

Cable: Commo Training AMWARM 1 Completed 9 Oct. Record: 104-10103-10384. CIA, October 10, 1963.

CIA Files on Eusebio Azcue Lopez, 1960–1970, as Reviewed by Ed Lopez. Document ID: 1994.03.07.15:38:13:120007. Agency File: 80T01357A. CIA, March 7, 1994, 117.

Report on Cuban Operations for Period 1-15 September 1961. Record: 104-10227-10153. CIA, September 26, 1961.

Chief of Station, JMWAVE. *Dispatch-Operational/Typic AMKNOB-1 Information on Cuban Matters.* HSCA Segregated CIA Collection (Microfilm – Reel 2: Artime – Barker), Record: 104-10181-10299, File: 80T01357A. CIA, September 10, 1963.

———. *Transmittal of Operational Plan for AMTRUNK VII.* Record: 104-10216-10148. CIA, January 28, 1964.

Director of Central Intelligence. *Cuban Government Involvement in Drug Trafficking: Interagency Intelligence Memorandum.* File: NI IIM 84-10010. CIA, December, 1984.

Director of Intelligence. *Smuggling Colombian Marijuana: A High-Profit Venture: An Intelligence Assessment.* Document: GI 82-10211. CIA, September, 1982.

JMWAVE. *JMWAVE Cable – Cuban Cabinet Changes.* Record: 104-10076-10393. Agency File: 80T01357A. CIA, December 13, 1963.

———. *JMWAVE Cable – Possible Sabotage of Cubana Aviation Aircraft.* Record: 104-10076-10188. Agency File: 80T01357A. CIA, December 8, 1963.

Office of Legislative Counsel, Central Intelligence Agency. *Photos of Individuals Possibly Identifiable with Persons Cited in*

Antulio Ramirez Ortiz' Manuscript (Attachments A, B – Tabs 1–26). Record: 1993.08.04.18:39:12:810059. CIA, April 7, 1978, 28.

FBI Reports

Subjects: Michael McLaney. Record: 124-90154-10214. FBI, February 3, 1967.

Blackmer, S. Jonathan. *Re: Summary of Victor Espinosa Deposition Taken June 7, 1978 in Washington, DC*. Record: 180-10078-10271. Agency File: 013151F. FBI, 1978.

Doerner, Jr., Fred W. *Crime Conditions in the Miami Division*. Record: 124-10208-10000. Agency File: 62-9-29-743. FBI, November 15, 1963, 124.

Hoover, John Edgar. *Braulio Alfonso Martinez Internal Security – Cuba*. Memo to CIA Director. Record: 124-90140-10021. Agency File: CR 100-413737-270. FBI, October 24, 1963, 3.

Labadie, Stephen J. *Santo Trafficante, aka*. Record: 124-10215-10002. Agency File: 92-2781-1047. FBI, August 7, 1964.

———. *Santo Trafficante, Jr., aka T. Labadie*. Record: 124-10211-10211. Agency File: 92-2781-938. FBI, December 11, 1963.

Marshall, Jack L. *Charles Tourine, aka*. Record: 124-90096-10034. Agency File: 92-2989-221. FBI, December 14, 1964.

Mexico Legal Attaché. *Samuel M. Giancana, aka*. Record: 124-10208-10121. Agency File: 92-3171-2066. FBI, August 4, 1967.

Scranton, Paul A. *Alleged Gambling Aboard the Wappen Von Hamburg, aka "Empress of Bahamas" In Subjects: Michael McLaney*. Record: 124-90154-10197. Agency File: CR 45-10253-11. FBI, January 10, 1963.

Special Agent in Charge, Miami Field Office. *Criminal Intelligence Program, Miami Division*. Record: 124-10207-10008. Agency File: 62-9-29-608. FBI, December 10, 1962.

———. *Criminal Intelligence Program, Miami Division*. Record: 124-10207-10027. Agency File: 62-9-29-626. FBI, January 25, 1963.

Special Agent in Charge, Tampa Field Office. *Santo Trafficante, JR. aka*. Record: 124-10206-10156. Agency File: 92-2781-668. FBI, January 11, 1963.

Verica, Joseph A. *Angelo Bruno, aka Angelo Bruno Annaloro (True Name). Russo, Ange*. Record: 124-10225-10352. Agency File: 92-2717-815. FBI, October 11, 1962, 36-37.

State Department Cables

American Embassy in Bogota. *Subject: Auction of US Flag Vessel "Coral Rock" by Colombian Court*. Cable to U.S. Secretary of State. Reference: 74BOGOTA3303. Department of State, April 19, 1974.

———. *Subject: Status Fishing Vessel Mil-Mar I*. Cable to U.S. Secretary of State. Reference: 1973STATE137518. Department of State, July 17, 1973.

American Embassy in Panama. *Subject: C1-75-0517, DA6-M2, Harold Derber (V)*. Cable to U.S. Secretary of State. Reference: 76PANAMA2883. Department of State, May 11, 1976.

Securities and Exchange Commission. *Subject: Investigation of Harold Derber and Rayhavem [sic] Adiel*. Cable to American Embassy in Panama. Reference: 1976STATE112381. Department of State, May 8, 1976.

U.S. Secretary of State. *Subject: Movements of Mil-Mar aka San Gregorio*. Cable to American Consul in Curacao. Reference: 1975STATE033349. Department of State, February 13, 1975.

Miscellaneous Government Reports

Secret Service Final Survey Report Miami, FL 11/18/63. RIF #: 154-10002-10422. Secret Service, November 18, 1963.

Bibliography

Califano Jr., Joseph A. *Report of Sub-Committee on Cuban Subversion on Progress Made During April-June Period in Curbing Cuban Subversion in Latin America*. Record: 198-10007-10022, Califano Papers, Box 2, Folder 26. United States Army, July 18, 1963.

Court Cases

Albernaz v. United States. No. 79-1709, 450 U.S. 333. U.S. Supreme Court. March, 1981.

Canaveral International Corporation v. Commissioner of Internal Revenue. Docket No. 2576-69, 61 T.C. 520, United States Tax Court. January 29, 1974.

Derber v. Candelaria. 15 A.D.2d 654, New York Supreme Court, Appellate Division. January 30, 1962.

Roth, Arthur vs Lake, Sandra. Local Case #: 1977-020008-CA-01, Dade County Court. June 29, 1977.

Seaboard Caribbean v. Hafen-Dampfschiffahrt. No. 20647, 329 F.2d 538, United States Court of Appeals, Fifth Circuit. March 31, 1964.

Sparkman McLean Co. v. Derber;. Court of Appeals of Washington, Division Two; 4 Wash. App. 341; 481 P.2d 585. February 25, 1972.

Talco Capital Corp. v. Canaveral Int'l. Corp. Civ. No. 63-125, 225 F. Supp. 1007, United States District Court S. D. Florida, Miami Division. January 23, 1964.

United States v. Cadena. Court of Appeals for the Fifth Circuit. Citations: 585 F.2d 1252. January 16, 1979.

United States v. Edward Rodriguez, A/K/A Rick et al. Court of Appeals for the Fifth Circuit. Citations: 585 F.2d 1234. Docket Number: 77-5339. November 20, 1978.

United States v. James R. Monaco and Eugene O. Hicks. 702 F.2d 860, 13 Fed. R. Evid. Serv. 248. United States Court of Appeals, Eleventh Circuit. March 7, 1983.

Government Publications

Congressional Record. Proceedings and Debates of the 88th Congress. First Session. July 16, 1963 to August 2, 1963. Volume 109 – Part 10. Washington, DC: United States Government Printing Office, 1963.

Drugs and Terrorism, 1984: Hearing Before the Subcommittee on Alcoholism and Drug Abuse of the Committee on Labor and Human Resources, United States Senate, Ninety-Eighth Congress, Second Session, on the Investigation of the Link Between Drugs and Terrorism. Government Publishing Office, August 2, 1984.

Securities Activities of First Jersey Securities, Inc., and Robert Brennan, Owner and Former Chairman. A Staff Report Prepared for the Use of the Subcommittee on Oversight and Investigations of the Committee on Energy and Commerce U.S. House of Representatives. Vol. 4, Washington, DC: U.S. Government Printing Office, 1987.

Hach, Steve. *Cold War in South Florida: Historic Resource Study.* Edited by Jennifer W. Dickey. U.S. Department of the Interior, National Park Service, Southeast Regional Office, Cultural Resources Division, October, 2004.

Johnson, Lyndon B. *Remarks at the Signing of the Immigration Bill, Liberty Island.* Public Papers of the Presidents of the United States: Lyndon B. Johnson, 1965. Volume II, Entry 546, October 3, 1965. Washington, DC: United Stated Government Printing Office, 1966, 1037–1040.

Russell, David. "Overview of Coast Guard Operations." In *Local Drug Abuse: Trends, Patterns and Issues*, edited by Community Correspondents Group, Planning and Human Systems, Inc, 161–71: Forecasting Branch, Division of Data and Information Development, National Institute on Drug Abuse, 1981.

United State Congress, Senate. *Role of Cuba in International Terrorism and Subversion, Hearings Before the Subcommittee on Security and Terrorism of the Committee on the Judiciary, February 26, March 4, 11, and 12, 1982. NCJ Number 89991.* Washington, DC: U.S. Government Publishing Office, 1982.

United States Congress, House. *Coast Guard Drug Interdiction. Hearings Before the Subcommittee on Coast Guard and Navigation of the Committee on Merchant Marine and Fisheries, House of Representatives, Ninety-fifth Congress, Second Session, on H.R. 10371 and H.R. 10698...* Washington, D.C.: U.S. Government Printing Office, July 19, 1978.

United States Congress, House. Select Committee on Assassinations. *Investigation of the Assassination of President John F. Kennedy.* Hearings Before the Select Committee on Assassinations of the U.S. House of Representatives, Ninety-fifth Congress, Second Session · Volumes 3–4. U.S. Government Printing Office, 1978.

United States Congress, Senate. *Stopping 'Motherships' – A Loophole in Drug Enforcement.* Hearing Before the Senate Subcommittee to Investigate Juvenile Delinquency, 95th Congress, 2nd Session On S. 3437. NCJ Number 62095. Superintendent of Documents, Government Publishing Office, August 22, 1978.

United States Congress, Senate. Committee on the Judiciary. Subcommittee on Security and Terrorism. *The Cuban Government's Involvement in Facilitating International Drug Traffic: Joint Hearing Before the Subcommittee on Security and Terrorism of the Committee on the Judiciary and the Subcommittee on Western Hemisphere Affairs of the Foreign Relations Committee and the Senate Drug Enforcement Caucus, United States Senate, Ninety-eighth Congress, First Session, on the Cuban Government's Involvement in*

Facilitating International Drug Traffic, Miami, Fla. Vol. 4, Washington, DC: U.S. Government Publishing Office, April 30, 1983.

United States House Select Committee on Assassinations. *Investigation of the Assassination of President John F. Kennedy Hearings before the Select Committee on Assassinations of the U.S. House of Representatives, Ninety-Fifth Congress, Second Session.* Testimony of Senor Eusebio Azcue Lopez, Former Cuban Consul in Mexico City. JFK Exhibit F-437. Washington, DC: U.S. Government Printing Office, 1978.

Books

Arab-Israeli War

Alexander, Zvi. *Oil: Israel's Covert Efforts to Secure Oil Supplies.* Jerusalem: Gefen, 2004.

Firth, Sidney. *Allegiance Under Three Flags – A Memoir.* Independent, 2021.

Rosenne, Daniel. גדעונים: מפעילי הקשר האלחוטי בשירות המדינה שבדרך. Gideonim: Wireless Operators in the Service of an Emerging State. Israel: Association for the Commemoration of the Fallen Soldiers of the IDF Signal Corps, 2018.

Cuba

Aguilera, César Reynel. *El Sóviet Caribeño: La Otra Historia de la Revolución Cubana.* Buenos Aires: Independent, 2019.

Bon Tempo, Carl J. "'They Are Proud People': The United States and Refugees from Cuba, 1959–1966." In *Americans at the Gate: The United States and Refugees during the Cold War*, 106-32: Princeton University Press, 2008.

Castañeda, Jorge G. *Compañero: The Life and Death of Che Guevara.* New York: Knopf Doubleday Publishing Group, 2009.

Colhoun, Jack. *Gangsterismo: The United States, Cuba, and the Mafia 1933–1966*. New York: OR Books, 2013.

Cuban American National Foundation. *Castro's Narcotics Trade*. Washington, DC: Cuban American National Foundation, 1983.

García, María Cristina. *Havana USA: Cuban Exiles and Cuban Americans in South Florida, 1959–1994*. Berkeley: University of California Press, 1996.

Hinckle, Warren, and William W. Turner. *The Fish is Red: The Story of the Secret War Against Castro*. New York: Harper & Row, 1981.

Johnson, Haynes. *The Bay of Pigs: The Leaders' Story of Brigade 2506*. New York: Norton, 1964.

Latell, Brian. *Castro's Secrets: Cuban Intelligence, the CIA, and the Assassination of John F. Kennedy*. New York: Palgrave Macmillan, 2013.

LeoGrande, William M., and Peter Kornbluh. *Back Channel to Cuba: The Hidden History of Negotiations Between Washington and Havana*. Chapel Hill: The University of North Carolina Press, 2015.

MacDonald, Scott. *Dancing on a Volcano: The Latin American Drug Trade*. New York: Praeger, 1988.

Masùd-Piloto, Felix Roberto. *From Welcomed Exiles to Illegal Immigrants: Cuban Migration to the U.S., 1959–1995*. Totowa, N.J: Rowman & Littlefield, 1996.

Nordelo, Gerardo Hernández, et al. *Welcome Home: Torturers, Assassins, and Terrorists in Refuge in the US*. Havana: Editorial Capitán San Luis, 2007.

Pérez-Cisneros, Pablo, John B. Donovan, and Jeff Koenreich. *After The Bay of Pigs: Lives and Liberty on the Line*. Miami: Alexandria Library, 2007.

Pina Tabío, Víctor. *Una Vida, Dos Pasiones: Revolución y Aviación: Víctor Manuel Pina Cardoso*. Cuba: Ruth Casa Editorial, 2023.

Rasenberger, Jim. *The Brilliant Disaster: JFK, Castro, and America's Doomed Invasion of Cuba's Bay of Pigs*. New York: Scribner, 2011.

Rovner, Eduardo Sáenz. *Conexión Colombia: Una Historia del Narcotráfico Entre los Años 30 y los Años 90*. Bogotá: Editorial Planeta Colombiana S.A., 2021.

———. *The Cuban Connection: Drug Trafficking, Smuggling, and Gambling in Cuba from the 1920s to the Revolution*. Chapel Hill: University of North Carolina Press, 2008.

Torres, María de los Angeles. *In the Land of Mirrors: Cuban Exile Politics in the United States*. Ann Arbor: University of Michigan Press, 1999.

Finances

Brennan, Robert E. *Brennan: The Record Stands*. Independent, 2023.

Griffin, Sean Patrick, and Alan A. Block "Penny Wise: Accounting for Fraud in the Penny-Stock Industry." In *Contemporary Issues in Crime and Criminal Justice: Essays in Honor of Gilbert Geis*, edited by Henry N. Pontell and David Shichor, 97–120. Upper Saddle River, N.J.: Prentice Hall, 2001.

Kwitny, Jonathan. *The Fountain Pen Conspiracy*. New York: Alfred A. Knopf, January 1, 1973.

Jewry

Dee, David. *The 'Estranged' Generation? Social and Generational Change in Interwar British Jewry*. London: Palgrave Macmillan, 2017.

Dobkin, Monty. *Tales of Manchester Jewry and Manchester in the Thirties*. Manchester: Neil Richardson, 1986.

Dobkin, Monty, and Robert Hodes. *150 Years of King David Schools, formerly Manchester Jews School, 1838-1988 5598-5748*. Manchester: Jewish Telegraph, 1988.

Kadish, Sharman. *'A Good Jew and a Good Englishman': The Jewish Lads' & Girls' Brigade, 1895-1995*. London; Portland, Or.: Vallentine Mitchell, 1995.

Livshin, Rosalyn. "Acculturation of Immigrant Jewish Children 1890–1930." In *The Making of Modern Anglo-Jewry*, edited by David Cesarani. Oxford: Blackwell, 1990.

Rosenthal, Jack, and Maureen Lipman. *By Jack Rosenthal: An Autobiography in Six Acts*. London: Robson, 2005.

Unowsky, Daniel. *The Plunder: The 1898 Anti-Jewish Riots in Habsburg Galicia*. Palo Alto, CA: Stanford University Press, 2018.

Williams, Bill. *Jewish Manchester: An Illustrated History*. Derby: Breedon Books, 2008.

———. *'Jews and Other Foreigners': Manchester and the Rescue of the Victims of European Fascism, 1933-1940*. Manchester: Manchester University Press, 2011.

Kennedy Administration

Bigger, Phillip J. *Negotiator: The Life and Career of James B. Donovan*. Bethlehem, Pennsylvania: Lehigh University Press, 2006.

Bird, Kai. *The Color of Truth: McGeorge Bundy and William Bundy: Brothers in Arms*. New York: Simon & Schuster, 2000.

Goodwin, Richard N. *Remembering America: A Voice from the Sixties*. New York: Harper & Row, 2014.

Hinckle, Warren. *Deadly Secrets: The CIA–Mafia War Against Castro and the Assassination of J.F.K.* New York: Thunder's Mouth Press, 1992.

Weberman, Alan J., and Michael Canfield. *Coup d'État in America: The CIA and the Assassination of John F. Kennedy.* New York: Quick American Archives, 1992.

Manchester

Cooper, Glynis. *Manchester at War 1939–45.* Barnslay, South Yorkshire: Pen and Sword Military, 2018.

Gillman, Peter and Gillman, Leni. *Collar the Lot! – How Britain Interned & Expelled its Wartime Refugees.* London: Quartet Books, 1981.

Hayes, Cliff. *Our Blitz: Red Skies Over Manchester.* Manchester: Memories, 1999.

Hodgson, Guy. *War Torn: Manchester, its Newspapers and the Luftwaffe's Blitz of 1940.* Chester, England: University of Chester Press, 2015.

Monkhouse, Allan. *Farewell, Manchester.* London: M. Secker, 1931.

Phythian, Graham. *Blitz Britain: Manchester and Salford.* Cheltenham: The History Press, 2015.

Smith, Peter J.C. *Luftwaffe Over Manchester: The Blitz Years 1940-1944.* Manchester: Neil Richardson, 2003.

Marijuana Trafficking

Britto, Lina. *Marijuana Boom: The Rise and Fall of Colombia's First Drug Paradise.* Oakland: University of California Press, 2020.

Ehrenfeld, Rachel. *Narco-terrorism.* New York: Basic Books, 1990.

Fuss, Charles M. *Sea of Grass: The Maritime Drug War, 1970–1990.* Annapolis, Maryland: Naval Institute Press, 1996.

Gately, William, and Yvette Fernández. *Dead Ringer: An Insider's Account of the Mob's Colombian Connection*. New York: Donald I. Fine, 1994.

Goldman, Albert. *Grass Roots: Marijuana in America Today*. New York: Harper & Row, 1979.

Gonzales, Manuel, Kevin McEnery, Thomas Sheehan, and Susan Mellody. *America's Habit: Drug Abuse, Drug Trafficking, and Organized Crime: President's Commission on Organized Crime*. Diane Pub Co, 1998.

Messick, Hank. *Of Grass and Snow: The Secret Criminal Elite*. Englewood Cliffs, NJ: Prentice-Hall, 1979.

Traub, James. *The Billion-Dollar Connection: The International Drug Trade*. New York: J. Messner, 1982.

Merchant Navy and Radio Officers

Anderson, Alex. *Hunter to Hunted – Surviving Hitler's Wolf Packs: Diaries of a Merchant Navy Radio Officer, 1939–45*. Independent, 2023.

Beckman, Morris. *Flying the Red Duster: A Merchant Seaman's First Voyage Into The Battle Of The Atlantic 1940*. Stroud: The History Press, 2011.

Carroll, Olive J. *Deep Sea 'Sparks': A Canadian Girl in the Norwegian Merchant Navy*. Vancouver: Cordillera Publishing Company, 1993.

Chandler, R.W. *Sparks at Sea: The Experiences of a Ship's Radio Officer*. Newton Abbot: David & Charles, 1973.

Good, Timothy S. *The Allied Air Campaign Against Hitler's U-Boats: Victory in the Battle of the Atlantic*. Barnslay, South Yorkshire: Pen and Sword, 2022.

Great Britain Post Office. *Handbook for Wireless Telegraph Operators Working Installations Licensed by His Majesty's Postmaster-General*. H.M. Stationery Office, 1913.

Greenlaw, Joanna. *The History of the Radio Officer in the British Merchant Navy and on Deep-Sea Trawlers*. Llandybie, Wales: Dinefwr Publishers Ltd, 2002.

Malcolm, Ian M. *Merchant Navy: Letters from a Radio Officer: Brocklebank, Marconi, Redifon, Crown Agents, Clan Line, RFA, Ferranti*. Independent, 2013.

Radio Officers' Association. *The Long Silence Falls: The Life and Times of the Merchant Navy Radio Officer 1900–2000*. Oxfordshire: Marston Book Services, 2015.

Scott, Harry. *The Radio Officer's War – Ships, Storms and Submarines*. Createspace Independent Publishing Platform, 2013.

Smith, William. *Churchill's Atlantic Convoys: Tenacity & Sacrifice*. Barnslay, South Yorkshire: Pen and Sword Maritime, 2023.

Sugarman, Martin. *Jews in the Merchant Navy in the Second World War: Last Voices*. Elstree: Vallentine Mitchell, 2018.

Syrett, David. *The Defeat of the German U-Boats: The Battle of the Atlantic*. Columbia, S.C.: University of South Carolina Press, 1994.

Whitfield, David John. *Marconi Radio Officer: The Convoys of a WW2 "Sparks"*. CreateSpace Independent Publishing Platform, 2015.

Miami

Burdick, Thomas, and Charles Mitchell. *Blue Thunder: How the Mafia Owned and Finally Murdered Cigarette Boat King Donald Aronow*. New York: Simon and Schuster, 1990.

Houghton, Vince, and Eric Driggs. *Covert City: The Cold War and the Making of Miami*. New York: PublicAffairs, 2024.

Miscellaneous

Canada Department of Transport. *List of Shipping: Being a List of Vessels on the Registry Books of the Dominion of Canada.* 1975.

LoBrutto, Vincent, and Harriet R. Morrison. *The Coppolas: A Family Business.* Santa Barbara, California: ABC-CLIO, 2012.

NOTES

Prologue

1. Douthat, Bill. "Man Murdered by Mistake in Drug Deal was Miamian." *Miami News*, February 3, 1977.
2. "Identity of Body Exhumed in Mesic Still Being Sought." *Pamlico County News*, May 27, 1976.
3. Watson Warrant.

PART I

1. Escape from Manchester

1. "The Jewish Lads' Brigade." *Jewish Chronicle*, June 16, 1899.
2. Film 3226, NWF.
3. "Mosley in Manchester. Anti-Nazis Ejected." *Jewish Chronicle*, October 27, 1939.
4. WO 364, NAUK.
5. Livshin, 82.
6. GB127.M66/126/2/2/6, MCL.
7. Kaplan, Edward. *Re: Harold Derber – A0-A10-096-029 App As – Film #185.* Letter to INS. FOIA USCIS Derber. January 7, 1959, 303.
8. "Manchester Jewish Evacuees to be Rebilleted: Plan for Series of Hostels." *Jewish Chronicle*, October 27, 1939.
9. RG 101/4254H/14, NAUK.
10. Gillman and Gillman, 156–157.

11. After his fruit grocery store went bankrupt in the early 1900s, Alter served six months in prison with hard labor for hiding assets from his creditors. HO 140/233, NAUK.
12. *Name: Alter Tuchverderber. Date of Birth: 1864. Place of Birth: Tarnow.* HO 396/93/286, NAUK. October 13, 1939.
13. Film 176, NWF.
14. *Manchester Evening News*, June 12, 1942.
15. Art.IWM PST 4039, IWM.
16. MMM.2000.31.1-121, MML.
17. Great Britain Post Office, 73–75.
18. Number 2817, NIMH.
19. NAID 4477487, NADC.

2. War

1. Mann, Peter. "The Status of the Marine Radioman: a British Contribution." *American Journal of Sociology* 63, no. 1 (1957): 39–41.
2. Convoy ONS.10, AHD.
3. Good, 118.
4. Number 2817, NIMH.
5. London-kort Hyman Tuchverderber, NAN.
6. BT 389/35/179, NAUK.
7. ADM 199/2190/62, NAUK.
8. Smith, 192–193.
9. Syrett, 207.
10. Hyman would later claim to have survived five torpedo attacks in the war. Glass, Ian. "Cuba Ferry Deal 'Stinks'." *Miami News*, November 3, 1963; and Cohen Memoir, 103. However, extensive searches of the UK, Norwegian, and Dutch archives found no evidence to suggest any of his ships had been torpedoed. Similarly, he would claim he broke both of his feet in "war operations" and suffered frostbite, resulting in permanent

paralysis of his toes. Transmittal of Copy of Legal Proceedings of Derber Trial at Port Antonio. FOIA USCIS Derber. November 2, 1963, 544. It's unclear whether Hyman's accounts were truthful but undocumented or audacious fabrications.
11. "Doctor's Report and Account," New York/London, AV/RA-S-4523/1/E/Ee/L0009, NAN.
12. New York-kort Hyman Tuchverderber, NAN.
13. M/T Østhav, AHD.
14. M/T Titania, AHD.
15. *London Gazette*, November 14, 1944.
16. BT 389/37/87, NAUK.

3. Questionable Ventures

1. BT 395/1/24515, NAUK.
2. "Appointments – Radio Officers." *Signal*, December, 1947.
3. *Harold Derber vs. Edward Ahrens.* Testimony of Harold Derber, Middle District Court of Florida, No. 63-195-Civil T., FOIA USCIS Derber. October 29, 1963.
4. "Globe-Trotter Runs into Cuba Plane Drama." *Manchester Evening News*, July 12, 1963.
5. Firth, 104.
6. Israel Immigration Lists, ISA; Ministry of Interior Letter to Author.
7. Rosenne, passim.
8. *Harold Derber (Immigration and Naturalization Service File No. A-10 096 029).* FOIA USCIS Derber. November, 1963, 1114–1122.
9. Le Breton, Edmond. "U.S. Hits Shipping to Reds: Legal Guns Aimed at 15 Vessels in Communist Trade." *San Pedro News-Pilot*, March 21, 1953.
10. Immigration and Naturalization Service. *Decision of the Special Inquiry Officer.* In Deportation Proceedings Under

Section 242 of the Immigration and Nationality Act, FOIA USCIS Derber. March 7, 1957, 351.

11. In 1953, the British government conducted a military coup of the democratically elected government of British Guiana. The resulting political confusion and British development plans created opportunities for prospectors. "MI5 Files Reveal Details of 1953 Coup That Overthrew British Guiana's Leaders." *Guardian*, August 26, 2011.

12. They made "promising finds of small stones in the alluvial silt of the Maú River and Echilebar Rivers." "Chance of Summer Afloat for Woman." *Coventry Evening Telegraph*, January 4, 1956.

13. United Press. "4 Claim Guiana Police Thwart Mining Plans." *Stars and Stripes (Pacific Ed.)*, February 4, 1954.

14. ———. "3 Complain of Treatment in British Guiana." *Miami Herald*, February 1, 1954.

15. Image 00015, NAB.

16. *Re: Harold Derber.* INS Memo. FOIA USCIS Derber. January 31, 1956, 371.

17. NAID 366526046, NADC.

18. NAID 4477230, NADC.

19. NAID 169474915, NADC.

20. *Harold Derber (Born in 1926, as Hyman Tuchverderber).* Document: AK1821/53. FO 371/168229, NAUK. July 18, 1963.

21. Kohler, F. Dudley. *Re: Harold Derber, British Resident.* Letter to the Honorable Commissioner of Immigration, New York, FOIA USCIS Derber. June 14, 1958, 328.

22. ———. *Re: Harold Derber, British Subject.* Letter to U.S. Immigration and Naturalization Service, FOIA USCIS Derber. May 21, 1960, 251.

23. American Orbitronics described itself as a high-technology aerospace components company that manufactured

"turbines, rotary wheels, nozzles, stators, jetevators and related missile components fabricated from exotic metals for use in solid and liquid propellant systems." "Orbitronics Acquires Monogram's Equipment." *Western Manufacturing*, August 1961.

24. FBI 124-90154-10197, 8.
25. "Orbitronics." *SEC News Digest* (August 17, 1961): 4.
26. "Local Firms Accused of Stock Fraud." *Washington Post*, August 17, 1961.
27. "Harold Derber Enjoined." *SEC News Digest*, no. 63-7-13 (July 18, 1963); "Orbitronics." *SEC News Digest* (August 17, 1961); Derber won a civil judgment against American Orbitronics' president, World War II flying ace Richard Candelaria. Derber v Candelaria.
28. Adiel's superior in the Israeli military was Michael Koll-Nesher, who would become the Israeli air attaché to Washington, D.C. Alexander, 87. Griffin and Block (p. 104) claimed that Adiel was the Israeli military attaché to Panama, but this could not be corroborated.
29. NAID 2848504, NADC.
30. The Coppola films were *The Peeper* and *Tonight for Sure*. They were produced by Searchlight Productions, which was co-owned by Derber and Adiel. FBI 124-90154-10197, 8; and LoBrutto and Morrison, 151.
31. Responding to the question about prior arrests on his U.S. visa application, Derber wrote, "Pending none [sic] criminal test case regarding diamond mining out of the wardens jurisdiction on international frontier of Brazil and British Guiana (Is a B.G. license required for mining in this area)." Form I-507. Application for Status as Permanent Resident. FOIA USCIS Derber, 354-357.
32. FOIA USCIS Derber. January 14, 1959, 293.

PART II

4. The Three-Mile Limit

1. Kohler, F. Dudley. *Re: Harold Derber, British Resident.* Letter to the Honorable Commissioner of Immigration, New York, FOIA USCIS Derber. June 14, 1958, 328.
2. Talco v Canaveral.
3. Canaveral v Commissioner of Internal Revenue.
4. FBI 124-90154-10197, 8.
5. Kwitny, 134.
6. "Crew of Fun." *Miami News*, June 28, 1962.
7. Wardlow, Jean. "Cruise Ship to Sail Daily for Bimini." *Miami Herald*, January 21, 1962.
8. In collaboration with the Greater Miami Israeli Association, the *Calypso Liner* hosted a "fun-raiser" for Wolf R. Lazarus, President of the Israeli state-owned shipping firm Zim Lines. The company evolved from the illegal refugee shipping fleets during the British Mandate. The soirée included members of the diplomatic jet set, such as Guatemala's General Counsel and Haiti's Vice Consul. "Cruise Con Consuls." *Miami Herald*, August 5, 1962.
9. *Miami Herald*, December 10, 1962.
10. FBI 124-10225-10352, 36-37.
11. Cohen Memoir, 50.
12. ———, 22-23.
13. Gottlieb Interview.

5. The New American Dream

1. Gottlieb Interview.
2. Cohen Memoir, 22-23.
3. Canaveral v Commissioner of Internal Revenue.
4. The *Empress*'s exquisite design would later earn her a cameo in James Bond's *From Russia with Love* as SPECTRE's

floating headquarters. Garrison, Jessica. "The 'Love Boat' faces a tragic ending in a lonely California slough." *Los Angeles Times*, November 22, 2024.

5. The CIA's newly established JMWAVE station in Miami contributed to the city's financial resurgence by placing hundreds of agents in the city, and funding hundreds of front companies, safehouses, and contractors. Eventually, JMWAVE became the Agency's largest station in the world and one of Miami's largest employers. Hach, 20.
6. FBI 124-90154-10214, 2.
7. Mike McLaney harbored a deep grudge against Castro for seizing his casino, to the point of sending multiple proposals to the CIA, outlining ways to assassinate the dictator. When the Agency didn't respond, McLaney took matters into his own hands and established the Lake Pontchartrain Training Facility in Lacombe, Louisiana. From there, he organized a mission to blow up the Shell Oil Refinery in Havana as an act of revenge. Fortunately, Robert F. Kennedy intervened and persuaded McLaney to abandon the plan. FBI 180-10078-10271, 4.
8. FBI 124-90154-10197, 83.
9. FBI 124-10207-10027, 3.
10. FBI 124-10207-10008, 2.
11. FBI 124-90154-10197, 21.
12. ———, 8.
13. ———, 69.
14. Weberman and Canfield, 491.
15. Hinckle, 224.
16. FBI 180-10078-10271, 4.
17. Sari's twin sister, Susan, also had a brush with the mob. Susan befriended the wife of Charlie White, also known as Charles ("The Blade") Tourine, a Genovese crime family capo, racketeer, and former co-operator of the Hotel Capri de Havana,

one of the first mob casinos in Cuba. The FBI was concerned with Susan's involvement with Tourine and interviewed her mother back in Bradenton. The Bureau informed Susan that Tourine was bad news and she broke off her association. FBI 124-90096-10034, 16.
18. FBI 124-10215-10002, 37.
19. Cohen Memoir, 46.
20. ———, 103.
21. ———, 50-52.

6. The Freedom Ferry

1. Samuels, Gertrude. "How Metadiplomacy Works: James Donovan and Castro." *Nation*, April 13, 1963.
2. Pérez-Cisneros et al, 62–65.
3. Wolfe, Jonathan. "What James Donovan Did After the Bridge of Spies." *New York Times*, November 26, 2015.
4. LeoGrande and Kornbluh, 53.
5. RFKAG-217-002, JFK.
6. Kraslow, David. "Red Cross to Help Ransom Captives." *Miami Herald*, December 14, 1962.
7. JFKNSF-402-003-p0091, JFK.
8. Meyer, Phil, and Al Burt. "Real Deal This Time? 'Ransom Ship' Sails." *Miami Herald*, December 18, 1962.
9. Springer-Auslandsdienst. "Castros Gefangene Schon Sonnabend in die Freiheit?" *Bild-Zeitung*, December 20, 1962.
10. TVN0724-2516-10, WLF.
11. "'Wappen von Hamburg' Wirft die Lienen loss." *Hamburger-Abendblatt*, December 28, 1962.
12. Southworth, George. "Ransom Plans All 'Go'; It's Up to Castro Now." *Miami Herald*, December 21, 1962.
13. FBI 124-90154-10197, 8.
14. Seaboard Caribbean v Hafen-Dampfschiffahrt.

15. Hoffmann, Egbert A. "Nur 88 Tage dauerte die Reise der ‚Wappen von Hamburg'." *Bild-Zeitung*, October 1, 1963.
16. Pérez-Cisneros et al, 201.
17. Glass, Ian. "Deported Derber in Mexico." *Miami News*, July 17, 1964.
18. Derber, Harold. *Letter to Robert A. Hurwitch, Deputy Coordinator of Cuban Affairs*. NAID 2059876, NACP. February 5, 1963, 42.
19. Referring to Derber and his lawyer, the Miami INS agent who reviewed their case said, "All in all, they seemed like a very dubious pair of fly-by-nights." Gidel, Louis T. *Subject: Plan for Havanna-Key West Ferry Service*. NAID 2059876, NACP, April 17, 1963, 38.
20. Summ, G. Harvey. *Letter to Mr. Gully*. NAID 2059876, NACP. May 8, 1963, 10–11.
21. Pina Tabío, passim.
22. Morales, Etienne. "'Un Orgullo de Cuba en los Cielos del Mundo.' Cubana de Aviación from Miami to Bagdad (1946–79)." *Journal of Transport History* 40, no. 1 (2019): 62–81.
23. Castañeda, 146.
24. "Memorial Cubano de la Denuncia Honra a Revolucionario Víctor Pina." *Prensa Latina*, June 27, 2018.
25. Pina was likely the CIA contact AMWARM-1, described in agency documents as "a civil aviation expert affiliated with the Ministry of Transportation, trained for intelligence work." (CIA 104-10076-10188) The CIA provided AMWARM-1 with a wireless set and clandestine communications training (CIA 104-10103-10384) and referred to him as "the principal agent of what remains of our intelligence net in Cuba" (CIA 104-10227-1015). The asset was recruited through the CIA's AMTRUNK program, which aimed to organize disaffected senior Cuban military officials to stage a coup against Castro. However, later evidence indicated that Cuban intel-

ligence had in fact turned AMTRUNK into a double agent operation against the CIA (CIA 104-10103-10097).
26. CIA 104-10181-10299, 3.
27. Commissioner of Police, Special Branch, Nassau Police. *Subject: Empress Lines Corp. Ltd.* FOIA USCIS Derber. June 25, 1963, 183–187.
28. Office Administering the Government of the Bahamas. *Bahamas. Intelligence Report for the Month of June, 1963.* Memo. 235, CO 1031/4762, NAUK. July 5, 1963.
29. Knight, Dick. "Havana Shuttle On–Maybe." *Miami Herald*, June 27, 1963.
30. District Director, Miami. *Subject: Harold Derber – A10 096 029 Possible Violation of Sec. 215 of the Immigration and Nationality Act.* Memorandum to Officer in Charge, Nassau, Bahamas, FOIA USCIS Derber. June 24, 1963, 203.
31. Auerbach, Stuart. "Nassau Blocks Ferry Promoter." *Miami Herald*, July 14, 1963.
32. The Bahamian government wrote, "[Derber's operation] constitutes at least an embarrassment to the Government of Bahamas, and for obvious reasons, it is undesirable for Bahamians to get involved." Memo. 393, CO 1031/4762, NAUK.
33. Office Administering the Government of the Bahamas. *Complaint of Mr. Derver [sic], a Br Subject, After Being Refused Entry into the Bahamas.* CO 1031/4859, NAUK. June 25, 1963.
34. MI5 first became aware of Harold Derber when he was barred from the Bahamas. MI5 Letter to Author.
35. TVN0725-2667-1, WLF.
36. "Acusa al Gobierno de los Estados Unidos." *El Informador*, June 30, 1963.
37. TVN0725-2668-5, WLF.
38. Associated Press. "1,000 Cuban Refugees Land at U.S. Port." *Palm Beach Post*, July 4, 1963.

39. United Press International. "Last Cuban Refugees Arrive in Florida." *Bradenton Herald*, July 3, 1963.
40. Kenny, Matthew T. "1204 Cuban Refugees Arrive, End Ransom Episode." *Philadelphia Inquirer*, July 4, 1963.

7. We Will Not Be Stopped by Military Force

1. Nordelo et al, passim.
2. Document: 64, SFA B.521. June, 1963, 331.
3. Knight, Dick. "Cuba-to-Florida Ticket Agent Held." *Miami Herald*, June 25, 1963.
4. Winfrey, Lee. "Police Close Ticket Office of the 'Refugee Cruise Ship'." *Miami Herald*, June 23, 1963.
5. Agreement between Harold Derber and Irenaldo Garcia Baez, FOIA USCIS Derber. June 19, 1963, 715–721.
6. Associated Press. "Refugee Is Accused Over Ticket Scheme." *Tallahassee Democrat*, June 25, 1963.
7. TVN0763-2663-4, WLF.
8. TVN0772-2685-5, WLF.
9. Chase, Gordon. *Subject: Ferry Service Between Miami and Havana for Cuban Refugees.* JFKNSF-056-010, JFK. July 13, 1963.
10. Congressional Record, 88:1 (1963), 13566.
11. *Briefing Paper for the President's Press Conference. Subject: Ferry Boat Service.* JFKNSF-056-010, JFK. August 1, 1963.
12. Klosson, Borris H. *Telegram from U.S. Embassy in Jamaica to Secretary of State.* Number: 64, JFKNSF-056-010, JFK. August 17, 1963.
13. Porter, William M. "Government Should Honor State Department Visas." *Miami Herald*, November 1, 1963.
14. "Exile Ferry Skipper Called Risk." *Miami News*, October 30, 1963.
15. TVN0777-2699-9, WLF.

16. *Memorandum for Mr. McGeorge Bundy: The White House.* B30, LBJ. August 14, 1963, 89–92.
17. Chase, Gordon. *Memorandum to McGeorge Bundy.* Document 705, Keefer et al., August 9, 1963.
18. Associated Press. "Refugee Ferrying Delayed." *El Paso Times*, June 30, 1963.
19. Knight. "Havana Shuttle On–Maybe."
20. Winfrey, Lee, and James Buchanan. "Stop the Cuba Voyage, Panama Tells U.S." *Miami Herald*, June 28, 1963.
21. Associated Press. "Cuban Assets Frozen to Block Subversion: Provision Exempts Refugees." *Miami Herald*, July 9, 1963.
22. Tucker, William. "Ferry Owner Will Defy U.S." *Miami News*, July 14, 1963.
23. Sneigr, Denis. "Caymanians Block Cuba Plane." *Miami News*, July 12, 1963.
24. When news of the Cayman mob incident reached England, the press asked Derber's family in Manchester to comment on why Harold was trying to reach Cuba. "Honestly, we have no idea what Harold is doing in Cuba," his sister, Sybil, noted. "He sent us a cable at the week-end saying he was flying from Cuba to Mexico and that a letter would be following." The letter was the first news home since "quite a few months." She admitted he was "a very adventurous boy." "Globe-Trotter Runs into Cuba Plane Drama." *Manchester Evening News*, July 12, 1963.
25. Sandys, Duncan. *Cayman Islands Monthly Intelligence Report July and August 1963.* CO 1031/4768, NAUK. September 7, 1963.
26. Auerbach, Stuart. "Promoter Barred in Nassau." *Miami Herald*, July 13, 1963.
27. Associated Press. "Castro Denies Sending Spies." *Tallahassee Democrat*, July 12, 1963.

28. "Desmienten Infundio de los EE.UU." *El Mundo*, July, 1963.
29. Wilkinson, Mary Louise. "Cuba to Free 85,000 in Jail." *Miami News*, July 27, 1963.
30. United Press International. "Castro May Free Prisoners." *Miami Herald*, July 17, 1963.
31. Associated Press. "U.S.–Cuba Ship Trips Set to Go." *Fort Lauderdale News*, August 8, 1963.
32. TVN0775-2692-9, WLF.
33. Doherty, William C. *Memorandum from U.S. Ambassador to Jamaica to Secretary of State. Reference: EMBTEL 49.* JFKNSF-056-010, JFK. August 13, 1963.
34. ———. *Memorandum from U.S. Ambassador to Jamaica to Secretary of State. Reference: EMBTEL 51.* JFKNSF-056-010, JFK. August 14, 1963.
35. "Boat for Refugee Run Held at Pt. Royal." *Daily Gleaner*, August 17, 1963.
36. JFKNSF-123-004, JFK.
37. "Teacher Dismissed." *Stornoway Gazette and West Coast Advertiser*, July 22, 1958.
38. United Press International. "Jamaica Arrests Crew of Bolting Cuba Ferry." *Miami Herald*, August 18, 1963.
39. Bonafede, Dom. "Fidel Blames U.S. in Exile Air Raid." *Miami Herald*, August 20, 1963.
40. Associated Press. "British Yacht Slips Officials to Attempt Refugee Pickup." *Miami Herald*, August 18, 1963.
41. Davis, Miller. "Jamaican Warplanes Intercept Exile Ferry." *Miami News*, August 18, 1963.
42. Luedtke, Kurt. "Lawyer Raps 'Hogwash' on Cuba Shuttle." *Miami Herald*, August 18, 1963.
43. *Cable No 279*. Document: 3. [Translated from French]. SFA B.72.0.2. August 14, 1963, 1.
44. TVN0777-2699-9, WLF.
45. "Refugee Yacht Held." *Daily Herald*, August 19, 1963.

46. The interception of the *Nana* was the inaugural mission of the Jamaican Air Wing. The pilots were told the ship was a ganja boat. The Official Website of the Jamaica Defence Force. https://www.jdfweb.com/jdf-air-wing/.
47. Herald Wire Services. "Jamaica Police Seize Cuba Ferry, Jail Crew." *Miami Herald*, August 18, 1963.
48. United Press International. "CIA in Cuban Refugee Case, Jamaica Hears." *Daily Press*, August 19, 1963.
49. Klosson, Borris H. *Telegram from U.S. Embassy in Jamaica to Secretary of State*. Number: 68, JFKNSF-056-010, JFK. August 19, 1963.
50. "Bateando Bolas de Afuera." *Noticias de Hoy*, August 20, 1963.
51. "Ferry Will Try It Again." *Miami News*, August 20, 1963.
52. Rose, Brian. *Report of Derber's Interview with Diggines*. Document: AK1821/93, FO 371/168231, NAUK. October 1, 1963.
53. *Briefing Paper for the President's Press Conference. Subject: Ferry Boat Service to Cuba*. NAID 77414843, NACP. August 20, 1963, 3.
54. Chase, Gordon. *Memorandum to White House Regarding Jamaica*. B58, LBJ. December 20, 1963, 122.
55. Associated Press. "Briton is Accused in Yacht Trespass." *Tallahassee Democrat*, September 12, 1963.
56. American Embassy, Jamaica. *Transmittal of Copy of Legal Proceedings of Derber Trial at Port Antonio*. FOIA USCIS Derber. November 2, 1963, 501-574.
57. *Derber*. No. 406 Confidential. Document: AK1821/48, FO 371/168228, NAUK. August 26, 1963.
58. "'Nana' Owner Threatens $1M Suit Against Govt." *Daily Gleaner*, August 20, 1963.
59. TVN0777-2700-12, WLF.
60. Luedtke, Kurt. "First Cuba Shuttle Due in State Today." *Miami Herald*, October 24, 1963.

Notes

61. MacLeese, Alan. "Refugees Protest Halt of Ferry." *Miami News*, August 19, 1963.
62. Associated Press. "Boat Men Guilty of Assault." *Miami Herald*, September 15, 1963.
63. "Kicked on Hand by Derber, Capt. Tough Tells Court." *Daily Gleaner*, September 4, 1963.
64. "RM Rules There is Case to Answer." *Daily Gleaner*, September 11, 1963.
65. Chase, Gordon. *Subject: Ferry Service Between Havana and Miami*. JFKNSF-056-010, JFK. October 24, 1963.
66. The State Department wrote to the ICCA that they had "Blocked initiation of an ocean ferry service between Habana and Florida by employing various delaying and obstructing tactics." State also informed the Join Chiefs of Staff that there were "Continued inter-Departmental efforts to prevent resumption of ferry service between Cuba and the U.S. which a British citizen, Harold Derber, has been attempting to establish during the past several month [sic]." ARMY 198-10007-10022.
67. Glass, Ian. "Ferry Deal Lambasted." *Miami News*, November 3, 1963.
68. "M.V. Nana Sails to Pt. Royal." *Daily Gleaner*, September 17, 1963.
69. Associated Press. "Boat to Ferry Cuban Exiles Slips From Jamaica Harbor." *Miami Herald*, September 30, 1963.
70. Burt, Al. "U.S. Suspects Fidel Supplied New 'Nana' When Other Sank." *Miami Herald*, November 6, 1963.
71. "Pestiferous Persistence." *Miami Herald*, October 25, 1963.
72. Buchanan, James. "Jury Told Derber Used Cuban Ship." *Miami Herald*, December 18, 1963.
73. Cavendish, Henry. "Derber Acquittal Denied by Judge." *Miami News*, December 18, 1963.
74. Swiss Embassy in Havana. *Aide Memoire. Cuba No. 2327*. Document: 36, SFA B.521. October 25, 1963, 133.

8. The Exile Runner

1. Tucker, William. "Cuba Ferry Boarded." *Miami News*, October 24, 1963.
2. Buchanan, James, and Don Ediger. "23 Cubans Arrive in 'Exile Runner'." *Miami Herald*, October 25, 1963.
3. Associated Press. "Refugees Say Castro Boats Escorted Their Ship Out." *Tampa Tribune*, October 29, 1963.
4. "23 Exiles, Ferry Held for Decision On Entry." *Miami News*, October 25, 1963.
5. Assistant/District Director for Travel Control Miami, Florida. *Subject: Arrival of the M/V 'NANA' at Key West, Florida.* FOIA USCIS Derber. October 28, 1963, 438–441.
6. McLaughlin, Leighton. "Derber, 3 Crewmen Still Held." *Miami Herald*, October 28, 1963.
7. *Re: Sarah Elizabeth Cohen, also known as Sari Cohen, Mrs. Cooper W. Thorne.* FOIA FBI Cohen. October 26, 1963, 5–6.
8. *Affidavit, Immigration and Naturalization Service.* FOIA USCIS Cohen. October 24, 1963, 5-6.
9. TVN0772-2750-15, WLF.
10. Associated Press. "Cuban People Really Hungry, Refugee Says." *Pensacola News Journal*, October 30, 1963.
11. O'Connor, Tom. "U.S. Insists on Holding Skipper of Refugee Ship." *Tampa Tribune*, October 30, 1963.
12. ———. "Skipper is Taken to Miami." *Tampa Tribune*, October 31, 1963.
13. Nageley filed a writ of habeas corpus, a constitutional safeguard against unlawful detention without criminal charges. However, the judge dismissed the writ, asserting, incorrectly, that habeas corpus rights were reserved for U.S. citizens. "U.S. Files Suit Against Ferry." *Miami News*, October 28, 1963.
14. "Exile Ferry Skipper Called Risk."

15. Associated Press. "Ferry From Cuba Friendly Service – Or Threat?" *Atlanta Journal*, October 30, 1963.
16. TVN0792-2751-9, WLF.
17. "Leave U.S., Derber Told." *Miami News*, November 12, 1963.
18. Letter from British Consulate in Miami to British Embassy in Washington, D.C., FO 371/174120, NAUK. December 31, 1963, 6–7.
19. *Harold Derber vs. Edward Ahrens and Guy Hixon*. Transcript of Proceedings, Southern District Court of Florida, No. 63-618-Civ-Ec, FOIA USCIS Derber. November 4, 1963, 2344.
20. Labadie, Stephen J. *Santo Trafficante, Jr., aka T. Labadie.* Record: 124-10211-10211. Agency File: 92-2781-938. FBI, December 11, 1963.
21. Glass. "Cuba Ferry Deal 'Stinks'."
22. ———. "Ferry Deal Lambasted."
23. "Derber Will Face 10 Charges." *Miami Herald*, October 31, 1963.
24. Associated Press. "Skipper of Ferry Will Be Arraigned." *Tampa Tribune*, October 31, 1963.
25. JFKPOF-061-006-p0159, JFK.
26. Cavendish, Henry. "Derber Slapped with Tax Lien." *Miami News*, November 18, 1963.
27. ———. "Derber Names JFK in Suit." *Miami News*, November 19, 1963.
28. Buchanan, James. "Derber Names JFK in Suit, Cites Orange Bowl Promise." *Miami Herald*, November 20, 1963.
29. Harold Derber at al vs John F. Kennedy. United States District Court, Southern District of Florida, FOIA USCIS Derber. November 18, 1963, 1164–1168.
30. Sneigr, Denis. "Derber Released by Mistake." *Miami News*, November 4, 1963.

31. Cavendish, Henry, and Denis Sneigr. "Derber Troubles Mount." *Miami News*, November 4, 1963.
32. Authorities also sought to prosecute Sari for being part of a subversive conspiracy and for critical comments she had made about U.S. policy while in Jamaica. After avoiding two federal subpoenas, she eventually testified to Derber's grand jury but was ultimately never charged. "Marshals Seeking Derber Secretary." *Miami News*, November 6, 1963; and "Secretary Talks to Grand Jury in Derber Quiz." *Miami News*, November 7, 1963.
33. Cavendish, Henry. "Derber Would Like Wedding, Citizenship." *Miami News*, November 30, 1963.
34. Buchanan, James. "Derber Pleads Innocent." *Miami Herald*, November 23, 1963.
35. "Jamaica Bans Derber." *Daily Gleaner*, December 18, 1963.
36. Secret Service 154-10002-10422.
37. During its investigation of JFK's assassination, the United States House Select Committee on Assassinations requested Derber's FBI file. Electronic Files of Joan G. Zimmerman, Senior Analyst. JFK Assassination Records Review Board.
38. Buchanan, James. "Jury Told Derber Used Cuban Ship." *Miami Herald*, December 18, 1963.
39. Cavendish, Henry. "Derber Acquittal Denied by Judge." *Miami News*, December 18, 1963.
40. Associated Press. "Jury Fails to Agree on Exile Ferry." *Tallahassee Democrat*, December 19, 1963.
41. Cavendish, Henry. "Derber Admits 2 Nanas." *Miami News*, December 18, 1963.
42. Buchanan, James. "Jury Split, Derber Case is Mistrial." *Miami Herald*, December 19, 1963.
43. Auerbach, Stuart. "Ferryboat Captain Acquitted." *Miami Herald*, January 14, 1964.

44. Kenny, Matthew T. "Rules Tightened for Exiles' Entry." *Miami Herald*, December 20, 1963.
45. Department of Justice, Immigration and Naturalization Service. *Trial Brief.* FOIA USCIS Derber. 1451–1472.
46. Glass, Ian. "Miami Bids a Farewell to Derber." *Miami News*, January 21, 1964.

9. Love and Hate and Humanitarian Solutions

1. "Deported Man Tells Story at Shannon." *Irish Weekly and Ulster Examiner*, January 25, 1964.
2. Getty fs210164012_0.
3. Derber faced extensive financial difficulties. He received multiple court judgments for overdue payments on the *Calypso Liner* and catering services. *Miami News*, June 19, 1964. The *Nana*'s crew won a lawsuit for back wages. *Miami News*, October 30, 1963. One hundred and fifty Cubans gathered in a Miami federal building, demanding refunds for their ferry tickets. *Miami News*, June 24, 1964. The rightful owner of the new *Nana* charged Derber with boat theft. *Miami News*, October 30, 1963. The Diner's Club sued for back payments. *Miami News*, November 21, 1964. The INS fined him $23,000 ($1,000 per passenger) for not providing twenty-four-hour notice of the *Nana*'s arrival, despite the charges being dropped. *Tampa Tribune*, March 3, 1964. A fisherman bought the *Nana* for $47,000 at a federal auction. *Miami Herald*, August 1, 1964. Sarah Cohen testified he was out of money. *Miami News*, March 4, 1964. One of his ex-business partners in Manchester said Derber was "flat broke." *Miami News*, October 22, 1964. Nageley withdrew as Derber's counsel. *Miami News*, May 28, 1964.

4. Derber, Harold. Letter to Braulio Martinez. June 26, 1965.
5. ———. Letter to Víctor Pina. March 14, 1964.
6. ———. Letter to U.S. Departments of State, Immigration & Naturalization Service, and Public Health Service. NAID 77414843, NACP. February 26, 1964, 7.
7. The UK Foreign Office confirmed Derber had acuired new ships, notifying the British Embassy in Washington: "[Derber has] secured two vessels for the transport of Cubans to the United States which are already on their way from the U.K. to Havana." Sutherland, I.J.M. Memorandum to J.M. Brown. Document: AK1821/9, March 13, 1964. FO 371/174120, NAUK, March 13, 1964.
8. The Estrada versus Ahrens decision was a pivotal court ruling that gave non-resident alien plaintiffs standing to seek mandamus relief in their immigration cases. The court reasoned that the Administrative Procedure Act afforded aliens the right to judicial review.
9. Office Administering the Government of the Bahamas. *Bahamas. Intelligence Report for the Month of November, 1963*. Letter Regarding Empress Lines Limited to Abba P. Schwartz, Administrator Bureau of Security and Consular Affairs, Department of State. Document: AK1821/11, FO 371/174120, NAUK. March 13, 1964, 51–52.
10. Cavendish, Henry, and Ian Glass. "Derber Says He'll Bring 500 More Cubans Here." *Miami News*, March 2, 1964.
11. "2 Derber Boats on the Way to Pick Up Exiles in Cuba." *Miami Herald*, March 14, 1964.
12. *Text of a Broadcast by Ralph Renick over WTVJ (Channel 4)*. Document: AK1821/5, FO 371/174120, NAUK. February, 1964, 27.
13. The British Embassy in Havana speculated Derber could evade U.S. law by exploiting the three-mile limit: "[O]ne way round the American regulations may be for Derber to have his pas-

sengers transferred into little boats while still outside American territorial waters and arrive, so to speak, under their own steam and complete with visa waivers." Hitch, B. *Memorandum to J.M. Brown.* Document: AK1821/12, March 31, 1964, 54–55, FO 371/174120, NAUK. March 31, 1964, 54–55.

14. Glass, Ian. "Derber's 'Defender' Wants to Quit Case." *Miami News*, May 28, 1964.
15. Derber's precise whereabouts during this period are unclear. "He has now disappeared, so far as we are concerned. If he plans to return to Havana, I doubt whether he will be considerate enough to let us know beforehand so I do not rate the prospects of our being able to give Havana advance warning very high." Brown, J.M. *Memorandum to I.J.M. Sutherland.* Document: AK1821/4, FO 371/174120, NAUK. January 29, 1964, 22. "H.M. Consul Miami telephoned me this afternoon to report that he had heard from what he regarded as a reliable source, that Derber would be back in Havana within 10 days." Sutherland, I.J.M. *Memorandum to J.M. Brown.* Document: AK1821/4(A), FO 371/174120, NAUK. January 24, 1964, 23. Reports indicated he was coordinating directly with the Cuban embassy in London. Shanley, Wallace D. *Subject: Harold Derber.* NAID 1254233, NACP. March 11, 1964, 33.
16. "Derber Ships Off to Cuba." *Miami News*, March 13, 1964.
17. Swiss Embassy in Havana. *Bemühungen in Angelegenheit Derber.* Document: 5. [Translated from German], SFA B.521. April 1, 1964, 7–11.
18. Chase, Gordon. *Subject: Cuba – Miscellaneous.* Memorandum for Mr. Bundy, B30, LBJ. March 17, 1964, 55.
19. The State Department pressured the British Foreign Office to stop Derber. However, since he was not violating UK law, the Foreign Office declined to intervene: "We ... would be reluctant to question him about them particularly as, if they are as

described in your telegram, they would not necessarily involve anything illegal." *Telegram 3480.* Document: AK1821/6, March 6, 1964, FO 371/174120, NAUK. March 6, 1964.
20. Zumwalt, M.G. *Movement of Cuban Refugees.* B30, LBJ. March 15, 1964, 52.
21. Derber, Harold. Letter to Commercial Attaché at British Embassy in Mexico. Document: AK1821/21, FO 371/174120, NAUK. June 26, 1964, 62.
22. Slater, Richard M.K. *Memorandum to David H. T. Hildyard.* Document: AK1821/23, FO 371/174120, NAUK. July 21, 1964, 69.
23. Johnstone, R.E.L. *Memorandum to G.E. Hall.* Document: AK1821/21, FO 371/174120, NAUK. July 2, 1964, 61.
24. Glass, Ian. "Deported Derber in Mexico." *Miami News,* July 17, 1964.
25. United Press International. "Fidel Seen Moving to Free Cubans." *El Paso Herald-Post,* July 27, 1964.
26. While in Havana, Derber told the Cuban Commerce Secretary he had the backing of Fidel Castro and his brother Raul, now Vice Premier and Minister of the Armed Forces. Sutherland, I.J.M. *Letter to John Crimmins.* NAID 77414844, NACP. April 27, 1965, 4–5.
27. FBI 124-90140-10021.
28. CIA 1993.08.04.18:39:12:810059.
29. District Director, Miami. *Derber, Harold: A10 096 029.* Letter to Richard E. Foster, Deputy District Director, FBI, Vermont. FOIA USCIS Derber. March 2, 1965.
30. Embassy of the USA in Switzerland. *Cuba No. 3473.* Document: 3, SFA B.521. June 15, 1965, 5.
31. State issued cables to embassies in Athens, Buenos Aires, London, Monrovia, Madrid, Ottawa, and Nassau, requesting any information on Derber's ships. Rusk, Dean. B30, LBJ. June 3, 1965, 90–94.

32. Derber, Harold. Letter to Víctor Pina. December 27, 1965.
33. Herald Wire Services. "Fidel: Cubans Can Go to 'Yankee Paradise'." *Miami Herald*, September 29, 1965.
34. "Castro Tells Rally Cubans Are Free to Leave Cuba." *New York Times*, September 30, 1965.
35. Castro, Fidel. *Ceremony for Return of Cuban Athletic Delegation*. Havana Domestic Radio and Television Services in Spanish, Latin American Network Information Center, University of Texas at Austin. June 30, 1966.
36. Johnson, Lyndon B. *Remarks at the Signing of the Immigration Bill, Liberty Island*. Public Papers of the Presidents of the United States: Lyndon B. Johnson, 1965. Volume II, Entry 546, October 3, 1965. Washington, DC: United Stated Government Printing Office, 1966, 1037–1040.
37. Castro, Fidel. *Castro Addresses CDR Main Event on Plaza de la Revolucion*. Havana Domestic Radio and Television Services in Spanish, Latin American Network Information Center, University of Texas at Austin. September 28, 1971.
38. Noble, Dennis L. "Lessons Unlearned: The Camarioca Boatlift." *Naval History Magazine* 23, no. 4 (August, 2009).

PART III

10. Shipping Interests

1. "Con $343,750 Resultó Defraudado un Bancode la Capitalde la Nación." *El Informador*, November 6, 1967.
2. Associated Press. "Retired Officer Held in Mexico on Fraud Charge." *Guam Daily News*, November 18, 1967.
3. The bad checks were possibly not all written by Derber. In one case, a fraudulent check was allegedly submitted by his former *Empress* partner, Mike McLaney, who purported to be a representative of Derber's company. Harold Derber vs

Mike McLaney et al, United States Court for Southern District of Florida, FOIA USCIS Derber. July 1967, 1965–1972.
4. FBI 124-10208-10121.
5. Carroll, Margaret. "Banned Exile Smuggler Arrested at Airport." *Miami Herald*, October 2, 1968.
6. "I wouldn't be surprised if he decided to fight to stay in the country," his former attorney, Nageley, commented. "It's always been Harold against the world." Glass, Ian. "Cuban 'Ferryman' Booted to Nassau." *Miami News*, October 2, 1968.
7. "Ferryman's Deportation Barred." *Miami News*, October 4, 1968.
8. Derber was a defendant in a lawsuit involving a shopping plaza in Washington state. Sparkman McLean Co. v Derber; and "Shopping Plaza to Be Sold at Sheriff's Sale." *Port Angeles Evening News*, January 24, 1969.
9. Glass, Ian. "Derber and Pan American Hope He's Freed Tomorrow." *Miami News*, October 16, 1968.
10. "Refugee Smuggler Visit OK." *Miami Herald*, November 2, 1968.
11. Vancouver Police Department. Various Investigation Reports, FOIA USCIS Derber. 1925–1935.
12. Gardner, Michael J. "Maritime Drug Smuggling Conspiracies: Criminal Liability for Importation and Distribution." *William & Mary Law Review* 27, no. 1 (1985): 217–43.
13. Brendel, Joseph R. "The Marijuana on the High Seas Act and Jurisdiction Over Stateless Vessels." *William & Mary Law Review* 25, no. 2 (1983): 313–40.
14. "Se fugaron cuatro pesqueros de E.U." *El Tiempo*, February 20, 1971.
15. Samuel. "Marinos Relatan "Toma" de Pesquero de EE.UU." *El Tiempo*, April 4, 1971.
16. Mesa, Ben Levi Pechthal, and Narciso Castro Y. "Estafador Extranjero Demanda a la Nación." *El Tiempo*, March 2, 1973.

Notes

17. 1973STATE137518, State.
18. 1975STATE033349, State.
19. "Como Se Planeó y Se Frustró el Robo del Barco Milmar-1." *El Universal*, March 8, 1973.
20. "Continúan Detenidos Sindicados del Robo Frustrado de un Barco." *El Universal*, March 11, 1973.
21. De Avila, Luis. "Tormenta Judicial en Torno al Frustrado Robo de un Barco en Cartagena." *El Universal*, March 7, 1973.
22. Greve, Frank. "Night Train to Start New Career." *Miami Herald*, February 26, 1977.
23. The British Consul in Honduras scrubbed Derber's passport of all his trips to Cuba. RG 46.238, GAN.
24. Derber's visa extension was approved by the INS Deputy District Director for Miami, Louis Gidel. "Application to Extend Time of Temporary Stay." FOIA USCIS Derber. April 22, 1974, 1875; May 29, 1974, 1874; October 15, 1974, 1871.
25. Markowitz, Arnold. "Ex-Hallandale Mayor Testifies in Drug Scheme." *Miami Herald*, February 10, 1978.

11. The Night Train

1. Eidge, Frank. "Agents Hunted Ship More Than 2 Years." *Florida Today*, February 4, 1977.
2. Burdick and Mitchell, 243–244.
3. Cigarette powerboats became the preferred vessels for pickups. Manufacturers even began designing models specifically for mothership operations, featuring stripped-down interiors and large storage compartments. Florida boat shops soon started renting out Cigarette boats exclusively for mothership runs. Burdick and Mitchell.

4. Moody, Sid. "Business Runs High in Haven for Smugglers." *Orlando Sentinel*, December 30, 1979.
5. "Trafficante wanted to do a minimum of fifty tons. He thought anything less wouldn't be economically feasible" in Marks, 174. "'The lowest weight you could have in order to make a [maritime] marijuana shipment profitable [was] around three hundred quintals [approximately thirty-three tons].'" Britto, 108. For an analysis of the mothership business model, see CIA GI 82-10211.
6. Greve. "Night Train to Start New Career."
7. Clifford, Tom. "Drug Smugglers Move North to Carolina." *Wilmington Morning Star*, December 13, 1977.
8. United Press International. "The Night Train." *Fort Lauderdale News*, February 4, 1977.
9. "Geography of Coast Gives Edge to Criminal." *State*, February 3, 1981.
10. Russell, 163.
11. "Marijuana Ship History Reveals Checkered Past." *Miami Herald*, March 6, 1977.
12. "Marijuana Ship Has Link to Canada." *Leader-Post*, February 7, 1977.
13. Canada, *List of Shipping*.
14. Hamill, Pete. "The Man Whose Invention Really Fertilized the Grass." *Daily News*, June 1, 1979.
15. Charles Fuss, a Special Agent with the Office of National Drug Control Policy wrote, "The most nefarious development was the advent of marijuana motherships. Former Royal Navy officer Harold Derber is credited with introducing the marijuana mothership in 1974 ... The modus operandi for transporting large volumes of marijuana to the United States was irrevocably changed." Fuss, 31. Another law enforcement official remarked, "No doubt about it. Harold Derber is the man who moved

marijuana smuggling into the big time." Hamill. In *Of Grass and Snow*, a seminal account of the dawn of the drug industry, the author wrote, "It was Derber the former sailor who had reintroduced the concept of 'the mothership,'" citing the Rum Runners of the Prohibition Era as the first practitioners of the technique. Messick, 64. The Associated Press wrote, "A technological breakthrough credited to one Harold Derber, was the use of a mothership ..." Moody. "Business Runs High in Haven for Smugglers."

16. Markowitz, Arnold. "Ex-Hallandale Mayor Testifies in Drug Scheme." *Miami Herald*, February 10, 1978.
17. Purdy, Matthew. "First Jersey's Paper Empire and Its Origins." *Philadelphia Inquirer*, April 13, 1986.
18. Carpenter, James. *Fatal Shooting of Harold Derber.* Inter-Office Memorandum from Police Investigator Carpenter to Lieutenant L. F. Gracey, Derber Murder File 615994. May 30, 1976.
19. Goldman, 206.
20. "New U.S. War to Collar Drug Smugglers." *Fort Lauderdale News*, September 17, 1978.
21. Coram, Robert. "The Colombian Gold Rush of 1978." *Esquire*, September 12, 1978.

12. Operation Zebra

1. Associated Press. "Bikini-clad Narc Reveals Pot Operation in Keys." *Miami News*, September 20, 1974.
2. Burdick and Mitchell, 243–244.
3. FBI 124-10208-10000.
4. Harrell, Ken. "Ex-Mayor Finds Truck, Drugs and Trouble." *Fort Lauderdale News*, September 21, 1974.

5. Booking record for Harold Deb, County of Dade Police, FOIA USCIS Derber. September 19, 1974, 1881.
6. FBI Identification Record on Harold Derber, FBI Record #: 3959200, FOIA USCIS Derber. October 16, 1975, 1882–1883.
7. Oglesby, Joe. "Drug Hunt Questioned." *Miami Herald*, December 20, 1974.
8. ———. "Arrest Search Illegal." *Miami Herald*, January 25, 1975.
9. Akey Interview.
10. Amlong, William R. "Their Legacy: Air-Sea Drug Network." *Miami Herald*, April 18, 1978.
11. Scholz, Jane. "Broward Ex-Official Called in Bloody Boat Probe." *Miami Herald*, May 20, 1975.
12. Raynor, Jerry. "Record Drug Raid Made Last Sunday in Mesic." *Pamlico County News*, January 15, 1976.
13. Hall, Michael J. "N.C. Viewed as Focal Point for Importing Illegal Drugs." *Evening Telegram*, January 12, 1976.
14. Allegood, Jerry. "15 Tons of Marijuana Seized on N.C. Coast." *News and Observor*, January 12, 1976.
15. Sentinel Wire Reports. "25-Ton Pot Haul Shows N.C. Key Pickup Spot." *Sentinel*, January 12, 1976.
16. Goldman, 206.
17. Allegood, Jerry. "Man's Body Found at Pot Raid Site." *News and Observer*, May 20, 1976.
18. United Press International. "Gunmen Shot Wrong Man, Police Say." *Fort Lauderdale News*, June 10, 1976.
19. ———. "Authorities Link Death, Smuggling." *Sentinel*, May 20, 1976.
20. Associated Press. "Remains of Man Identified." *Winston-Salem Journal*, February 3, 1977.
21. Charles V. Wilson, previously arrested with Derber in Key Largo for marijuana possession, and James Alexander Wat-

son were charged as accessories to murder after the fact. They were in the trailer during Watkins' murder and buried his body and the evidence. Allegood, Jerry. "2 Face Hearing in Drug Slaying." *News and Observer*, March 23, 1977.

22. Associated Press. "Man Names 7 in Marijuana Smuggling Trial." *Charlotte News*, April 6, 1976.
23. Bernish, Paul. "Coastal N.C. Called Ideal for Smuggling." *Charlotte Observer*, April 12, 1976.
24. Kornbluth, Jesse. "Poisonous Fallout from the War on Marijuana." *New York Times*, November 19, 1978.
25. Britto, passim.
26. Amlong, William R. "Drug Smugglers' Lifestyle: Big Money and Big Risks." *Miami Herald*, April 19, 1978.
27. Gately and Fernández, 21.
28. ———, passim.
29. Crumbo, Chuck. "Jury Indicts Five in R.I.-Broward Drug Smuggling." *Fort Lauderdale News*, September 1, 1977.
30. Messick, 89-107.
31. United States v Monaco and Hicks.
32. Goodgame, Danny. "Suspected Drug Smuggler Mastermind Turns Self In." *Miami Herald*, September 2, 1977.
33. Boyd Interview.
34. Messick, 65–67.
35. Adams, Nathan M. "Havana's Drug-Smuggling Connection." *Reader's Digest*, July, 1982.
36. The public would not learn of Cuba's role in the drug trade until years later, when testimony from two U.S. government witnesses disclosed that drug smuggler Jaime Guillot Lara had met with Cuba's Ambassador to Colombia, Fernando Ravelo-Renedo, and entered a guns-for-drugs trade deal. U.S. authorities would eventually arrest Lara for trafficking massive amounts of marijuana to America. He transported 200 tons of weapons to Colombia's Marxist 19th of April

Movement (M-19) guerrillas on the return trips. At the time of Lara's arrest, a classified U.S. government report said the case was "only the tip of the iceberg of Cuba's ultrasecret involvement in the drug trade." Cuba was shortly after placed on the list of state sponsors of terrorism. The U.S. would later indict four Cuban officials, including Ravelo-Renedo, and prepare indictments against many top Cuban leaders, including Raul Castro and Piñeiro. Satchell, Michael, et al. "Narcotics: Terror's New Ally." *U.S. News & World Report*, May 4, 1987; Buchanan, Edna. "Miami drug smuggler ran guns for Castro to guerrillas, agents say." *Miami Herald*, January 24, 1982; McGee, Jim. "U.S. Indicts Four Castro Officials on Drug-trafficking Conspiracy." *Miami Herald*, November 6, 1982.

37. Richard, Randall, and Irene Wielawksi. "Ring Pays for Drugs with Guns and Cash." *Providence Sunday Journal*, August 28, 1977.
38. Carpenter, James. *Fatal Shooting of Harold Derber.* Inter-Office Memorandum from Police Investigator Carpenter to Lieutenant L. F. Gracey, Derber Murder File 615994. May 30, 1976.

13. Vast Opportunities

1. Derber's Miami banks were Capital Bank and Flagship National Bank. He purchased $2.5 million in certificates of deposit and made regular cash deposits, including one for $130,000. He deposited $502,500 in the account of an unidentified R. C. Gomez. Derber wrote three checks to an unknown Jairo Diaz, deposited them into three separate accounts, and endorsed them in three different handwriting styles. Derber deposited cash into the Ocean Explorations Corp business account and issued cashier's checks, many

Notes

of which went to First Jersey Securities. Amlong. "Their Legacy."
2. Brennan Interview.
3. Welling, Kathryn M. "The Bottom Line: Murder." *Barron's*, April 9, 1979.
4. "Decisions in Administrative Proceedings." *SEC News Digest* 6, 14, no. 74-219 (November 12, 1974).
5. Purdy. "First Jersey's Paper Empire."
6. Welling, Kathryn M. "New Kid on the Block: How First Jersey Securities Makes a Bundle in Low-Priced Stocks." *Barron's*, April 9, 1979.
7. Securities Activities of First Jersey Securities, Inc., 7.
8. Derber purchased shares in URT, which then underwent a three-for-one split. The share price did not fall proportionally, as is typical after a stock split, because First Jersey propped up the price with self-trades, which they could do because they controlled most of the outstanding shares. Derber sold his shares six weeks later to Brennan and First Jersey for an enormous profit, who in turn, sold the shares to the public. ADA Navigation was a Panamanian company controlled by Derber. Brennan self-dealed in the company's shares to inflate the price and generate an enormous profit for Derber and Brennan's father. Again, the public provided the exit liquidity. Derber purchased 50% of the charter shares in Chefs International, a New Jersey-based restaurant group, a month after its incorporation. The company acquired a chain of La Crepe Restaurants. His investment increased more than twenty-fold months later when the company offered shares to the public. He also purchased a $180,000 Chefs International bond that paid 10% interest. Through his company, Ocean Explorations Corp, Derber loaned $300,000 to a leather handbag firm called Leather Orr. Adiel was chairman and had a stake in the company. Derber bought a $235,000 certificate

of deposit from the First Israel Bank in New York marked "for Leather-Orr." When Leather Orr announced plans to go public as Empire Orr, the loan was converted into shares for Derber on preferential terms. Amlong "Their Legacy."; Welling. "The Bottom Line: Murder."; Purdy.

9. Amlong. "Their Legacy."
10. Hamill. "The Man Whose Invention Really Fertilized the Grass."
11. The companies included Ocean Explorations, Atlanta Sea Highway, ADA Navigation, Magic City Shipping, Leather Orr, Outer Island Shipping, and Investors Transcontinental. Welling, "Bottom Line: Murder."; 76PANAMA2883, State; and Gaceto Oficial Organo del Estado, Año 78, No. 19.364, July 20, 1981, 4.
12. Derber Murder File 615994.
13. Derber's girlfriend, Sandra Lee Bill, claimed she and Derber married in Colombia in 1975. She stated that she gave her lawyer the marriage certificate, yet she was unable to produce it during Derber's estate hearing. Roth v Lake.
14. Kelly, Maureen. "Killers Got Wrong Man the First Time." *Miami News*, June 10, 1976.
15. Associated Press. "U.S. Investigating Brennan for Stock, Election Violations." *Record*, April 16, 1986.
16. Brennan, 90.
17. 1976STATE112381, State.
18. This theory is further supported by the DEA denying the author's Freedom of Information Act request for Derber's file, citing the need to protect their techniques and procedures. Additionally, the DEA could not provide the author with the report on Derber it had previously supplied to Congress.
19. Buchanan, James. "Slain Fortune-Hunter 'Was Into Everything'." *Miami Herald*, March 24, 1976.

20. Coram, Robert. "2 Reports Indicate Russians May Be Aiding Narcotics Flow." *Atlanta Constitution*, June 29, 1981.
21. Richard, Randall, and Irene Wielawksi. "Discovering the 'R.I. Connection' in Drugs." *Evening Bulletin*, November 30, 1977.
22. Inclan, Hilda. "Slain Adventurer Had Many Enemies." *Miami News*, March 23, 1976.
23. Lopez, M. Incident Report for Harold Derber. Derber Murder File 615994. March 23, 1976.
24. Derber Autopsy.

Epilogue

1. O'Toole, Thomas. "Satellites Used to Round Up U.S.-Bound Marijuana Ships." *Washington Post*, July 11, 1978.
2. Akey Interview.
3. Goldman, 206.
4. Messick, 89–107.
5. "High-Seas Drama When Night Train Was Seized." *U.S. News & World Report*, March 27, 1978.
6. United States v Cadena.
7. Laliberte, Daniel A. "End of the Line for the Night Train." *Naval History Magazine* 32, no. 4 (August, 2018).
8. "U.S. Claims Big Pot Seizures After Satellite Tracks Ships." *Miami Herald*, July 11, 1978.
9. Riordan, Patrick. "Elusive Pot Ship, Record Cargo, Were Seized in Sea Duel." *Miami Herald*, April 18, 1978.
10. United States v Rodriguez.
11. Teel, Leonard Ray. "Court Backs High Seas Pot Seizure." *Atlanta Journal*, November 21, 1978.
12. Sosin, Milt. "Federal Agents' Role in Drug Bust Detailed." *Miami News*, February 15, 1977.